'Welding together the discussion of crisis and migration turns out to be an inspired intervention, taking us fittingly far from the prosaic categories of policy analysis.'

Robin Cohen, University of Oxford, UK

'This book deftly probes the links between migration and crisis, destabilizing the normative assumptions that migration *is* crisis. The authors conceptualise crisis and migration not as isolated events but rather as co-constituted processes understood in relation to colonialism, nation-state formation, industrialisation, and urbanization. And crisis migration, they argue, precipitates crisis management. A compelling read.'

Jennifer Hyndman, Centre for Refugee Studies,
York University, Canada

T0376652

Crisis and Migration

Crisis and migration have a long association, in popular and policy discourse as well as in social scientific analysis. Despite the emergence of more nuanced and even celebratory accounts of mobility in recent years, there remains a persistent emphasis on migration being either a symptom or a cause of crisis. Moreover, in the context of a recent series of headline-hitting and politically controversial situations, terms like 'migration crisis' and 'crisis migration' are acquiring increasing currency among policy-makers and academics.

Crisis and Migration provides fresh perspectives on this routine association, critically examining a series of politically controversial situations around the world. Drawing on first-hand research into the Arab uprisings, conflict and famine in the Horn of Africa, drug cartel violence in Latin America, the global economic crisis, and immigration 'crises' from East Asia to Southern Africa to Europe, the book's contributors situate a set of contemporary crises within longer histories of social change and human mobility, showing the importance of treating crisis and migration as contextualised processes, rather than isolated events.

By exploring how migration and crisis articulate as lived experiences and political constructs, the book brings migration from the margins to the centre of discussions of social transformation and crisis; illuminates the acute politicisation and diverse spatialisations of crisis–migration relationships; and urges a nuanced, cautious and critical approach to associations of crisis and migration.

Anna Lindley is a Lecturer in the Department of Development Studies at SOAS, University of London, UK.

Routledge Studies in Development, Mobilities and Migration

This series is dedicated to the growing and important area of mobilities and migration within Development Studies. It promotes innovative and interdisciplinary research targeted at a global readership.

The series welcomes submissions from established and junior authors on cutting-edge and high-level research on key topics that feature in global news and public debate.

These include the Arab Spring; famine in the Horn of Africa; riots; environmental migration; development-induced displacement and resettlement; livelihood transformations; people-trafficking; health and infectious diseases; employment; South–South migration; population growth; children's well-being; marriage and family; food security; the global financial crisis; drugs wars; and other contemporary crises.

Gender, Mobilities and Livelihood Transformations
Comparing indigenous people in China, India and Laos
Edited by Ragnhild Lund, Kyoko Kusakabe, Smita Mishra Panda and Yunxian Wang

Intimate Economies of Development
Mobility, sexuality and health in Asia
Chris Lyttleton

Crisis and Migration
Critical perspectives
Edited by Anna Lindley

Crisis and Migration
Critical perspectives

**Edited by
Anna Lindley**

Routledge
Taylor & Francis Group

LONDON AND NEW YORK

First published 2014
by Routledge

Published 2016 by Routledge

2 Park Square, Milton Park, Abingdon, Oxon, OX14 4RN

and by Routledge
711 Third Avenue, New York, NY 10017

Routledge is an imprint of the Taylor & Francis Group, an informa business

First issued in paperback 2015

© 2014 selection and editorial material, Anna Lindley; individual chapters, the contributors

The right of Anna Lindley to be identified as author of the editorial material, and of the individual authors as authors of their contributions, has been asserted by her in accordance with sections 77 and 78 of the Copyright, Designs and Patents Act 1988.

All rights reserved. No part of this book may be reprinted or reproduced or utilised in any form or by any electronic, mechanical, or other means, now known or hereafter invented, including photocopying and recording, or in any information storage or retrieval system, without permission in writing from the publishers.

Trademark notice: Product or corporate names may be trademarks or registered trademarks, and are used only for identification and explanation without intent to infringe.

British Library Cataloguing in Publication Data
A catalogue record for this book is available from the British Library

Library of Congress Cataloging-in-Publication Data
Crisis and migration : critical perspectives / [edited by] Anna Lindley.
pages cm. -- (Routledge studies in development, mobilities and migration)
Includes bibliographical references and index.
1. Emigration and immigration. 2. Migration, Internal. 3. Crises. I. Lindley, Anna.
JV6035.C75 2014
304.8--dc23
201305019

ISBN13: 978-0-415-64502-7 (hbk)
ISBN13: 978-1-138-64700-8 (pbk)

Typeset in Times New Roman
by Taylor & Francis Books

Contents

Notes on contributors	viii
Acknowledgements	xi

1 Exploring crisis and migration: concepts and issues   1
ANNA LINDLEY

2 Migration and 'crisis' in the Middle East and North Africa region   24
PHILIP MARFLEET AND ADAM HANIEH

3 Histories and contemporary challenges of crisis and mobility in
Somalia   46
ANNA LINDLEY AND LAURA HAMMOND

4 Criminal violence and displacement in Mexico: evidence,
perceptions and politics   73
LAURA RUBIO DÍAZ-LEAL AND SEBASTIÁN ALBUJA

5 The global economic crisis and East Asian labour migration: a
crisis of migration or struggles of labour?   93
DAE-OUP CHANG

6 Crisis, enforcement and control at the EU borders   115
JULIEN JEANDESBOZ AND POLLY PALLISTER-WILKINS

7 The social construction of (non-)crises and its effects: government
discourse on xenophobia, immigration and social cohesion in
South Africa   136
IRIANN FREEMANTLE WITH JEAN PIERRE MISAGO

8 Imagined threats, manufactured crises and 'real' emergencies:
the politics of border closure in the face of mass refugee influx   158
KATY LONG

9 Crisis? Which crisis? Families and forced migration   181
TANIA KAISER

Index   203

Contributors

Sebastián Albuja is Head of the Africa and Americas Department at the Internal Displacement Monitoring Centre (IDMC) of the Norwegian Refugee Council in Geneva. He has published extensively on forced migration, human rights, and public policy. He previously practised law in his country of origin, Ecuador. He holds a PhD in Law and Public Policy from Northeastern University, the USA, where he was a Fulbright scholar and taught on various undergraduate courses.

Dae-oup Chang is a Senior Lecturer in Development Studies at SOAS, University of London, and specialises in labour relations, transnational corporations and the political economy of East Asia. He has published widely on these issues, including *Capitalist Development in Korea: Labour, Capital and the Myth of the Developmental State* (Routledge, 2009). He has a PhD in Sociology from the University of Warwick and previously taught at the University of Hong Kong, and worked as a research co-ordinator for Asia Monitor Resource Centre, an NGO specialising in labour issues.

Iriann Freemantle is a researcher based at the African Centre for Migration and Society at the University of the Witwatersrand in Johannesburg, South Africa. With a background in sociology, ethnic and migration studies, her doctoral project focused on cosmopolitanism, and her recent research explores the social construction of difference, xenophobia, nationalism and social cohesion in policy and practice in South Africa.

Laura Hammond is a Senior Lecturer and Head of the Department of Development Studies at SOAS, University of London. Her research interests include food security, conflict, forced migration and diasporas, and she has published widely on these issues, including *This Place Will Become Home: Refugee Repatriation to Ethiopia* (Cornell University Press, 2004). She has worked in the Horn of Africa for the past 20 years, and been a consultant for a wide range of development and humanitarian organisations. She has a doctorate in Anthropology from the University of Wisconsin-Madison and held previous lectureships at Clark University and the University of Reading.

Contributors ix

Adam Hanieh is a Senior Lecturer in the Department of Development Studies at SOAS, University of London. His specialist areas include political economy, labour migration and Middle Eastern politics. His publications include *Capitalism and Class in the Gulf Arab States* (Palgrave Macmillan, 2011). He is on the editorial board of the journal *Historical Materialism*, on the management committee of the Council for British Research in the Levant, and a member of the advisory committee for the Centre for Palestine Studies at SOAS.

Julien Jeandesboz is an Assistant Professor in the Department of Politics at the University of Amsterdam. His research explores the politics of security and technology in Europe, focusing on border control, and the relationship between security and surveillance. He previously worked as a Research Associate at the Department of War Studies, King's College London, and earned his PhD in Political Science and International Relations from Science Po, Paris.

Tania Kaiser is a Senior Lecturer in Forced Migration Studies in the Department of Development Studies at SOAS, University of London. Her research interests are in forced migration and refugee experiences, violence, conflict and gender, and in culture, aesthetics and social change. Her ethnographic work has focused on the socio-cultural and political/protection consequences of displacement for conflict-affected populations of Southern Sudanese refugees in Uganda from 1996 to the present, and she has published numerous articles in journals, including the *Journal of Refugee Studies*, *Mobilities* and the *Journal of East African Studies*. She holds a DPhil in anthropology from the University of Oxford.

Anna Lindley is a Lecturer in the Department of Development Studies at SOAS, University of London, working on migration, livelihoods and remittances; conflict and displacement; and migration and refugee policy issues. She is the author of *The Early Morning Phone Call: Somali Refugees' Remittances* (Berghahn, 2010), and previously worked as a researcher at the Refugee Studies Centre and the Centre on Migration, Policy and Society at Oxford University, where she completed a doctorate in Development Studies.

Katy Long is a Lecturer in International Development at Edinburgh University and a Visiting Scholar at Stanford University. Her research focuses on the politics of migration and the meaning of citizenship. She is the author of *The Point of No Return: Refugees, Rights and Repatriation* (Oxford University Press, 2013). She was previously a lecturer at the London School of Economics, and has worked as a researcher for the Refugee Studies Centre, Oxford, and the United Nations High Commission for Refugees. She holds a PhD in History from Cambridge University.

Philip Marfleet is Professor of Migration and Refugee Studies at the University of East London. He has published widely on globalisation and migration, mass displacement, Europe and exclusion, and social and political change

x   *Contributors*

in the Middle East. He is the author of *Refugees in a Global Era* (Palgrave, 2006) and *Egypt: The Moment of Change* (Zed Books, 2009), and recently edited a special issue of the *International Journal of Contemporary Iraqi Studies* on Iraq's displacements (2011).

Jean Pierre Misago is a researcher and PhD candidate at the African Centre for Migration and Society at the University of the Witwatersrand, Johannesburg, South Africa. His research focuses on xenophobic violence, xenophobia and the effects of migration and displacement on identity and belonging. His most recent work was on developing an 'early warning system' for xenophobic violence able to predict, address and contain violence against foreign nationals in its early stages.

Polly Pallister-Wilkins is an Assistant Professor of International Relations at the University of Amsterdam. Her previous research while a PhD researcher at SOAS, looked at the resistance to the separation barrier in the Occupied Palestinian Territories. Her current research focuses on the wider political sociology of walls and fences more generally, while maintaining her regional interest in the Middle East-Mediterranean-European relations regarding security practices and border controls. Her most recent field research has focused on the Evros borderland in Greece where she investigated both the newly built border fence and the daily working practices of Greek and FRONTEX border guards.

Laura Rubio Díaz-Leal is Professor in the Department of International Studies at the Instituto Technológico Autónomo de México (ITAM), Mexico City, Mexico. Alongside recent work on displacement and migration in Mexico, she specialises in foreign policy and human rights, particularly in relation to Asia. She has a PhD in History from Manchester University.

Acknowledgements

Thanks first and foremost to the contributors. I have found working with them an immensely rewarding process. At SOAS, Paolo Novak, Parvathi Raman and John Campbell offered useful feedback at various stages; Giulia Baldinelli provided some terrifically competent research assistance; and the insights of many other Development Studies colleagues and students have filtered into the process one way or another.

An initial workshop in summer 2012 was funded by the SOAS Centre of Migration and Diaspora Studies and the Department of Development Studies, and was ably assisted by Sibel Balci Saner, Anna Seecharan and Nathifa Hall.

I am also grateful to Oliver Bakewell, Mark Bradbury, Maurice Herson, Nando Sigona and Nicholas Van Hear for their constructive engagement. Aside from her own contribution to the book, Katy Long provided help at a crucial stage.

At Routledge, warm thanks are due to Khanam Virjee for her initial encouragement, and to Charlotte Russell, Helen Bell and Siobhán Greaney for their editorial support.

On a personal note, thank you to Jenny and Isabel for bringing such joy and to Martin for being so steadfast. And also to Fadumo, my 'mum friends', Julie and the much-loved Lindley family, for their support during the period this book was in development.

1 Exploring crisis and migration

Concepts and issues

Anna Lindley

Crisis and migration have a long association, in popular and policy discourse as well as in social scientific analysis. Many crisis situations are associated with significant out-migration and displacement, and in-migration is often associated with tensions or conflict at destination. Moreover, there is a deep well of sedentarist thinking, which in some sense frames migration *as* crisis, and staying put as the natural and desirable human condition. Despite the relatively recent emergence of more nuanced and even celebratory accounts of mobility, the tendency to link migration with crisis in a strongly negative fashion remains deeply entrenched and vigorously persistent.

Since the mid-2000s, alongside protracted conflict situations, a series of new crises with strong migratory elements have hit the headlines, from the uprisings across the Arab world, the global economic crisis, the East African drought, to mega-disasters like the Haitian earthquake and the typhoon in the Philippines. Meanwhile, tensions around migration are mounting, sometimes culminating in severe backlashes, from Kuala Lumpur to Johannesburg to Athens, and with daily tragedies in the Mediterranean, the Sahara and other border zones. Terms like 'crisis migration' and 'migration crisis' are acquiring increasing and renewed currency among academics and policy-makers alike.

Notions of crisis and migration have some intriguing parallels. Both are often viewed as exceptional phenomena – crisis as occurring beyond the realms of 'normal' development and change, migration as occurring across the borders that structure politics, society and thinking about the social world. Both are often viewed as threatening, crisis as jeopardising social systems and human welfare; migration as undermining the integrity of the nation-state and bounded identities. At the same time, both are often described as characteristic of the contemporary world: scholars proclaim that we are in an 'age of crisis' and an 'age of migration' (Castles and Miller, 2009; Solimano, 2010). Together, crisis and migration have a powerful contemporary resonance.

Our aim in this book is to provide some fresh perspectives on this routine association, taking a critical look at how crisis and migration articulate, as lived experiences and as political constructs, by examining a range of situations around the world. As a first step, this opening chapter explores ways of

2   Anna Lindley

conceptualising crisis and migration, sketching out key issues and inter-linkages; and then outlines the approach, structure, and emerging themes of the book.

Crisis?

Crisis is a concept both loud and vague. It demands our attention, communicating a sense of danger and urgency, implying the overturning of normal life, racing to the top of political agendas, demanding social scientific scrutiny. At the same time, rhetorically inflated, analytically unspecific 'crisis-talk' abounds (Holton, 1987). Crisis means different things to different people: the identification of a crisis often depends critically on the perceptions and pronouncements of dominant actors, which may reflect to a rather variable extent objectively measurable indicators and people's real-life experiences (Boin, 2004). However, two particular qualities frequently recur in descriptions of crisis situations: (1) that they are not normal; and (2) that they are bad. These merit some discussion.

First, crises are typically defined in relation to a notion of normality, implying some form of marked discontinuity, a 'breaking point in a patterned process of linearity' (ibid.: 167). The assumption is that the discontinuity is marked, even dramatic, clearly distinguishable from both incremental processes of change, and from on-going situations of threat and embedded vulnerability. Crises are often viewed as critical turning points in history (Habermas, 1976).[1] They may be rapid onset situations (involving a sudden rupture with the normal pattern), or slower onset (in the form of a cumulative intensification/crescendo of events, or a trend of change reaching a critical threshold or tipping point). Trajectories vary. Some crises teeter on the edge and are averted, the threatened damage not inflicted; others blossom into full-blown disasters. Some are short-lived; others become protracted over long periods of time. Generally the use of the term crisis implies the expectation or possibility in principle of an ending, where normality is re-established. This may involve the restoration of the old status quo or it may involve a wholesale transformation, or selective reform/reorganisation. Whatever their particular shape, however, crises are conventionally viewed as, by definition, an exceptional turn of events.

The second recurring quality in conventional descriptions of crisis is the idea that they are bad: that they entail a severe threat or damage to important human needs and goals. Crises are often conceptualised in relation to entire social systems: as the moment when due to external disturbances and/or inherent internal contradictions, a social system cannot continue to exist as before: its essential structures are under threat (Boin, 2004). Here, the identity and survival of 'society as we know it' are under threat. But crises not only affect social systems writ large, but may also be identified unfolding at various other scales and in various realms of human affairs. The threat may concern the physical, material, psychological welfare or security of a particular individual, family or population group. Or particular economic, social or political institutions may be in jeopardy: often we talk about a crisis in the markets, of the

Exploring crisis and migration   3

family, of government regimes, or the nation-state itself. Some crises are humanitarian emergencies, overwhelming people's capacity to cope without external assistance. Others are more political in nature, and may or may not translate into major suffering among the population. However, the term crisis generally implies a threat of some severity and pervasive impact across various scales and dimensions of human life and may be seen as 'ill-structured messes' of policy problem (Mitroff *et al.*, 2004: 175; Vigh, 2008).

Clearly, these key elements are subject to nuance and debate. Empirical facts 'require an *interpretative framework* for actors to make sense of them, and for specific events to be recognised as representing a "crisis"' (Broome *et al.*, 2012: 11). Different branches of social theory take rather different views of crisis.

Crises are a central and recurring feature of the painful progression of capitalism in Marxist analysis, part of its characteristic dialectic of creation and destruction (Marx, 1995; Harvey, 2011). Processes of primitive accumulation dispossess producers and force them to work as wage labourers, forming a cheap and flexible 'reserve army of labour' that facilitates industrial expansion, and the management of recurrent crises of accumulation. Debate continues about how cumulative crises can generate class struggle and alternatives to capitalism (Saad Filho, 2011).

By contrast, functionalist understandings of modern social order stretching back to Durkheim have interpreted the increasingly complex division of labour in industrial societies as leading to a new style of social integration, sometimes generating *anomie* and conflict as a temporary result of the rapid pace of change, but generally producing social systems that tend to be self-regulating and harmonious, underpinned by shared values and interdependent elements and practices (Giddens, 1971; Preston, 1996).

When post-Second World War optimism that the rest of the world could emulate Western-style modernisation began to run aground, neoclassical economics provided a modified, but still basically functionalist vision of development, emphasising the free movement of capital, goods and labour as ultimately leading to equilibrium and convergence (Friedman, 2002). Facing early resistance to their policy prescriptions of privatisation, deregulation and state reduction, neoliberal policy advocates concluded that: 'Only a crisis – actual or perceived – produces real change' (ibid.: xiv). Time and again, economic 'shock therapy' has been administered in contexts of crisis, transition, states of emergency, authoritarian rule and fragile post-conflict situations (Cramer, 2006; Klein, 2008; Van Hear, 2006). While providing lucrative opportunities for some, such reforms were experienced as a crisis by many people around the world. Nevertheless, crisis is often conceptualised within this framework as a disruption best managed by deepening neoliberal reform, rather than fundamentally challenging to the overall development vision (Williamson, 1994).

Thus, contrasting theories of social change and development critically shape understandings of crisis. The same system modification may be viewed as either triggering dissolution and system collapse, or as a learning process

4   *Anna Lindley*

and system modification, depending on the degree of importance the observer attaches to the maintenance of a static system identity (Habermas, 1976). Moreover, whereas the broadly 'developmentalist' approaches described above tend to conceptualise crisis in relation to progressive, on-going processes of change, others think about crisis rather as punctuating extended periods of statis viewed as characteristic of complex social systems (Baumgartner and Jones, 1993).

Approaches to studying crisis vary, but there are several broad lines of enquiry, albeit somewhat overlapping. They variously focus on triggers and exceptionality; wider structural processes; lived experiences; and political constructions of crisis. Conventional approaches tend to view crisis as an exceptional event disrupting normal liberal development pathways. This tends to go with a focus on specific triggers and consequences of crisis, as a necessary foundation for some form of pre-emptive or remedial policy response (Broome *et al.*, 2012). Efforts focus on the objective measurement of particular variables deemed to reflect discontinuity and threat, often at quite high levels of geographic aggregation. Use is made of some form of crisis threshold on continuous scales of measurement, deemed to approximate significant social shifts.[2] A basic challenge here is uncertainty: in severe crisis situations, data systems are often disrupted and there is a limited statistical evidence base (Boin, 2004).

While there is a strong association of crisis with more acute, rapid onset situations, these often have longer build-up periods and deeper structural causes that are not always fully acknowledged. Revisionist work challenges the notion of crises as exceptional events, and urges us to put crisis into context, taking a more process-oriented approach (Rosenthal, 2003). This requires tracking back from the triggering event(s), to understand underlying structural factors, processes of disintegration, and exploring the internal dynamics of crisis (Roux-Dufort, 2007). It shifts the focus from coping with consequences and victims to addressing causes and culprits (ibid.).

This kind of difference – between emphasising triggers and exceptionality, or structural processes – is reflected in contrasting analyses of violent conflict. For example, Collier *et al.* conceptualise civil war as 'development in reverse' (2003: i), an aberration of development with damaging consequences at home and abroad; they focus on identifying risk factors for conflict through analysis of large-scale datasets. More process-oriented political economy analysis suggests that violence may not be an aberration, but rather 'actually existing development', arising from the structural difficulties of late transitions to capitalism in a particular kind of global economic and political setting (Cramer, 2006; Duffield, 2007: 183).

A second approach focuses on the lived experiences and practices of people on the ground and on their perceptions and narratives of crisis, through 'bottom-up' research. This has contributed to a much more nuanced understanding of threats and their differentiated impact. Research shows how issues of entitlement and vulnerability shape people's experience of famine and violence (de Waal, 1997; Collinson, 2003). Even 'natural' disasters do not automatically

Exploring crisis and migration 5

translate into personal crises: much depends on people's capacity to cope, which in turn is mediated by policy responses (Wisner *et al.*, 1994; Hyndman, 2011). A micro-level view highlights that crises may produce opportunities as well as threats – in the course of disruption (for those able to successfully navigate or turn a profit from turmoil) or through the wider transformation of social frameworks and possibilities (e.g. reinforced status or upward/downward mobility of particular groups) (Lautze and Raven-Roberts, 2006).

Micro-level analysis also puts notions of discontinuity under the spotlight. If we consider 'what constructions of "normal times" conceal' (Greenhouse, 2002: 9), we may discover hidden crises affecting particular population groups, not broadcast by the media and political actors, showing that distinctions between entrenched vulnerability and a crisis situation are often highly political. Conversely, the crisis label may conceal significant continuities or the emergence of new normalities and routines for people on the ground. For example, while violent conflict is generally viewed as involving events which suspend normal social processes, the unpalatable truth is that, for many people, protracted conflict and displacement become '*the* normal – in the sense of "expected" – context for the unfolding of social life' (Lubkemann, 2008: 1). This highlights the dual aspect of normality, which is used to refer to what generally happens (a predominant state of affairs), and also reflects ideas about what *should* happen (a normative state of affairs) (Vigh, 2008).

In a discipline-shaping departure from anthropology's traditional emphasis on 'order and imponderability', a rich seam of ethnographic work has emerged examining experiences of crisis and upheaval (ibid.: 12). This has opened up the possibility of viewing crisis as a condition, focusing on the fragmentation of coherence and control which is the daily reality for many people around the world, rather than an interruption of an otherwise 'normal' existence (Greenhouse, 2002). Prolonged crisis creates high levels of uncertainty, displacing not only only people, but also familiar social processes and signifiers (ibid.). Thus, while physical mobility is a key element in many ethnographic accounts of crisis, arguably people whose social worlds radically change under their feet may effectively experience displacement without moving (Lubkemann, 2008). The goal shifts from putting crisis *in* context, to understanding crisis *as* context, as 'a terrain of action and meaning rather than an aberration', a point of departure for fine-grained focus on agency and how people seek new bearings in highly constrained circumstances (Richards, 2005; Vigh, 2008: 8).

Studying crisis from the 'bottom up', rather than based on 'objective' measures and indicators, may be viewed as complementary to, or prompt a critique of the latter. For example, in some cases, formal declarations of war, or much-vaunted transitions to peace, are relatively insignificant markers for people on the ground, for whom experiences of official armed conflict may be hard to clearly distinguish from endemic structural and social violence (Goodhand, 2006; Marriage, 2013).

A third approach puts the emphasis on unpacking the political construction of crisis. We can think about crisis not only as an analytical category, but also

6   *Anna Lindley*

as a category of practice and as part of the apparatus of governmentality (Burchell *et al.*, 1991; Jeandesboz and Pallister-Wilkins, Chapter 6 in this volume). Iterative acts of framing and interpretation by key actors link discrete events together to construct a crisis, imposing a form of cognitive order on instability, and rationalising it as exceptional (Broome *et al.*, 2012). Complex power relations underlie the processes of defining and identifying threats and keeping different forms of security in place (Fierke, 2007).

Political actors may be very active in the construction of a crisis, typically because it serves to justify, or reorient the dominant policy agenda in ways they deem desirable (Boin, 2004). A classic example is the 'moral panic', where politicians and the media identify a particular condition, episode, person or group as posing a threat to basic societal values and interests (Cohen, 2002). Research on mugging has shown how, in 1970s Britain, youth, crime and race were articulated into a crisis, based on questionable evidence, legitimating calls for a more coercive 'law-and-order' role for the state in a period of growing societal tension and conflict (Hall *et al.*, 1978). Immigrants, refugees and asylum-seekers have been the target of similar moral panics across Europe since the early 1990s (Cohen, 2002).

A more subtle aspect of the political construction of crisis is the use of depoliticising analogies of medical or psychological trauma, implying the need for therapeutic response to prevent pathological reactions, rather than political action (Brassett and Vaughan-Williams, 2012). Another common analogy is the extreme weather event, for example, the global financial crisis is often likened to a hurricane, diverting attention from the political reality of finance as 'the ongoing product of social interactions within structures of power' (Brassett and Vaughan-Williams, 2012: 25). Such metaphors imply that crisis is exceptional, unexpected, and outwith the control of political actors. On another track, there is a tendency in Western discourse to construct poorer countries as endemically crisis-ridden – without appreciating either the high level of people's resilience and adaptation to adverse conditions, or the global structural sources of the threats that they face (Bankoff, 2001; Duffield, 2007).

On the other hand, political actors may promulgate a 'business-as-usual' or non-crisis discourse, seeking to deny or minimise empirical experiences and objective indicators of severe threat and discontinuity, for instance, terrible and systematic violence may be dismissed as just crime by insulated elites. This is often the case where marginalised population groups (such as migrants) are disproportionately affected, or if dominant actors feel that declaring a crisis would undermine their authority or do little to help them deal with the situation. Thus, definitions and interpretations of normality and crisis take us to the heart of the politics of the time.

Popular cultural perceptions may align or conflict with state-political constructions of (non-)crisis. It is often hard to discern to what extent politicians are following or trying to shape public opinion in talking about crisis, particularly in relation to political references to an 'immigration crisis'. While the voices of ordinary people are quite often marginalised in the loud politics of crisis, social

Exploring crisis and migration 7

criticism and grass-roots counter-discourses may also deploy crisis terminology to problematise and politicise the status quo, highlight the discontinuity of social change, and draw attention to the significance of particular moments and decisions (Holton, 1987).

How key actors define and narrate crisis is often highly suggestive of what constitutes an appropriate response. The use of the term crisis typically implies a call to action which 'under time pressure and highly uncertain circumstances – necessitates making critical decisions' (Rosenthal *et al.*, 1989: 10). In this sense, the distinction between crisis identification and response may seem artificial: 'crisis *is* governance' as Brassett and Vaughan-Williams neatly put it (2012: 19). Responses to crisis situations may be formulated at the level of individuals, families and communities, or at wider institutional level, by local authorities, non-governmental organisations, businesses, government bodies, international organisations, or foreign states. Crisis management has become a flourishing commercial and policy field (Roux-Dufort, 2007). Responses may involve pre-emptive risk management or insurance (for example, household income diversification, instigation of drought early warning systems, or programmes to increase the resilience of vulnerable population groups). Often more obvious, however, are the ex-post, reactive interventions or coping strategies which attempt to address the immediate and worst consequences of the crisis (from household asset depletion to humanitarian interventions, border closures and bank bail-outs). Here, political actors may argue for exceptional measures as legitimate responses to exceptional threats (Bigo, 2002). Longer-term strategies to get out of the crisis may also unfold (for example, household livelihood adaptations; economic recovery policies; peace processes and reconstruction; refugees' durable solutions). These may focus on rebuilding pre-crisis forms of order, or on building alternative futures and addressing the structural causes of the crisis. Some actors may also use the designation of a crisis strategically to open up, reinforce or close down particular avenues of policy action (Broome *et al.*, 2012).

Migration?

Elements of exceptionality and threat also characterise common understandings of migration, as we shall see. In relation to the social world, 'migration' is conceptualised as human movement articulated in a particular way across space and time. Like all mobility, migration is a spatial phenomenon involving movement between distinct *places* – locations imbued with meaning and power (Cresswell, 2006: 3). Migration more specifically refers to people changing their *place of residence*, where they live on a habitual basis, embracing not only the actual physical structure, but also in some sense the wider community in which they live (Skeldon, 1997). Thus, the term is associated with the crossing of some kind of socially significant frontier.

Migration is clearly located in time as an identifiable event which occurs when a person moves physically from one place to another, though this act is

8   *Anna Lindley*

embedded in an array of earlier and subsequent social processes which are also viewed as facets of migration. Indeed, for migration to have occurred, a stay of some substantial duration is deemed necessary: rather than just visiting, the migrant is establishing some kind of a regular life in the place of destination, whether on an open-ended or more temporary basis (King *et al.*, 2010). Of course, individual migration trajectories vary: beyond the simplest pattern, of movement followed by permanent stay, migration also may involve return; back-and-forth, circular movements between places; step-wise, onward movement from place to place over time; and the construction of simultaneous translocal/transnational worlds (Skeldon, 1997).

Also central to understandings of migration is the purpose, or cause of movement. People move for a wide range of reasons. Migration for labour market opportunities is crucially important and is probably most prominent in academic and policy discussions. But family considerations, educational opportunities and adventure, climate and cultural preference, and very basic and immediate physical security issues can also drive migration. In crisis situations, the latter are often very salient. Typically, various factors come into play over time in shaping migration decisions, from more structural elements, to predisposing factors, immediate triggers, and intervening factors including social networks and immigration regimes elsewhere (Van Hear, 1998).

Although the precise boundaries of migration as a concept are somewhat blurred, there is a core of meaning which in some ways is easier to pin down than with the concept of crisis. However, this does not mean that the phenomenon is not highly politicised. Institutional frameworks powerfully shape how we understand migration in terms of space and time. Spatially, migration is commonly characterised by reference to a range of framings – internal/international, rural/urban, South/North – moulded by developmental and national thinking. The 'durable stay' element of migration is refined bureaucratically in national contexts (for example, some countries only classify a visitor as a migrant if they stay for a year or more) in ways that also influence data collection and research.[3]

Migration is heavily problematised, by contrast with immobility and more micro-mobilities (Carling, 2002; Cresswell, 2006). Migrant identity is often assumed to be a key explanatory variable in social processes and experiences, where in fact other distinctions (gender, age, race, class) may be more or equally important. Some people on the move (refugees and asylum-seekers, low-skilled workers, racialised minorities) are positioned as more migrant than others (business elites, highly skilled workers) (Guild, 2005). A commonly noted weakness of migration studies is the tendency to privilege policy categories ('temporary migrant worker', 'industrial trainee', 'refugee', 'internally displaced person', 'unaccompanied minor', and so on) as a starting point for research. For example, research on forced migrants has disproportionately focused on people living in refugee camps where they are visible to state bureaucracies and aid agencies. This 'constrain[s] the questions asked, the objects of study and the methodologies and analysis adopted' (Bakewell, 2008a: 432).

Exploring crisis and migration 9

Against this background, the chapters that follow try to illuminate the 'mobility environment' broadly speaking, including well-recognised and emphasised migration patterns, but also offering insights into immobility, people's diverse micro-negotiations of space and routine, and politically less visible migration patterns. We also try to move 'outside the policy box', often including as an object of analysis the institutional frameworks, policy processes and bureaucratic categories that tend to frame so powerfully how we see migration; and to some extent exploring migrants' negotiation of these frameworks, processes and categories.

The heavy institutional influence on thinking about migration makes sense in the context of a long history of viewing migration as dangerous, deviating from a spatial order which naturalises people's connections to place (Cresswell, 2006). This 'sedentarist metaphysics' represents migrants as rootless, politically suspect and potentially contagious, not domesticated within local forms of order or protection, posing a threat to otherwise cohesive families and communities (Malkki, 1992; Cresswell, 2006; Anderson, 2013). Nation-state formation and European colonialism gave strong impetus to this paradigm, with clearly demarcated borders territorialising identities and rights, albeit often through crisis and conflict (Arendt, 1951; Marfleet, 2006). While mobility (in the form of sedentarisation or expulsion of nomads and groups marginal or troublesome to the national narrative, the circulation of military and civil servants, and migration towards industrialising urban centres) was integral to these processes, at the same time, states work hard to fix people to place in ways that made them 'legible' and facilitated key state functions such as taxation, conscription and provision of services (Scott, 1998). Elevated mobility might be an inevitable and necessary part of the shift to a modern social order, but is also associated with the spectre of socio-political crisis. Migrants are still viewed as often poorly integrated into urban/national culture, emblematic of anomic existence, and a challenge to the cohesion of national political communities (Anderson, 1983; Papastergiardis, 2000; Favell, 2001). Refugees are particularly anomalous in the 'national order of things' (Arendt, 1951; Malkki, 1992).

In Marxist-influenced analysis, the link between migration and crisis is also very apparent, though theorised differently. The process of primitive accumulation is characterised by crisis and displacement, and migrants are a vital part of the 'reserve army' of labour, filling gaps in the labour market, keeping wages down, easily recruited or dismissed in response to fluctuations in the economic cycle helping to avert or manage crises (Cohen, 2006; Castles and Miller, 2009). Migrants are prominent in the precarious, flexible workforce, with employers seeing them as more pliable than local workers due to their more insecure political status (Standing, 2011). Thus migration is viewed as a symptom of uneven global development, tending to serve the interests of capital.

The rise of neoclassical economics marked the beginning of a series of more 'mobility positive' theoretical developments. Neoclassical economic theory assumes that the free movement of labour allows individuals to rationally

10   *Anna Lindley*

pursue their economic interests, enabling them to move in response to wage differentials, maximising their utility (Harris and Todaro, 1970). The revisionist micro-economic theory known as the 'new economics of labour migration' nuanced this considerably, suggesting that migration decisions were often made at the household level, and driven not only by income maximisation, but also often by the need to diversify income to manage shocks and crises (Taylor, 1999). This also put the spotlight on remittance flows, often deemed more stable (even counter-cyclical) in contexts of economic and political crisis than other financial flows (World Bank, 2006).

Critical reviews temper both downbeat and more celebratory accounts of migration, suggesting that it is best viewed as part and parcel of global processes of social transformation (Castles, 2010). Empirical research suggests that migration has highly context-specific, socially differentiated and policy contingent impacts 'back home' (de Haas, 2010). Meanwhile, studies of labour market demand and segmentation, and its combination with national social protection policies and other contextual factors, challenge the simplistic notion that migrant workers 'take local workers' jobs' in a zero-sum game (Ruhs and Anderson, 2010). Different scales and patterns of movement have complex and differentiated impacts in home and host areas, and on the migrants themselves.

On a distinct track, a blossoming of more agency-sensitive and inter-subjective approaches in the social sciences has enriched understandings of migration (Papastergiardis, 2000). More nuanced accounts of the association of people and place emerged in the 1990s, using concepts of identity formation, emplacement, transnationalism, mobilities, cosmopolitanism and hybridity, which go beyond conventional, territorially-bound and singular forms of family, identity and home (Basch *et al.*, 1994; Papastergiardis, 2000; Vertovec and Cohen, 2002; Hammond, 2004). These ideas challenge traditional scholarly notions of migration as precipitating a crisis of identity or alienation in the migrant, and as necessarily having an unsettling effect on the social milieu in which the migrant moves. The notion that migration necessarily causes a crisis of the family, for instance, has confronted studies of how people maintain family roles and relationships in the absence of physical cohabitation (Bryceson and Vuorela, 2002). At the wider social level, instead of being necessarily a disruptive phenomenon, migration can be seen as an 'on-going constitutive process within modernity' (Papastergiardis, 2000: 13), providing a counterpoint to analyses of 'high modernity' that emphasise the state pursuit of spatialised order (Scott, 1998; Cresswell, 2006).

These more recent mobility-positive strands of thinking combined in the 2000s to forge a new policy consensus on migration among international development policy-makers. Migration was distanced from notions of crisis, or indeed lauded as a bottom-up solution to long-term difficulties and recurrent crises faced in poor parts of the world and the crisis of development financing. The notion of migrants as development protagonists has appealed to diverse constituencies in development politics, but has received powerful impetus

Exploring crisis and migration 11

from neoliberal policy institutions, particularly the World Bank, consistent with their focus on deregulating markets and more recent emphasis on the role of civil society in development (World Bank, 2006; Faist, 2008). Policy-makers have emphasised market-based solutions to channel remittances, as part of broader processes of financialisation. Diaspora business and investment forums, and knowledge networks are assiduously promoted. Home town associations are viewed as a key element in transnational civil society, able to convey cash and ideas directly to the grassroots. More recently the development of temporary migrant worker programmes has been a key focus.

Overall the focus is on leveraging migrants' contributions to development 'back home', often with the underlying assumption that development in places of origin will eventually end migration (de Haas, 2007; Bakewell, 2008b). Less is said about freedom of movement, and little about migrants' rights. While passionate advocates of the deregulation of trade and finance, neoliberal reformers are less vocal about the free movement of labour: as Milton Friedman put it: 'About immigration, the least said the better' (quoted in Munck, 2008: 1239). The 'migration and development' policy agenda has emerged in ways heavily circumscribed by the interests of richer destination countries, which still fiercely guard migration control.

Many national policy-makers still view migration as a temporary and disruptive phenomenon, something that needs to be carefully managed, albeit with some useful and redeeming effects. In the context of a globalising economy progressively eroding state control of economic affairs, and faced with the structural unease of citizens on the hard end of neoliberal globalisation, states' control of foreigners' movement across territorial boundaries has become all the more important as a marker of authority and legitimacy (Bigo, 2002). With hermetically sealing borders unfeasible and economically undesirable, states focus instead on 'managing migration' by filtering migrants into different policy categories subject to distinct measures of control, surveillance and rights.

Many remark on the gap between rhetoric and reality when it comes to migration control, often viewing this as indicating a failure – indeed, even a crisis – of immigration policy. Some analysts suggest that immigration policies fail due to the inexorable forces of globalisation and constant migrant innovation, combined with policy-makers' misconceptions, ignorance or liberal constraint (Castles, 2004). Some suggest that states have in fact been extremely successful in their underlying goal of 'securitising' migration (formulating it as security issue, to be dealt with beyond the normal political arena, justifying exceptional measures) as a vehicle to reassert state authority and relevance in the face of global forces, regardless of the often deadly consequences to migrants (Bigo, 2002). Other research emphasises that immigration is like all areas of public policy: there is often a gap between public discourse and policy on paper; clear implementation of policies on paper is far from guaranteed; governments often deliberately fudge distinct and irreconcilable priorities into inconsistent policy packages; and the extent to which implemented policies affect migration is often uncertain, with a high degree of

12   *Anna Lindley*

opportunistic credit-taking for outcomes (Boswell and Geddes, 2010; Czaika and de Haas, 2013).

Crisis is a defining feature of understandings of forced migration. The concept of forced migration does not represent a clear analytical category, but rather brings together groups with some kind of 'family likeness': people displaced by persecution, conflict, natural disasters, development projects, and so on, who have diverse needs but a special moral claim on our attention (Castles, 2003; Turton, 2003). The causes of forced migration are often viewed as overwhelming, unpredictable and hard to theorise, and of interest primarily from a legalistic perspective, so as to locate the migrant within institutional frameworks (Bakewell, 2008a). However, there is growing interest in understanding better the interplay between structure and agency in processes of displacement, challenging the crude dichotomy of economic/voluntary versus forced/political migration (Monsutti, 2005; Lubkemann, 2008; Lindley, 2010).

While generally entry policies and packages of rights are determined by a combination of economic demand and domestic/regional politics, international and regional refugee law and human rights law carve out an important exception. People moving in the context of a well-founded fear of persecution for reasons of race, religion, nationality, social group or political opinion, or the threat of armed conflict, serious disturbances to public order or serious harm, are generally entitled to some form of refugee or related protected status, though coverage and practice vary considerably (Gibney, 2004). Thus, *particular types of crises* where the state is no longer willing or able to guarantee basic protections to its citizens may trigger special international protection.

A major contemporary issue is that in contexts of protracted conflict and displacement, instead of obtaining the 'durable solutions' of repatriation, resettlement or local integration, refugees are often warehoused in camps for many years, with a stifling effect on their rights and life goals. But though refugees are still often portrayed as aid-dependent victims, many are clearly active – and mobile – in the pursuit of a better life (Monsutti, 2005; Horst, 2006; Lubkemann, 2008).

Another issue is the 'protection gaps' that arise from inadequate coverage or implementation of existing refugee and human rights provisions, or from situations where people are driven to migrate by overwhelming factors which nevertheless fall outside protection frameworks, such as severe economic stress, or slow-onset environmental change (Van Hear, 2009). For example, the concept of 'survival migration' was introduced to refer to international migration resulting from a range of crises – environmental crisis, livelihood collapse, and state fragility – which pose an existential threat, and for which migrants have no domestic remedy (Betts, 2010).

It is in this context that notions of 'crisis migration' and 'migration crisis' are acquiring strong currency.[4] The notion of 'crisis migration' embraces classic disaster and conflict situations but also widens the focus outwards. It was used, for example, to describe the Albanian exodus in the 1990s, where some 20 per cent of the population emigrated in the wake of the challenges of

Exploring crisis and migration   13

the post-communist transition, poverty and economic instability, surging criminality and disastrous pyramid selling (King and Mai, 2008). The term has also been used to describe the massive out-migration prompted by Zimbabwe's economic free-fall, soaring inflation and unemployment, political oppression, public service collapse and spiralling poverty (Crush and Tevera, 2010). The 'Crisis Migration Project' at Georgetown University focuses on movement in the context of *humanitarian crises* where there is 'a widespread threat to life, physical safety, health or basic subsistence that is beyond the coping capacity of individuals and the communities in which they reside', as a point of departure for exploring normative and implementation gaps in the protection of vulnerable people on the move (Martin *et al.*, 2014: 5).

A Christian Aid report used the term 'migration crisis' to draw attention to diverse patterns of forced movement, to rally policy action (Christian Aid, 2007). The International Organisation for Migration (IOM), an inter-governmental organisation, uses the term 'migration crisis' to describe

> large-scale, complex migration flows due to a crisis which typically involve *significant vulnerabilities* for individuals and communities affected. A migration crisis may be sudden or slow in onset, can have natural or man-made causes, and can take place internally or across borders.
>
> (IOM, 2012: 9, emphasis added)

IOM has reoriented a major plank of its thinking and operations around the notion of 'migration crises', trying to integrate humanitarian and migration management frameworks in their response.

While these approaches tend to foreground the vulnerabilities of people on the move, references to migration crises which threaten communities and social systems in destination areas are also increasingly salient. Conflict and displacement are increasingly seen as potential sources of regional instability (Loescher *et al.*, 2008). Often large numbers of migrants are seen to increase pressure on jobs, public services and natural resources, fuelling popular and political backlashes against immigration and migrants themselves (Anderson, 2013). The key contours of Weiner's 'global migration crisis' (Weiner, 1995) – including a perception of weakening control over entry, difficulties 'absorbing' migrants, tensions arising over migration in international relations and regimes, and acute moral dilemmas between human rights and national interest – are live concerns among policy-makers today.

Approach and themes

This book engages critically with the articulation of migration and crisis in different settings. It is an attempt to bring together some thought-provoking perspectives, rather than a comparative research project with a single conceptual and methodological framework, which might focus on a particular type of crisis/ migration interface or a particular scale of analysis. Across diverse settings,

14   *Anna Lindley*

we investigate two broad questions. First, what is the nature of the association that people make between migration and crisis, and who responds to the 'crises of migration' identified, and how? Second, what do the 'crises of migration' identified reveal about the wider processes and politics of change, crisis and migration?

There are two common elements in our approaches. First, we examine how concepts of crisis and migration unfold and coalesce in the contexts we study, rather than taking these for granted: this means paying close attention both to how people actually experience the 'crises of migration' identified and how these situations are structured and constructed politically. Second, the contributions are empirically and historically grounded: drawing on first-hand research into key contemporary contexts, the authors situate their analysis in the context of longer histories of social change and mobility in the places affected.

Chapters 2–4 begin by exploring how crises generate migration. With recent Arab migrations cast as a threat in European destinations, Philip Marfleet and Adam Hanieh turn the tables in Chapter 2, charting the history of the 'migration-crisis nexus' in the Middle East and North Africa. This highlights the often over-looked role of external influence (in the form of colonial, neoliberal and recent politico-military interventions) in shaping processes of regional change and migration over the last 200 years. They also explore socially differentiated experiences of migration, particularly in Egypt, revealing how temporary migration has become a permanent survival strategy for vulnerable people.

Questions of timeframes are also critical in Chapter 3, in which Laura Hammond and I challenge the dominant narrative of Somalia as being in 'constant crisis', which lurked behind representations of the massive movement which occurred in the context of the 2010–11 drought. Based on contradictory evidence of dramatically shifting socio-political landscapes over the past 25 years, they highlight the political functions of a 'constant crisis' framing for various international and domestic actors. Meanwhile, they show how evidence on Somali mobility – multi-causal, differentiated, strategic and central to social change – challenges conventional framings of movement in conflict-affected settings. As hopes for political consolidation spark a focus on return, they suggest how these insights might inform contemporary policy-making.

While the Somali situation has long been seen as catastrophic, in Chapter 4, Laura Rubio Díaz-Leal and Sebastián Albuja focus on a crisis downplayed. Challenging the dominant view of Mexican migration as economically motivated movement northwards, they highlight the major internal displacement associated with a surge in violence and insecurity which has been generated by confrontations between the government and the drug cartels since 2007. Their chapter uses opinion polls and narrative research to show how this violence has been experienced as a major crisis by ordinary citizens across Mexico, and presents statistical evidence linking the violence to significant new trends in internal migration. Despite all this, the government has

Exploring crisis and migration 15

systematically denied the severity of the situation, in an attempt to protect its domestic political legitimacy and international credibility. The resulting policy inertia means that the crisis continues: people continue to be displaced, and receive minimal assistance, transmitting pressures to receiving areas.

Chapters 5–7 turn, broadly speaking, to destination settings. In East Asia, Dae-oup Chang focuses on the impact of the global economic crisis on migrant workers. He questions the common notion that migration is a temporary feature easily halted or reversed in the context of economic crisis, challenging early expectations that the global economic crisis would trigger a reverse migration crisis in East Asia. Instead the regionalising circuit of capital in East Asia has ensured continued structural demand for migration. Echoing evidence from the Asian financial crisis of 1997–98, there is evidence of some effect on migration indicators in major labour-importing countries, but this is less significant or prolonged than one might expect, or the government rhetoric suggests. Meanwhile, a much-overlooked aspect of the recent crisis is the strong additional impetus it has provided to the on-going development of a more assertive political subjectivity among migrant workers.

Also dissecting host state responses to migration, in Chapter 6, Julien Jeandesboz and Polly Pallister-Wilkins set out how the Arab uprisings were immediately constructed as an immigration crisis for the European Union. They argue that political emphasis on crisis enables the adoption and practice of emergency measures, while in fact masking the continuation of routine practices of immigration control. Further, they show how crisis labelling sets particular spatio-temporal limits on migrant experiences, which veil the wider forms of structural inequality that drive much contemporary mobility.

By contrast, in Chapter 7, Iriann Freemantle and Jean Pierre Misago examine how the South African government framed the wave of anti-outsider violence in 2008 as a 'non-crisis' or 'just crime', denying the existence of xenophobia as a major structural problem, despite the displacement of some 100,000 people. At the same time, the government claims the country is facing an immigration crisis, positioning foreigners as antagonistic to South Africa. It formulates social cohesion as a problem of inherited racial division, effectively denying the relevance of other forms of politicised difference. The authors argue that these stances ignore important evidence, and together work to legitimise xenophobic violence, allowing social instability to fester and recur.

The final two chapters, Chapters 8 and 9, engage specifically and directly with the institutional frameworks dealing with refugee movements. In numerous instances, mass influxes of crisis-induced migrants are met with claims of migration-induced crisis, and border closures. In Chapter 8, Katy Long looks at why and how states close their borders in these situations, and the consequences. Focusing on three border closures – Turkey/Northern Iraq in 1991, Macedonia/Kosovo in 1999, and Kenya/Somalia from 2007 to 2011 – she argues that the language of national refugee crisis is often deployed by governing elites to mask and manage subnational discontents. However, in the very real humanitarian emergencies that can result from these situations, the international community

16   *Anna Lindley*

often fails to challenge the border closure itself, instead responding with new and ingenious programmes (such as in-country safe zones and humanitarian evacuation). Humanitarian action thus serves to mask the politics of border closure, and hide the role that nation-state structures play in producing refugee flows.

Finally, based on ethnographic research in a protracted refugee situation, in Chapter 9, Tania Kaiser focuses on how the notion of crisis is articulated in relation to the family, by different social actors. Humanitarian and institutional actors typically frame crisis in terms of the immediate physical and security needs of refugee groups, responding with technical and material solutions. Restoring family unity is seen as a key goal. By contrast, this chapter shows how Sudanese refugees both experience and manage crisis through the family, transforming and adapting family relations in protracted displacement, even dispersing further in pursuit of individual and collective goals.

Together, these chapters suggest that wherever the terms crisis and migration are linked, some pause for nuanced and critical reflection is worthwhile. Among the many issues addressed, four broad themes emerge, which should inform future research: social change and transformation; politicisation; spatialisation; and nexus hazards.

Social change and transformation

Crisis and migration do not appear here as isolated, anomalous events, but as processes firmly embedded in wider patterns of social change and transformation. The crisis–migration dynamics explored connect closely with, for example, histories of colonialism, nation-state formation, de-agrarianisation, industrialisation, urbanisation, deregulation of trade, financialisation, labour market flexibilisation, global and regional geopolitical shifts, demographic shifts, and climate change. We look beyond immediate triggers, and explore combinations and culminations of factors that produce and shape crisis and migration. This often involves putting aside common typologies of crisis and migration as 'economic', 'political' or 'environmental' to explore issue interconnections and complex causation.

Crisis analysis often overlooks migration, recognising it as a consequence of crisis, but seeing it as marginal to how crisis unfolds, a side issue to be relegated to the attention of specialists in migration, human rights and humanitarian issues. By contrast, these chapters show how migration is central to how people experience and respond to crisis – showing how individuals, families and communities use mobility in sometimes pre-emptive, often reactive, and other times more strategic fashion. Thus, mobility becomes an important lens through which we can understand crisis. Crisis may disrupt, intensify, or otherwise shape routine social and migration patterns, practices and differentiation, and may have changing effects as it unfolds. At policy level, crisis-mode responses may either reflect or provide a break with predominant modes of governing migration. In retrospect, legacies become clear: crises may simply

Exploring crisis and migration   17

punctuate or build on fairly stable migration patterns and practices; or they may mark a major turning point in a migration system (see also Van Hear, 1998).

Politicisation

The intensely political construction of the relationships between crisis and migration is a strong theme running through the book. Time and again, governments make strenuous efforts to construct migration situations as crises, for example, scapegoating or securitising migrants as a means of channelling domestic discontent and cementing the power of dominant elites. At the same time, depoliticising analogies abound, with migration in contexts of crisis frequently compared to extreme weather events (floods, tsunamis, avalanches of people on the move), portraying the situation as exceptional and unexpected, tending to disassociate political actors from responsibility for causing it. The language of humanitarian response, in focusing on dealing with needs and consequences, rather than addressing causes, also often functions to divert attention from questions of domestic and international responsibility.

Crisis construction is often a prelude to securing political consent or material support for emergency migration measures: draconian immigration restrictions, border closures, mass deportation, protracted encampment, discretionary protected statuses, or humanitarian interventions. Gaps between rhetoric and reality are common: evident both in instances where restrictive, crisis rhetoric is belied by the permeability of borders on the ground, as well as in instances where much-vaunted liberal human rights principles are belied by deaths at the border and denial of protection (see also Boswell and Geddes, 2010; Castles, 2004).

Meanwhile, the contributors also highlight the existence of 'business-as-usual' discourses in contexts as diverse as South Africa, Mexico and Somalia, normalising crisis, downplaying aspects of migration experiences, especially where acknowledgement would undermine the domestic legitimacy and international credibility of political leaders, or reveal the damaging or inadequate nature of international responses.

Moreover, in the face of these rather well-mapped stances on the part of dominant actors, Chang's and Kaiser's chapters show that more research is needed on the responses of migrants to crisis and categorisation. These situations may be scenes not only of suffering, but also of the emergence of new dimensions of political subjectivity, agency and resistance (see also Zetter, 1991; Novak, 2007; Polzer and Hammond, 2008).

Spatialisation

Research and policy tend to link crisis and migration in two key ways: focusing on migration in the wake of a crisis in the country of origin; and migration as generating crisis in a place of destination. But our contributions highlight a range of less-emphasised 'spatialisations'. Viewed from places of

18   *Anna Lindley*

origin, the immobilising effect of crises is often overlooked. People may be unable or afraid to leave conflict-ridden territories, or come up against heightened political restrictions on internal or international mobility imposed as a result of crisis (see also Lubkemann, 2008).[5] Out-migration may act as a safety valve, dispersing the unemployed and the politically restive, helping to *avert* a crisis, or alternatively may be viewed as contributing to a crisis of labour or skills shortages, disarticulation of families and communities. While repatriation is often taken as a signal that a crisis is over, it may itself help consolidate or rather put untimely pressure on precarious political settlements (Long, 2013).

What happens when crises hit migrants' places of residence also merits investigation. As jobs disappear, or as the environment becomes insecure, often migrants return 'home', or move onwards. Many states engage in strong migration restriction and deportation to ensure this occurs, in an attempt to mitigate the impact of crisis on the local population. However, evidence suggests that in many difficult situations, substantial numbers of migrants actually do stay put, and try to weather hard times: they may hope things will look up, and fear that if they leave, it could be expensive and difficult to come back; often because of the structural demand for migrant labour, they are still able to work. Indeed, in many major host areas an exodus of migrants would substantially undermine the economic model, public services and social stability.

Several contributions highlight the significance of the 'spatial fixing' of crisis, which often occurs in methodologically nationalist ways, and how by shifting this, other realities are brought into focus. For example, by focusing on an immigration crisis, we may overlook the much more severe and 'real' forms of crisis-generating movement. Camps, while providing a site of initial refuge, may become a site of crisis themselves. Migrants in transit and migrants displaced by crisis in their place of *residence* are often omitted from analysis. Regionalising our analysis may reveal how migration and migrants' transnational connections can act as a transmission belt, displacing the impact of crises rapidly across space. At the same time, in some instances similar processes – be it regional drought or global recession – affect home and host areas, generating complex migration pressures and counter-pressures.

Nexus hazards

Finally, reading through these chapters will tend to encourage a circumspect approach to notions of 'crisis migration' and 'migration crisis'. To its credit, the term crisis migration has an intuitive resonance and draws attention to the often complex causation of migration in difficult contexts. It forces us to think across and beyond the standard policy categories which so strongly structure thinking about migration in difficult settings, and may yet prompt innovation in policy approaches aiming to support the vulnerable (Martin *et al.*, 2014).

On the other hand, to the extent that the crisis at the root of a migration pattern remains a nebulous and complex phenomenon, this may effectively

Exploring crisis and migration 19

depoliticise migration, masking causes and responsibility. As with the shift from 'refugees' to 'forced migration', the looser notion of 'crisis migration', even when intended to highlight protection gaps, is not underwritten by a clear international legal framework, and may tend to resonate more with controlled-oriented migration management agenda rather than rights-based protection approaches (Hathaway, 2007).

It is significant that much of the emerging policy work on crisis migration is driven by the challenges of migration in countries of *destination* – indeed 'crisis migration' and 'migration crisis' are often used interchangeably in policy literature – the mobility of the crisis is part of what puts it on the international agenda (IOM, 2012; Koser, 2012). Migration undoubtedly in some instances exerts major pressures in destination areas: these are complex and differentiated, and systematic assessments are often thin on the ground. However, the chapters that follow also point to the diverse functions of 'immigration crises' from the point of view of political actors. Time and again the resulting restrictions constrain people's attempts to cope with crisis through mobility. All this underscores the real dangers of uncritical approaches to articulations of crisis and migration.

Notes

1 In medicine, crisis usually refers to a decisive point in the course of an illness.
2 For example: one definition of civil war proposed that it must *inter alia* cause 500–1,000 deaths in the first year (sustained at 1,000 for the next two years), involve politically and militarily organised parties with identifiable leadership and publicly stated objectives, and include the government as a combatant (Sambanis, 2002; cited in Cramer, 2006).

   The UN definition of an 'acute food and livelihood crisis', used in the monitoring of food security, includes a crude mortality rate of 0.5–1/10,000 per day, acute malnutrition affecting 10–15 per cent of the population, as well as accelerated and critical depletion or loss of access to livelihood assets. (The two worst food security classifications outlined by the Food and Agriculture Organisation's 'Integrated Phase Classification' are humanitarian emergencies and famine.)

   While the term economic crisis is often used in a rather imprecise fashion, economists typically define a recession as two successive quarters of falling GDP, and depression as a more sustained, long-term downturn where real GDP declines more than 10 per cent or the recession lasts more than three years (*The Economist*, 2008).
3 This narrow definition tends to exclude a considerable amount of movement – for example, on a seasonal basis – that we commonly refer to as migration (King *et al.*, 2010).
4 A rather earlier academic reference to 'migration crises' interestingly defined these as acute disruptions to a *migration order* (an otherwise reasonably stable configuration of factors underlying migration), often triggered by catastrophic events, and entailing 'sudden, massive, disorderly population movements' (Van Hear, 1998: 23).
5 Another neglected pattern – not addressed in this book, but worth more exploration – is the specialist immigration of aid workers, medical personnel, military and 'disaster capitalists', which may be small numerically but significant politically (Klein, 2008).

20   *Anna Lindley*

References

Anderson, B. (1983) *Imagined Communities: Reflections on the Origins and Spread of Nationalism*. London: Verso.

——(2013) *Us and Them? The Dangerous Politics of Immigration Control*. Oxford: Oxford University Press.

Arendt, H. (1951) *The Origins of Totalitarianism*. New York: Harcourt Brace and Company.

Bakewell, O. (2008a) 'Research Beyond the Categories: The Importance of Policy-Irrelevant Research into Forced Migration', *Journal of Refugee Studies* 21: 432–53.

——(2008b) '"Keeping Them in their Place": The Ambivalent Relationship Between Development and Migration in Africa', *Third World Quarterly* 29: 1341–58.

Bankoff, G. (2001) 'Rendering the World Unsafe: "Vulnerability" as Western Discourse', *Disasters* 25: 19–35.

Basch, L., Glick Schiller, N. and Szanton Blanc, C. (1994) *Nations Unbound: Transnational Projects, Postcolonial Predicaments and Deterritorialized Nation-States*. London: Routledge.

Baumgartner, F. and Jones, B.D. (1993) *Agendas and Instability in American Politics*. Chicago: University of Chicago Press.

Betts, A. (2010) 'Survival Migration: A New Protection Framework', *Global Governance* 16: 361–82.

Bigo, D. (2002) 'Security and Immigration: Toward a Critique of the Governmentality of Unease', *Alternatives: Social Transformation and Humane Governance* 27: 63–92.

Boin, A. (2004) 'Lessons from Crisis Research', *International Studies Review* 6: 165–94.

Boswell, C. and Geddes, A. (2010) *Migration and Mobility in the European Union*. Basingstoke: Palgrave Macmillan.

Brassett, J. and Vaughan-Williams, N. (2012) 'Crisis is Governance: Subprime, the Traumatic Event, and Bare Life', *Global Society* 26: 19–42.

Broome, A., Clegg, L. and Rethal, L. (2012) 'Global Governance and the Politics of Crisis', *Global Society* 26: 3–17.

Bryceson, D. and Vuorela, U. (2002) *The Transnational Family: New European Frontiers and Global Networks*. London: Berg.

Burchell, G., Foucault, M., Gordon, C. and Miller, P. (eds) (1991) *The Foucault Effect: Studies in Governmentality*. Chichester: Harvester Wheatsheaf.

Carling, J. (2002) 'Migration in the Age of Involuntary Immobility: Theoretical Reflections and Cape Verdean Experiences', *Journal of Ethnic and Migration Studies* 28: 5–42.

Castles, S. (2003) 'Towards a Sociology of Forced Migration and Social Transformation', *Sociology* 37(1): 13–34.

——(2004) 'Why Migration Polices Fail', *Ethnic and Racial Studies* 27: 205–27.

——(2010) 'Understanding Global Migration: A Social Transformation Perspective', *Journal of Ethnic and Migration Studies* 36(10): 1–22.

Castles, S. and Miller, M.J. (2009) *The Age of Migration: International Population Movements in the Modern World*. Basingstoke: Palgrave Macmillan.

Christian Aid (2007) *The Human Tide: The Real Migration Crisis*. London: Christian Aid.

Cohen, R. (2006) *Migration and its Enemies: Global Capital, Migrant Labour and the Nation-state*. Aldershot: Ashgate.

Cohen, S. (2002) *Folk Devils and Moral Panics*. London: Routledge.

Exploring crisis and migration 21

Collier, P., Elliot, V., Herge, H., Hoeffler, A., Reynal-Querol, M. and Sambanis, N. (2003) *Breaking the Conflict Trap*. Washington, DC: World Bank.

Collinson, S. (2003) 'Power, Livelihoods and Conflict: Case Studies in Political Economy Analysis for Humanitarian Action', *Humanitarian Policy Group Report*, No. 13. London: Overseas Development Institute.

Cramer, C. (2006) *Civil War Is Not a Stupid Thing: Accounting for Violence in Developing Countries*. London: Hurst.

Cresswell, T. (2006) *On the Move: Mobility in the Modern Western World*. New York: Routledge.

Crush, J. and Tevera, D. (eds) (2010) *Zimbabwe's Exodus: Crisis, Migration, Survival*. Cape Town: Southern African Migration Project.

Czaika, M. and de Haas, H. (2013) 'The Effectiveness of Immigration Policies', *Population and Development Review* 39(3): 487–508.

de Haas, H. (2007) 'Turning the Tide? Why Development Will Not Stop Migration', *Development and Change* 38: 819–41.

——(2010) 'Migration and Development: A Theoretical Perspective', *International Migration Review* 44: 227–64.

de Waal, A. (1997) *Famine Crimes: Politics and the Disaster Relief Industry in Africa*. Oxford: James Currey.

Duffield, M. (2007) *Development, Security and Unending War*. Bristol: Polity Press.

Faist, T. (2008) 'Migrants as Transnational Development Actors: An Inquiry into the Newest Round of the Migration-Development Nexus', *Population, Space and Place* 14: 21–42.

Favell, A. (2001) *Philosophies of Integration: Immigration and the Idea of Citizenship in France and Britain*, 2nd edn. Basingstoke: Palgrave.

Fierke, K.M. (2007) *Critical Approaches to International Security*. Cambridge: Polity Press.

Friedman, M. (2002) *Capitalism and Freedom*. Chicago: University of Chicago Press.

Gibney, M. (2004) *The Ethics and Politics of Asylum*. Cambridge: Cambridge University Press.

Giddens, A. (1971) *Capitalism and Modern Social Theory: An Analysis of the Writings of Marx, Durkheim and Weber*. Cambridge: Cambridge University Press.

Goodhand, J. (2006) *Aiding Peace? The Role of NGOs in Armed Conflict*. Rugby: Intermediate Technology Publications.

Greenhouse, C.J. (2002) *Ethnography in Unstable Places: Everyday Lives in Contexts of Dramatic Political Change*. Durham, NC: Duke University Press.

Guild, E. (2005) 'Cultural and Identity Security: Immigrants and the Legal Expression of National Identity', in E. Guild and J. van Selm (eds) *International Migration and Security*. London: Routledge, pp. 101–12.

Habermas, J. (1976) *Legitimation Crisis*. Oxford: Polity and Blackwell.

Hall, S., Critcher, C., Jefferson, T., Clarke, J. and Roberts, B. (1978) *Policing the Crisis: Mugging, the State, and Law and Order*. Basingstoke: Macmillan Press.

Hammond, L.C. (2004) *This Place Will Become Home: Refugee Repatriation to Ethiopia*. Ithaca, NY: Cornell University Press.

Harris, J.R. and Todaro, M.P. (1970) 'Migration, Unemployment and Development: A Two-Sector Analysis', *American Economic Review* 60: 126–42.

Harvey, D. (2011) *The Enigma of Capital and the Crises of Capitalism*. London: Profile Books.

Hathaway, J. (2007) 'Forced Migration Studies: Could We Agree Just to "Date"?'*Journal of Refugee Studies* 20(3): 349–69.

22　Anna Lindley

Holton, R.J. (1987) 'The Idea of Crisis in Modern Society', *The British Journal of Sociology* 38: 502–20.

Horst, C. (2006) 'Refugee Livelihoods: Continuities and Transformation', *Refugee Survey Quarterly* 25(2): 6–22.

Hyndman, J. (2011) *Dual Disasters: Humanitarian Aid After the 2004 Tsunami*. Sterling, VA: Kumarian Press.

IOM (2012) 'Moving to Safety: Migration Consequences of Complex Crises', Background Paper for the International Dialogue on Migration 2012, IOM.

King, R., Black, R., Collyer, M., Fielding, A. and Skeldon, R. (2010) *People on the Move: An Atlas of Migration*. Berkeley, CA: University of California Press.

King, R. and Mai, N. (2008) *Out of Albania: From Crisis Migration to Social Inclusion in Italy*. Oxford: Berghahn Books.

Klein, N. (2008) *The Shock Doctrine*. London: Penguin Books.

Koser, K. (2012) 'Protecting Migrants in Complex Crises', GCSP Policy Paper No. 2012/2. Geneva: Geneva Centre for Security Policy.

Lautze, S. and Raven-Roberts, A. (2006) 'Violence and Complex Humanitarian Emergencies: Implications for Livelihoods Models', *Disasters* 30: 383–401.

Lindley, A. (2010) 'Leaving Mogadishu: Towards a Sociology of Conflict-Related Mobility', *Journal of Refugee Studies* 23: 2–22.

Loescher, G., Milner, J., Newman, E. and Troeller, G. (eds) (2008) *Protracted Refugee Situations: Politics, Human Rights and Security Implications*. Tokyo: UN University Press.

Long, K. (2013) *The Point of No Return: Refugees, Rights, and Repatriation*. Oxford: Oxford University Press.

Lubkemann, S.C. (2008) *Culture in Chaos: An Anthropology of the Social Condition in War*. Chicago: University of Chicago Press.

Malkki, L. (1992) 'National Geographic: The Rooting of Peoples and the Territorialization of National Identity among Scholars and Refugees', *Cultural Anthropology* 7(1): 24–44.

Marfleet, P. (2006) *Refugees in a Global Era*. Basingstoke: Macmillan Press.

Marriage, Z. (2013) *Formal Peace and Informal War: Security and Development in Congo*. London: Routledge.

Martin, S., Weerasinghe, S.S. and Taylor, A. (eds) (2014) *Humanitarian Crises and Migration: Causes, Consequences and Responses*. London: Routledge.

Marx, K. (1995) *Capital: A New Abridgement*. Oxford: Oxford University Press.

Mitroff, I.I., Alpaslan, M.C. and Green, S.E. (2004) 'Crises as Ill-Structured Messes', *International Studies Review* 6(1): 165–94.

Monsutti, A (2005) *War and Migration: Social Networks and Economic Strategies of the Hazaras of Afghanistan*. London: Routledge.

Munck, R. (2008) 'Globalisation, Governance and Migration: An Introduction', *Third World Quarterly* 29: 1227–46.

Novak, P. (2007) 'Place and Afghan Refugees: A Contribution to Turton', *Journal of Refugee Studies* 20: 551–78.

Papastergiardis, N. (2000) *The Turbulence of Migration: Globalization, Deterritorialization and Hybridity*. Cambridge: Polity Press.

Polzer, T. and Hammond, L. (2008) 'Invisible Displacement', *Journal of Refugee Studies* 21(4): 417–31.

Preston, P.W. (1996) *Development Theory: An Introduction*. Oxford: Blackwell Publishers.

Exploring crisis and migration 23

Richards, P. (ed.) (2005) *No Peace, No War: An Anthropology of Contemporary Armed Conflicts.* Oxford: James Currey.

Rosenthal, U. (2003) 'September 11: Public Administration and the Study of Crises and Crisis Management', *Administration & Society* 35: 129.

Rosenthal, U., Charles, M.T. and t' Hart, P. (1989) 'The World of Crises and Crisis Management', in U. Rosenthal (ed.) *Coping with Crises: The Management of Disasters, Riots, and Terrorism.* Springfield, IL: Charles C. Thomas.

Roux-Dufort, C. (2007) 'Is Crisis Management (Only) a Management of Exceptions?', *Journal of Contingencies and Crisis Management* 15(2): 105–14.

Ruhs, M. and Anderson, B. (eds) (2010) *Who Needs Migrant Workers? Labour Shortages, Immigration, and Public Policy.* Oxford: Oxford University Press.

Saad Filho, A. (2011) 'Crisis in Neoliberalism or Crisis of Neoliberalism?', *Socialist Register* 47: 242–59.

Sambanis, N. (2002) *Defining and Measuring Civil War: Conceptual and Empirical Complexities.* New Haven, CT: Yale University, Department of Political Science.

Scott, J.C. (1998) *Seeing Like a State: How Certain Schemes to Improve the Human Condition Have Failed.* New Haven, CT: Yale University Press.

Skeldon, R. (1997) *Migration and Development: A Global Perspective.* Harlow: Longman.

Solimano, A. (2010) *International Migration in the Age of Crisis and Globalization.* Cambridge: Cambridge University Press.

Standing, G. (2011) *The Precariat: The New Dangerous Class.* London: Bloomsbury.

Taylor, E.J. (1999) 'The New Economics of Labour Migration and the Role of Remittances in the Migration Process', *International Migration* 37(1): 63–88.

The Economist (2008) 'Diagnosing Depression', 30 December.

Turton, D. (2003) 'Conceptualising Forced Migration', *Refugee Studies Centre Working Paper*, No. 12. University of Oxford.

Van Hear, N. (1998) *New Diasporas: The Mass Exodus, Dispersal and Regrouping of Migrant Communities.* London: UCL.

——(2006) 'Conclusion: Re-casting Societies in Conflict', in N. Van Hear and C. McDowell (eds) *Catching Fire: Containing Forced Migration in a Volatile World.* Lanham, MD: Lexington Books, pp. 213–22.

——(2009) 'Managing Mobility for Human Development: The Growing Salience of Mixed Migration', Human Development Research Paper, No. 20. New York: UNDP.

Vertovec, S. and Cohen, R. (2002) *Conceiving Cosmopolitanism: Theory, Context and Practice.* Oxford: Oxford University Press.

Vigh, H. (2008) 'Crisis and Chronicity: Anthropological Perspectives on Continuous Conflict and Decline', *ETHNOS* 73(1): 5–24.

Weiner, M. (1995) *The Global Migration Crisis: Challenge to States and to Human Rights.* New York: HarperCollins.

Williamson, J. (ed.) (1994) *The Political Economy of Policy Reform.* Washington, DC: Institute for International Economics.

Wisner, B., Blaikie, P., Cannon, T. and Davis, I. (1994) *At Risk: Natural Hazards, People's Vulnerability and Disasters.* London: Routledge.

World Bank (2006) *Global Economic Prospects 2006: Economic Implications of Remittances and Migration.* Washington, DC: World Bank.

Zetter, R. (1991) 'Labelling Refugees: Forming and Transforming a Bureaucratic Identity', *Journal of Refugee Studies* 4, 39–62.

2 Migration and 'crisis' in the Middle East and North Africa region

Philip Marfleet and Adam Hanieh

The Arab uprisings that erupted in late 2010 and early 2011 have been closely associated in public consciousness and policy-making circles with a series of migration crises within and beyond the Middle East (see Jeandesboz and Pallister-Wilkins, Chapter 6 in this volume). Population movements arising from upheavals in Tunisia, Egypt, Libya and Syria have been seen as a challenge to migration policies and to the well-being of 'receiving' societies. Some movements have been viewed not merely as crisis in themselves but as episodes that foreshadow the destabilisation of entire regions. In the case of migration across the Mediterranean from Tunisia in 2011, Italian government ministers declared a national emergency and warned that other European states – and the continent as a whole – were at risk. Italy's interior minister, Roberto Maroni, invoked imagery in use since the time of the Crusades, declaring that political change in North Africa had prompted 'an exodus of biblical proportions' (*Der Spiegel*, 2011). This, he pronounced, threatened the fabric of Italian society and would have 'devastating consequences' for Europe (BBC News, 2011a). Italian Prime Minister Silvio Berlusconi meanwhile warned that Milan was 'besieged by foreigners' and could turn into 'an Islamic city' (BBC News, 2011b). Other European leaders adopted a less apocalyptic tone but joined the Italians in enforcing new border controls directed primarily against people attempting to enter Europe from the Middle East and North Africa (MENA) region. For politicians who advocated these exclusions, cross-Mediterranean migrations were crises by definition: 'unplanned, unwelcome, destabilising and threatening' (Marfleet and Cetti, 2013).

In contrast to a perspective that sees migration as a danger arising within the region to threaten Europe's borders, this chapter shows how migratory movements in and from the Middle East are often associated with developments in which external actors play a key role. We describe this linkage as a *migration–crisis nexus*, in which mass movements of people are inseparable from major social, economic and political changes that have characterised the region since the colonial period. Approaching the movement of people in the Middle East in this context reframes the terrain of debate, revealing how such changes – and major migrations – are not an outcome solely of internal dynamics but are associated with wider influences, notably those of powerful states and corporate interests. The Middle East is not unique in this respect: linkages between mass migration and economic/political change have become more and more evident as an agenda for global development driven by neo-liberal principles is implemented worldwide. The Middle East is distinguished, however, by certain historic continuities: the legacy of European colonialism and its abrupt re-ordering of the region into nation-states, the focused interest of imperial and neo-imperial powers in energy resources, and a recent history of powerful external politico-military interventions. The outcome is a complex pattern of multiple migrations, including mass displacements within and across borders.

The term 'crisis' is used freely in daily discourse. It appears prominently in political debate and in mass media, where its associations with danger, difficulty, instability and uncertain outcomes make the word attractive for headline writers and for summary accounts of complex situations. All manner of developments become 'crises', especially when addressed in the widest contexts – 'international crisis', 'world crisis', 'global crisis'. Moore (2012: 1) notes the importance of migrants to contemporary crisis narratives which, she observes, 'populate news media around the world as emergencies and longer-term "migration crises"'. Since the emergence of the modern nation-state and of ideologies of nation associated with fixed borders, territorial integrity and a sedentary norm, most migrants have been viewed as transgressors (Marfleet, 2007a, 2013). This characterisation has recently become more marked – a development associated with globalisation and its influence on those who wish to exert authority locally and internationally/transnationally. The global order is – paradoxically – a world of disorder and increasing uncertainty. Baumann (2004: 66) suggests that 'uncertainty and anguish born of uncertainty are globalization's staple product'. States and international agencies which once acted with assurance have diminished powers and seek to assert themselves by new measures of control, especially in relation to migrants. The latter are an irresistible target. Migrants with bodily form (rather than those merely evoked as threat) have historically been people characterised by their vulnerability. Denied means to contest ideological and material measures used against them, they have often been 'a screen on to which all manner of evils can be projected' (Kundnani, 2001: 48).

Migration 'crises' have become focal points for the exercise of crisis management – interventions which aim to ameliorate global dangers and to restore order. This approach has had a profound impact on academic research in the field of migration, which is often dominated by institutional concerns and pressures to produce analyses which can serve policies of migration control. In the case of forced migration, argues Black (2001: 67), much research has been reduced to 'policy studies', producing work that is methodologically questionable, theoretically underdeveloped and 'fundamentally unsuited even to the task of influencing the policy world'.

In this chapter we consider migration in the MENA region in a different context, seeing migrants as social actors whose circumstances and experiences are integral to understanding patterns of movement. We ask: Who has moved?

26 *Philip Marfleet and Adam Hanieh*

What prompted their journey/s? What is the impact on their lives? What is the relationship between their movements and wider socio-economic and political forces? Here 'crisis' has an experiential character. For some migrants, changes that prompt their journeys are unwelcome or even threatening, and migration itself is undesired and dangerous; for others, change is positive, presenting new opportunities, including those offered by migration. For others, meanwhile, migration is a social practice associated less with change than with routines of family or community life. A distinguishing feature of migration in the MENA region is the evident link between political and economic change and large-scale migrations, among which many involve journeys under constraint. For almost 200 years the Middle East has witnessed multiple external interventions and mass migrations, among which some have repeatedly targeted vulnerable populations: the migration–crisis nexus is part of the dynamic of social life in an exceptionally turbulent region.

The analysis below begins with an overview of human mobility in the MENA region before European colonial intervention. It considers the impact of Europe and the long process by which colonial powers 'unmixed' people of the Middle East. The second part of the chapter turns to a more recent expression of the migration–crisis nexus – the relationship between political economies of neoliberalism and movements of people both within and from the region. Drawing upon an examination of Egypt's political economy and upon recent research in the Nile Delta, we discuss how migration has become both a survival strategy for vulnerable Egyptians and a mechanism transmitting new pressures to their communities of origin.

'Unmixing' of peoples

It is less than a century since colonial powers dismantled the structures of the Ottoman Empire and in their place created a swathe of new nation-states. Following the First World War, they divided the Ottoman regions of the Arab East, imposing new state borders on the basis of preferences determined entirely in London and Paris.[1] As elsewhere in the 'colonial' world, new borders violated all manner of economic and socio-political arrangements, including complex patterns of human movement. Pastoralism had been practised across vast areas of the MENA region, especially in semi-arid zones, and was integrated with the urban economy and with settled agriculture.[2] Major cities were linked by historic trade routes – part of ancient networks described by Abu-Lughod (1991) as 'circuits of commerce' that operated across Africa, Asia and Europe. At focal points within the MENA networks, cities such as Aleppo, Damascus, Alexandria, Cairo, Baghdad, Basra, Istanbul, Salonica and Tunis were at the hub of sub-regions that were also administrative units of the empire. Hourani (1991: 231) describes the empire as 'a vast trading area, in which persons and goods could move in relative safety, along trade routes maintained by imperial forces'. The major routes were pathways along which passed not only agricultural products, manufactured goods, livestock and

money, but also merchants, artisans, labourers, soldiers, sailors, imperial administrators, clerics, scholars and vast numbers of pilgrims. The Mediterranean in
particular was a commercial highway and a migratory path linking the Asian,
African and European portions of the empire and adjacent regions. One feature of
socio-cultural life was an associated 'cosmopolitanism' – an accommodation
of diverse ethno-religious and linguistic communities particularly characteristic
of the major cities and expressive of continuous migratory movements within
and beyond the empire (Zubaida, 1999; Chatty, 2010).

These arrangements were formalised by the Ottoman *millet* system. The
empire was ruled by Muslim dynasties in accordance with preferred versions
of Sunni tradition and *shari'a* but other religious groups – notably a host of
Christian and Jewish currents and sects – operated as semi-autonomous
communities linked to co-religionists elsewhere in the region. Ethno-religious
groups often undertook specific economic and socio-political roles. Ottoman
rulers conscripted boys from Christian villages of the Balkans whom they
enrolled in elite military forces (Janissaries) which served across the empire.[3]
In Anatolia and Mesopotamia, Christian communities – mainly Armenians,
Assyrians and Chaldaeans – were associated with fine artisan work of historic
importance to the trading networks. In major commercial centres, Jews –
including many Sefardim whose ancestors had been refugees from Spain and
Portugal – were prominent in finance and long-distance trade. Jewish
merchants of Alexandria, whose networks were based in the Maghreb, played
a key role in trading textiles and agricultural products (Reimer, 1997: 27). In the
case of Salonica, Mazower comments (2004: 53), '[Muslims] administered the
city, the Jews ran its economy. It was a division of labour that suited both sides
and the city flourished.' Human mobility across complex migratory networks
was integral to this system, which survived (albeit with numerous local
upheavals, secessions and re-integrations) for almost 400 years.

From the mid-nineteenth century the empire was under enormous pressure,
especially in its Balkan provinces. Most of western and central Europe had
already been 'nationalised' – divided among a series of modern states which
replaced the mosaic of local fiefdoms, monarchies and religious authorities of
the pre-modern era. By the 1820s, similar developments were affecting the
Ottomans' Balkan provinces, strongly encouraged by the European powers and
by the Russian Empire, which disputed Ottoman influence around the Black Sea
and in Caucasia. A long process of fragmentation began, with independent or
semi-independent states emerging successively in Greece, Romania, Serbia,
Bosnia, Montenegro and Bulgaria. Each state-making project involved new
migrations: these, however, were mass forced migrations undertaken by
people excluded from membership of new national collectives. The novelty of
the nation-state formation lay in assertion by those in authority (or who
aspired to such authority) of criteria for membership of the nation in relation
to which the state (or putative state) made claims on loyalty. This required
identification of distinct Others – external and internal enemies against whom
the national collective could be measured.[4] In the case of the Ottoman

28　*Philip Marfleet and Adam Hanieh*

Empire, with its diverse ethno-religious and linguistic groups, the impact was explosive. A series of secessionist movements achieved varying degrees of independence from the empire, each producing massive population displacements as 'non-national' groups were expelled en masse from 'national' territories. The experience was one of profound crisis – of eviction of large populations by means of what would later be called ethnic cleansing. Chatty (2010: 73) describes the impact in Bulgaria in the 1870s:

> Some 515,000 Muslims, almost all Turkish-speaking (generally now called Turks), were driven out of Bulgaria into other parts of the Ottoman Empire. They were the victims of a kind of state-sponsored programme of rape, plunder, and massacre by Bulgarian revolutionaries, Russian soldiers (especially Cossacks), and Bulgarian peasants. In the end, 55 per cent of the Muslims of Bulgaria were either killed or evicted.

Similar developments affected the northern Balkans and – under the impact of Russian military offensives – the southern Caucasus. During the 1870s, a million people were displaced within these regions. Statistics compiled by Ottoman officials also showed that, over the course of 20 years from 1876, a million refugees moved within the remaining territories of the empire: they included long-distance migrants such as expellees from the Balkans who travelled to Syria and large communities of Circassians (various Muslim groups from the Caucasus) who settled in the Jordan Valley (Chatty, 2010: 73–4, 99). British colonial administrator Lord Curzon was later to refer to these changes, and to the continuous displacements which followed, as 'the unmixing of peoples' – a redistribution, under the impact of nationalism and imperial rivalry, of diverse groups of people who had hitherto lived in amalgamated communities (Marrus, 1985: 41). It is in this sense that, in the nineteenth century, major migrations were associated with crisis – they were unwilled mass movements consistent with the appearance across the region of novel state structures and of strongly contested national ideologies and agendas for belonging.[5]

Chatty comments that, by the 1870s, mass displacement and forced migration had already become 'the characteristic mark of nationalism' across the Middle East (Chatty, 2010: 73). The process was given further impetus by the emergence of Turkish nationalism and the intervention of Britain and France during and after the First World War. Under the terms of the Sykes–Picot agreement of 1916 – a secret arrangement to divide the Arab East between the two powers – new states of Syria, Lebanon, Iraq and Trans-Jordan were to be established, with Palestine allocated an indeterminate status as a proto-state under British mandate authority. Turkish nationalists meanwhile succeeded in creating a new state entity in Anatolia and in a fraction of the Ottomans' European territories around Istanbul. The process was extraordinarily violent. Across Anatolia and in the neighbouring regions of the Arab East, there were intensive campaigns which aimed to remove unfavoured populations. In the Balkans, most victims of this process had earlier been Muslims; now most

Migration and 'crisis': Middle East, N Africa 29

were members of Christian and Jewish communities. Armenian communities experienced a genocidal offensive and there were repeated assaults on Assyrian Christians and members of the small heterodox Christian groups and syncretic sects of eastern Anatolia and northern Mesopotamia. Many of these 'minority' groups fled, seeking refuge in regions to the south which were soon divided among the new states planned by Britain and France and established formally in the early 1920s. In this chaotic situation some ethno-religious groups were privileged with 'national' or proto-national status; others were specifically denied such status. The settler Jews of Palestine, most of European origin, were offered a 'national home' by the British government;[6] the Armenians were denied a nation-state, as were the Kurds of the Zagros region at the eastern limits of the Ottoman Empire, whose resistance to centralised rule in the new state of Iraq met with sustained repression from British forces. In the new states, ruling groups (most led formally by a European-appointed monarch) set about policing new borders and inhibiting population movements which they viewed as a challenge to their authority. Key historic trading links were seriously affected: commercial centres such as Aleppo, Mosul, Beirut, Akka and Istanbul were separated by new territorial borders and the efforts of new rulers to develop centralised national economies and political structures. Cross-border movements in general were affected, so that the mobility of pastoral people was progressively inhibited, while pilgrims who had hitherto passed unhindered on journeys to shrines and sacred sites were confronted by multiple border controls. For those who enforced these measures, such people were important only to the extent that they provided means of asserting authority: they were, in effect, the human materials upon whom new borders were drawn.

The 'exchange' of peoples

Throughout the nineteenth and early twentieth centuries the most influential state actors in the region – Britain, France and Russia – worked energetically to support secession from Ottoman rule. Movements for independence were portrayed as reforming initiatives that challenged an enfeebled, backward empire. In this view, the nation-state project in the Balkans and the Middle East was relatively uncomplicated: it was an expression of Progress in the Enlightenment tradition, contesting reaction in general and Islamic 'backwardness' in particular. At the same time, the European powers were competitive, using the Middle East as an arena for playing out wider rivalries. Edward Said (1978: 191) comments:

> Standing near the center of all European politics in the East was the question of minorities, whose 'interests' the [European] Powers, each in its own way, claimed to protect and represent. Jews, Greek and Russian Orthodox, Druzes, Circassians, Armenians, Kurds and various small Christian sects: all these were studied, planned for, designed upon by the European Powers improvising as well as constructing their Oriental policy.

When ethno-religious conflicts emerged in the Arab East, rival powers were quick to intervene: in the case of Lebanon in the 1860s, France supported the Christians while Britain backed the Druze. The 'unmixing' of peoples was part of the colonial project in general *and* an expression of hostilities between European powers. Combining and eliding issues of nation, state and 'race', European governments also projected onto 'the East' their own problems of maintaining order among domestic populations (Turner, 1994).[7]

The impacts of state-making were felt for decades. In the 1920s, there were mass forced migrations across the Aegean – 'exchanges' of population that removed historic communities of Greek-speaking Christians from Anatolia and of Ottoman Muslims from mainland Greece and the Aegean islands. Almost 1.5 million people were reallocated to 'national' territories in projects of ethnic cleansing endorsed by international agreement in the form of the Treaty of Lausanne. This ended conflicts between the contending powers of the First World War that had continued after the failed Treaty of Sèvres; it also recognised new borders, formalising processes of ethnic cleansing. Migrations continued: hundreds of thousands of European settlers moved to Palestine and in Iraq British forces responded to Kurdish uprisings with strategies including village clearances – an important precedent for post-colonial campaigns of mass displacement. Rulers who had been imposed by the colonial powers meanwhile struggled to consolidate centralised control. Their efforts were typically organised around systems of patronage that drew on Ottoman models but were focused on privileging specific ethno-religious groups and networks within the apparatus of state. This approach had been used by European powers across the colonial world but was carried to new extremes in the MENA region. France placed a Christian sect – the Maronite Catholics – in positions of privilege in Lebanon, and Britain consolidated Sunni Muslim hegemony in Iraq.

Across the MENA region new diasporas were meanwhile in formation, reflecting further 'unmixing' of Ottoman society: Armenians, Assyrians, Kurds and Jews were among those who undertook multiple journeys and attempts at settlement. In Palestine, continuous displacements of the urban and rural populations as the result of European settlement culminated in the *nakba* of 1948, forcing some 750,000 Palestinians into neighbouring states.[8] A further nation-state entity appeared, with the Zionist movement establishing a Jewish enclave which excluded not only the majority of Palestinians (Muslims, Christians, Druze and others) but also former refugees such as Circassians who had been expelled by Russia over 50 years earlier.[9] 'Nationalisation' of the region had produced repeated mass displacement, so that forced migration was an integral feature of the process of political change.

Using oral histories of migrations of the early and mid-twentieth century, Chatty (2010) demonstrates that for those affected, these were life-changing experiences. Rendered highly vulnerable by their initial displacement, the Armenians, Palestinians and Kurds (and, to a lesser extent, Circassians and Chechnyans) became targets for state bodies that wished to assert their

Migration and 'crisis': Middle East, N Africa 31

authority over volatile populations. Many experienced multiple displacements, as forced migration became an instrument of control for regimes across the region. The migration–crisis nexus was experienced as a succession of migrations, sometimes repeated across the generations.

More migrations

A further series of migrations now took place: movements that were part of an intensive process of change associated with economic expansion following the Second World War. The epicentre was the Arab Gulf, where newly discovered oilfields represented a huge prize for those who could assert their influence in the region, notably corporations based in the United States and Western Europe. Here new states were also established, their construction facilitated in part by earlier mass migrations. They emerged at breakneck speed, with state infrastructure – civil administration, education and technical expertise – provided initially by Palestinians, especially those expelled in 1948. Ibrahim (1982: 45–8) comments:

> [Palestinians'] uprootedness and the usurpation of their country make it more likely for them to settle temporarily with their dependents wherever they happen to find employment. This ... has made them the most influential migrant community in oil-rich countries.

By 1970, more than half the total workforce in Kuwait, Bahrain, Qatar and the United Arab Emirates was composed of migrants, of whom the majority were Palestinians (ibid.: 49). Although this pattern was soon changed by mass immigration from South Asia and South-East Asia, Palestinian refugees played the key role in the early development of the petro-economies and continued to occupy important roles as professionals and administrators. This was an important precedent: if in the mid-nineteenth century mass displacement had become a key feature of the MENA region, 100 years later a new pattern was evident, that of 'mixed' migrations. These combined people who had been compelled to migrate by political upheavals – such as the Palestinians – with others who had more complex motivations, including those solicited by migration agencies to travel or to resettle in order to meet demands for labour.

Until the mid-1970s, most states of the Middle East inhibited what might broadly be called 'labour migration'. After decades of sustained efforts to construct new 'national' economies, those in authority were reluctant to release their citizens to travel outside state borders. In the case of Egypt, comments Lesch (1990: 93), highly restrictive migration policies reflected concern 'that all of Egypt's manpower was needed to promote economic and social development'. In 1967, just 80,000 Egyptians lived abroad, most as teachers and professionals (ibid.: 93). In that year, however, Arab states in general experienced major political shocks – an outcome of war with Israel

32   *Philip Marfleet and Adam Hanieh*

and of intense criticism of governments whose projects of national development had ended in military defeat and economic failure. Egypt was first to respond with efforts to stimulate emigration – a means to address economic problems and rising political anger, especially among the young. Within a decade, there were some 600,000 Egyptians working abroad: 10 years later the figure was 3.5 million (ibid.: 92). State incentives to migrate were aimed ostensibly at tackling Egypt's employment problems and at securing remittances; at the same time, suggests Ibrahim (1982: 93), they fulfilled a 'political venting function', taking 'restless elements' to states of the Gulf and to Libya, which was also experiencing oil-fed growth. Migrations associated with 'development' were now increasingly difficult to distinguish from those prompted by political instability. When, in 1980, Iraq invaded Iran, initiating a long war between the two countries, millions of Egyptians were recruited into the Iraqi workforce: in 1976, there had been 32,500 Egyptians in Iraq; by 1985, numbers had risen to 1.25 million (Lesch, 1990: 92).

The Iran–Iraq War was associated with profound problems of instability in post-colonial Iraq. Initiated by the Saddam Hussein regime, it was primarily a response to the impact in Iraq of the Iranian revolution of 1979. The Ba'thist regime which came to power in Iraq in 1968 had inherited a state shaped by the British in which ethno-religious difference was exploited by those in power to maintain networks of patronage serving certain Sunni Muslim networks at the expense of the wider population, especially Shi'a Muslims, Kurds, Christians and heterodox Islamic sects.[10] The Iranian revolution, with its appeal to Shi'a traditions of dissidence, prompted anxiety among Iraq's Sunni rulers, who responded with an invasion of Iran aimed at asserting Iraqi national unity. The war intensified mass migrations under way since the early 1970s, when the regime had used mass population displacement as a means to weaken Kurdish nationalist influence. During the conflict, millions of Kurds and Shi'a Muslims were moved forcibly from their regions of origin, sometimes replaced by 'loyalist' Sunni Muslims who occupied their homes and land. Struggling to cohere a national entity constructed upon sectarian privilege, the Ba'thists continued to use population displacement as an instrument of rule. When a coalition of forces under American leadership invaded Iraq in 2003, forcing a change in the balance of power from Sunni to Shi'a networks, they too prompted mass ethnic cleansing, for the architecture of the colonial state still influenced processes of political change.[11] Millions of Iraqis crossed state borders in the largest refugee movement since the *nakba* of 1948, demonstrating how external interventions continued to impact upon the region. Iraqis seeking security in Syria and Jordan found themselves alongside other historic refugee populations, including Palestinians, Armenians, Kurds and Circassians. In the case of Damascus, those who settled in the Muhajireen ('Immigrants') district discovered a quarter of the city that had been established 150 years earlier to accommodate migrants expelled from the Balkans and re-settled by the Ottoman authorities.

Neoliberal reform and poverty in Egypt

Mass movements of population have been part of the process through which the modern political order has emerged in the MENA region. In more recent times, the importance of migration to social processes has been accentuated by movements of people connected to the transformation of the region's economy. Over the last two decades, all countries in the region have moved (at varying speeds) to adopt neoliberal economic policies such as privatisation, labour market deregulation, accommodation of foreign direct investment, increasing integration into global financial markets, reduction of tariffs and other barriers to trade, and cuts to social spending. Neoliberalism has generated successive waves of instability, creating conditions under which millions of people have moved within states and across borders. In turn, migration movements have influenced the ways in which outcomes of neoliberal policy are experienced by broad swathes of the population.

Egypt provides the ideal vantage point from which to examine these processes. It has been the regional model for neoliberal reform – indeed, the Egyptian government under President Husni Mubarak was listed as one of the world's top ten 'best reformers' by the World Bank each year from 2006 to 2009. From the 1970s onwards, liberalisation produced sustained pressure on most Egyptians, with varying impacts according to socio-economic status, regional location, age and gender. One outcome was a massive level of internal and international migration. By 2009, according to World Bank figures, Egypt was the largest receiver of remittances in the Middle East (US$7.8 billion), making up around 5 per cent of the country's GDP (IOM, 2009).

Egypt had been deeply affected by the retreat of the colonial powers and the rise of Arab nationalism during the 1950s and 1960s. In 1952, a military coup led by Colonel Gamal Abdel-Nasser and the Free Officers Movement led to the ousting of British-backed King Farouk. By 1954, Nasser had gained control of the Egyptian state and instituted a series of measures aimed at nurturing the growth of a local state capitalism (Abdul-Fadil, 1980; Vitalis, 1995). The key focus of Nasser's policy was an attempt to weaken the power of the landed class through the redistribution of land, while simultaneously strengthening an emerging business elite that was closely connected to – and often overlapped with – the state apparatus itself. These measures received widespread popular support, and reinforced other policies aimed at establishing Egypt's definitive break with British colonialism (symbolised dramatically by the 1956 nationalisation of the Suez Canal). Politically the Nasser regime consciously destroyed mass political mobilisation through a twin strategy of institutional cooptation of opposition parties and trade unions into the state apparatus, and imposition of repressive laws that outlawed strikes and independent political organisations (Abdalla, 1985; Botman, 1988; Beinin, 1990). The majority of Egypt's population nonetheless experienced an improvement in living conditions and developed expectations of a better future.

34 Philip Marfleet and Adam Hanieh

Following Nasser's death in 1970, his successor Anwar Sadat launched a new set of policies that were known as *infitah* (opening). These marked the beginning of neoliberalism in Egypt: they focused on opening the economy to foreign investment through providing tax exemptions for joint ventures with international firms; liberalising foreign trade; and transferring state-run economic activities to a much more autonomous private sector (Bush, 1999; Mitchell, 2002; Wurzel, 2009). Those who benefited were segments of the Egyptian business elite favoured by the state in earlier years; the highest echelons of the state apparatus itself, notably top military officers; and a growing commercial business sector involved in import–export (Hanieh, 2011).

A particularly important focus of Sadat's policies was the rural sector. In 1970, he passed a decree aimed at returning ownership of land redistributed under Nasser to the private owners of the colonial era. Egypt's highest court, the Council of State, ratified this measure in 1974 and granted financial compensation or restitution of property to large landowners (Forte, 1978: 276). Laws remained, however, that limited the size of holdings allowed for any one individual – though this was circumvented by landowners who registered land in the names of family members. Sadat also changed the structure of rural cooperatives, so that farmers were no longer able to elect their own representatives, with the result that larger landholders enjoyed greater influence over decision-making in the countryside. Despite these measures, Egyptian tenants had rights to remain on the land and were guaranteed fixed and relatively low rents (Bush, 2004).

After Sadat's assassination in 1981, the situation in rural areas became increasingly precarious. Sadat's successor as president, Husni Mubarak, progressed steadily towards further neoliberal reform and in 1990 adopted a structural adjustment programme negotiated with the IMF which set the scene for more radical change. There were two main features of this policy as they related to agriculture (Hanieh, 2013). The first was the liberalisation of agricultural pricing mechanisms. Previous policies that capped prices for essential inputs such as fertilisers were abolished and the Egyptian government no longer guaranteed the purchase of crops at set producer prices. Private companies increasingly provided agricultural services and controlled the supply and distribution of rural products on the basis of market mechanisms. The second key feature was a sustained attempt to sell off state-owned or collective land to private farmers. The process was marked by the passage of Law 96 (1992), which allowed landlords to evict tenants and lifted caps on rural rents. Landlords were also permitted to sell land without informing or negotiating with tenants (Bush, 2004). As a result, rents increased by 300–400 per cent in some areas and over a third of all tenant families in Egyptian rural areas (around 1 million households) lost their rights to the land (USAID, 2010: 6). Law 96 was enthusiastically backed by the World Bank and the IMF as part of a general policy to establish a market in rural land and private property rights in agriculture. A USAID-sponsored study congratulated the Egyptian government for passing the law, which it saw as

Migration and 'crisis': Middle East, N Africa   35

doing away with 'more than 40 years of an imbalanced relationship between landlords and tenants' (RDI, 2000: 1).

Another set of neoliberal reforms aimed at dismantling Egypt's state sector. Before *infitah*, all university and secondary school graduates had been guaranteed work in state-owned enterprises (SOE). Under Sadat, this practice was abolished, though the state sector continued to employ the majority of formal workers until the early 1990s. As part of structural adjustment policies, however, many of these SOEs were privatised: one result was that the number of workers in public sector companies fell by half between 1994 and 2001 (Joya, 2008). In 2006, the IMF claimed that policies of privatisation had 'surpassed expectations' (IMF, 2006) – yet their effect on much of the Egyptian population was a severe decline in employment stability and general working conditions.

These measures brought significant change in rural areas – experienced as what might be called a 'permanent crisis' in agrarian relations. By 2010, 45 per cent of the smallest farmers owned only 10 per cent of the land, with an average holding of less than 1 feddan; among the largest landholders 3 per cent owned more than 10 feddan, controlling one-third of Egypt's entire agricultural area (AfDB, 2010: 10). When examined in the context of gender, these patterns are even more unequal, with females constituting only 5.72 per cent of the total number of landholders in the country (FAO, 2005: 284). Having enjoyed the most radical reforms in the Middle East during the Nasser era, Egypt's rural population was now confronted by inequalities in land ownership which were among the most striking in the Middle East.

Levels of rural poverty in Egypt rose sharply, becoming significantly higher than in urban areas – according to the World Bank, by 2000, rural poverty exceeded urban poverty by a factor of 2.4: by 2008, the figure was 2.8.[12] Some 60 per cent of the poor in Egypt live in rural areas – half in Upper Egypt. Much poverty is concentrated among agricultural labourers, landless farmers and farmers owning less than half a hectare (USAID, 2010: 6). Under the Mubarak regime, the deterioration in rural living conditions was compounded by very high levels of political violence that accompanied implementation of the new neoliberal agricultural measures, especially Law 96. According to figures provided by Egyptian NGOs, between January 1998 and December 2000, incidents associated with eviction of tenants resulted in 119 deaths, 846 injuries and 1409 arrests (Bush, 2004: 15). Violence has become a permanent part of rural life: one NGO, Sons of the Soil Land Center, recorded 270 people killed resisting dispossession from their land in 2010 – up from 197 in 2009 (Glain, 2012).

At the same time, social conditions deteriorated in urban areas. A June 2009 study by the Egyptian Centre for Economic Studies found that when the minimum wage was expressed as a percentage of per capita gross national product, it 'decreased from nearly 60% in 1984 to 19.4% in 1991/92 and further to 13% in 2007' (Abdelhamid and El Baradei, 2009: 9). This measurement of the minimum wage refers, moreover, to the formal sector, and thus significantly *overstates* the real wages received by much of the population. It was

36   *Philip Marfleet and Adam Hanieh*

nevertheless one of the lowest in the world – compared to 78 per cent in Turkey, 51 per cent in France and 26 per cent in Spain (ibid.: 10).

According to official Egyptian government statistics, the number of people living on less than $1.25 a day increased from 16.7 per cent to 21.6 per cent from 2000 to 2009 (Rashwan, 2010). This is a significant increase but official statistics need to be approached with caution. As a consequence of labour market deregulation, an estimated 40 per cent of Egypt's workforce is found in the informal sector, which is not well captured in official poverty measures (Ramalho, 2007: 61). Some estimates suggest that around 40 per cent of the Egyptian population earn less than $2 a day (Achy, 2010). The former head of the Economic Analysis Section of the United Nations Regional Office in Beirut, Ali Kadri, estimates that 'real' unemployment (including disguised, hidden and under-employment) surpasses 50 per cent (Kadri, 2011). There is a disproportionate impact on youth: conservative estimates suggest that some 60 per cent of the unemployed in Egypt are young people (IMF, 2011: 39).

'Permanent' migrations

It is in this context that migration has become a major mechanism of survival for millions of Egyptians. Migration grew rapidly during Sadat's *infitah*, which coincided with demands for labour from the Gulf states. Freedom to seek work overseas was made a constitutional right in 1971 and the requirement for exit visas for Egyptian nationals was abolished in 1974. Special training centres were set up under the 1978–82 Five Year Plan to equip potential migrants with the necessary skills and incentives put in place (such as special bonds for workers in the Gulf) to encourage investment of remittances. By 1979, overseas remittances had reached the same level as Egypt's combined earnings from cotton, the Suez Canal and tourism (Zohry, 2003). During this period migration involved skilled labour such as teachers, engineers, medical personnel and veterinarians, who travelled to Arab countries (particularly the Gulf states), as well as unskilled labour to countries such as Libya and Iraq (which hosted the largest number of Egyptian workers until the 1990–91 Gulf War). In 1976, between 10 per cent and 14 per cent of the Egyptian labour force was estimated to be working overseas: the absolute number of workers abroad doubled over the following decade (Collyer, 2004: 11). The vast majority of these temporary international migrants were males (at least 90 per cent according to an estimate provided in Zohry, 2005: 34). Large numbers of Egyptians also departed to Jordan where they worked in agriculture and construction (in part, filling the position of Jordanian residents who had left to go to the Gulf). In 1986, it was estimated that Egyptians constituted 87 per cent of all agricultural workers in the Jordan Valley (east of the Jordan River) (Chatelard, 2004). By the late 1990s, Arab migrant workers (mostly Egyptian) made up a fifth of Jordan's workforce (Abu Jaber, 1997: 86).

These sustained cross-border labour flows led to what has been termed 'the permanence of temporary migration' in Egypt (Farrag, 1999: 55). They

Migration and 'crisis': Middle East, N Africa 37

represented an attempt by millions of people to address pressing socio-economic problems; at the same time they were encouraged by successive regimes which sought to ameliorate potential social upheaval, for the state 'welcomed the activities of emigrants who concentrated on making money instead of making revolution' (Marfleet, 2006: 92). Despite fluctuations in migration outflows as a result of political developments in receiving states, Egyptian governments have continued to rely upon emigration as a key element in development strategy. The International Organisation for Migration (IOM) noted in 2011 that 3.9 million Egyptians were living abroad, some 5 per cent of the country's total population (IOM, 2011). Between 1970 and 2008, Egypt was the largest recipient of remittances from overseas workers of all countries in the MENA region (Naufal and Varga-Silva, 2012: 380).

It is difficult to compile statistical data on the place of origin of Egyptian migrants, especially as much migration takes place by means of multiple journeys. Nonetheless, it is clear that many journeys begin in rural areas. Severe pressure upon rural dwellers produced by neoliberal reform and by accompanying socio-political violence has been a crucial factor contributing to these movements (Adams, 1989). A study of undocumented child migration from Egypt's Delta region undertaken by Save the Children UK (SCUK) in 2012 confirms this relationship.[13] The project focused on villages from which an increasing number of unaccompanied minors have attempted to cross the Mediterranean Sea to Italy and other destinations in Europe. The charity's researchers recorded testimony of villagers in Oyun, Beheira Governorate. Here, they learned, rents had recently risen to 6,000 Egyptian pounds (LE) per feddan from the earlier relatively stable level of LE500. The cost of fertiliser had also increased sharply, while prices of Egyptian products for export had greatly decreased. As a result, they were told, young people were increasingly abandoning agricultural work to travel abroad. Among those who returned, some were able to buy agricultural land and build houses, a development perceived negatively by local residents. Sami, a young man from the neighbouring village of Itay-El Barud, said: 'At the time of Abdel-Nasser and Sadat, we used to plant so much. But now the lands have reduced because of greed. [Those] who have ... agricultural land ... build on it.' SCUK observes that the area available for agriculture is steadily being reduced, prompting more young people to migrate abroad and stimulating further building development (SCUK, 2012). Here are all the signs of disarticulation of a rural society in which, despite continuous processes of change, the *fellaheen* (cultivators) had for generations remained in contact with the land.

These migrations are associated with processes of cumulative causation, in which population movements reinforce a form of path-dependency that makes further migration more likely and strengthens transnational networks. In some villages of the Delta, migration has become a rite of passage, with communities expectant that young males will make cross-Mediterranean journeys to secure resources required not only for family survival but also for the *shabka* (wedding gift) and the dowry required to secure a bride.[14] In this

38   *Philip Marfleet and Adam Hanieh*

region – and in certain villages of Fayoum, south of Cairo, which has a similar tradition of migration to Europe – an increasing number of people speak Italian fluently and some have adopted both Italian styles of dress and architectural preferences (Civic Pole, n.d). Many take huge risks to cross the Mediterranean. Relatively safe, formal routes to the Gulf states are no longer an option: for most unskilled migrants of rural origin smuggling to Europe provides their only means of exit.

Egypt has also experienced very high levels of internal migration, closely connected to the outcomes of neoliberal reform. Zohry (2005: 23–4) comments:

> [R]ural youth who represent the surplus of the agricultural sector have no way to survive other than migrating to cities ... Cairo and Alexandria offer better wages (generally around triple those in rural Egypt), somewhat more regular work (and therefore more regular income), a more exciting lifestyle, and the chance to support family members in the home village.

This form of migration is not necessarily a permanent relocation of residence but typically involves circular migration in which migrants move for an extended period to urban areas. The vast majority are men who end up working in the informal sector. Typically they use family connections to help them find a job and a place to live, leading to the agglomeration of kin-based neighbourhoods in the large informal communities that surround Egypt's key cities (Ouda, 1974). Zohry (2005: 24) observes that migration is 'a "survival strategy" [aimed at] sustain[ing] the basic needs of migrants' families left behind'. He continues:

> Upper Egyptian laborers live a miserable life in Cairo in order to ensure a decent life for their families. This marginalised group, which is partially absorbed by the capital's large informal economy, has some similarities with refugees in Cairo in terms of living and working conditions.

For many decades, Cairo has been a hub for refugees. In 2008, there were refugees from some 40 countries, including communities such as the Armenians, Palestinians and Iraqis – whose presence is associated with historic mass displacements in the Middle East – and from the conflict zones of Sub-Saharan Africa.[15] In 2012, they were joined by large numbers of Syrians and by Palestinians displaced from the refugee camps of Syria. For many rural Egyptians, life in the city – as Zohry observes – has much in common with the circumstances of the most marginal refugees. Many former *fellaheen* are indeed 'survival' migrants, even if their legal status provides them with greater security than those viewed as refugees 'proper'.[16] Their predicaments say much about the impact of four decades of neoliberal policy, which has disembedded people from rural communities in ways that parallel processes of displacement associated with political upheaval across the MENA region.

The global economic crisis and the Arab uprisings

On the eve of the global economic crisis that erupted in 2008, some 6.5 million Egyptians were estimated to be living abroad – equivalent to around 8 per cent of the country's population (Zohry, 2009: 1). Most were workers based in the Gulf countries, in Libya and in Jordan (a combined total of 75 per cent) with the remainder largely located in North America and Europe. Links established between Egypt and the wider MENA region through these movements constituted one transmission mechanism for the global economic crisis. In the years preceding the crisis, remittances were equivalent to 4–5 per cent of Egyptian national GDP, and were to fall substantially as a result of mass layoffs and the economic contraction that spread in the wake of the global collapse. Egypt was particularly susceptible to this process because of migration flows (both documented and undocumented) to Southern Europe in sectors such as construction, agriculture and manufacturing. From 2008 to 2009, the country experienced a contraction of nearly 18 per cent in remittances inflows (World Bank, 2010: 142). The World Bank was to conclude that Egypt lost close to 1 per cent of GDP – the most severe decline among all states in the MENA region (ibid.: 369).

These impacts of global crisis – transmitted here through migration networks – are an important component of causes underlying mass mobilisations that led to the overthrow of Husni Mubarak in 2011 (Hanieh, 2011). The uprising was not simply a response to authoritarian rule but was linked to processes arising from neoliberal reform and ways in which the global crisis affected North Africa (Hanieh, 2013). Moreover, as revolt spread, Egyptian migrant workers were deeply affected by changes that ensued in the neighbouring countries. An important illustration was the overthrow of the Gaddafi regime in Libya in June 2011. Conflict in Libya led to displacement of an estimated 200,000 Egyptians – around 13 per cent of the total Egyptian migrant worker population in the country (Elmeshad, 2012). According to a survey carried out by the IOM, the majority of those who left Libya returned to impoverished rural zones in the Nile Delta and Upper Egypt. IOM observed that these areas 'face high unemployment rates especially among the youth and now struggle to absorb large numbers of returnees into their labor markets' (IOM, 2012). Most of those who returned were single males supporting dependants in Egypt, and poverty levels likely increased since remittances 'were primarily spent for direct household expenses and health care' (ibid.).

Although there has been no detailed study to date of impacts at the household level, it is likely that the reduction in remittances from abroad has had severe consequences for those who depend upon them for day-to-day existence. In 2008–2009, the largest sources of remittances to Egypt were the United States, Kuwait, Saudi Arabia and the United Arab Emirates. Given the fact that most workers in these states are higher-paid (or in the case of the USA are permanent migrants), and that the Gulf states have managed to overcome the worst effects of the global crisis, these migrants are likely to have been more resilient in terms of their remittance patterns. Poorer, low-paid migrants have tended to move to Jordan, Southern Europe and Libya – and it is reasonable to assume that these workers will find it more difficult both to maintain employment and to remit funds (particularly in the case of undocumented migrants in Southern Europe who tend to be found in sectors hardest hit by the crisis).

Conclusion

Colonialism left a specific imprint on the MENA region, establishing a series of novel state structures, centralised regimes associated with networks of patronage and ethno-religious particularism, and large displaced populations living as 'warehoused' refugees[17] or as 'minorities'. Forced migrants – notably Palestinians – have been dispersed widely across the region and especially in the Arab East, where there are complex diasporic networks. These communities live in a state of continuing instability, their lives profoundly affected by processes of change in 'host' states. Mass displacement remains a key feature of multicausal crises of the region – as demonstrated by recent events in Libya, from which there have been mass movements to Tunisia and Egypt, and in Syria, from which refugees have moved to Turkey, Lebanon, Jordan and Egypt. All these forms of migration show that it is impossible to appreciate fully the contemporary social and political dynamics of the Middle East without understanding the intersections of migration and of the processes of economic and socio-political change that are constitutive of the region itself.

A starting point to address these issues is recognition that change impacts differently across social groups. One group's crisis may be another's boon. In the MENA region, colonialism and later foreign interventions have brought wealth and power to some – but increasing marginalisation for most. This is particularly important in the context of neoliberalism, where the Egyptian case demonstrates an intensification of social inequalities. During the Mubarak era, there was a particularly acute convergence of multiple forms of constraint – economic, social and political – with migration pursued as one strategy among many that individuals and families adopted in order to survive. It has also been used by successive Egyptian regimes to displace crisis: here the 'safety valve' of international migration facilitated by the state has been part of the latter's own survival strategy. Migration has delivered diminishing returns, however, for it has also transmitted instabilities into Egypt, contributing to the 'permanent' crisis experienced by much of the population and intensifying pressures which eventually produced the uprising of January 2011.

These observations indicate the importance of giving due weight to migration in analyses of the socio-political phenomena in the MENA region. The movement and mixing of peoples that have characterised the region for over 150 years are sometimes viewed as an issue of historical interest but one that bears little contemporary relevance. The idea of a migration–crisis nexus

Migration and 'crisis': Middle East, N Africa 41

understood by reference to human experience helps to make history relevant to a region still in tumult.

Notes

1 For a usually frank 'insider' account of the process, see Monroe (1963).
2 Pastoralists did not operate in isolation solely in remote desert or semi-desert areas but as part of regional economic arrangements, supplying livestock and livestock products to urban centres and to settled cultivators. 'Nomads' had complex, reciprocal arrangements with cities, settled rural areas and those using trade routes. Some moved in and out of pastoral and trading activity, so that the distinction between those with a mobile, migratory lifestyle and the sedentary population was often blurred.
3 In some cases, this amounted to enforcement of a levy accompanied by transportation – a form of forced migration (Goodwin, 2006).
4 For an analysis of mass displacement in the making of the early nation-state, see Soguk (1999). On refugees and state-making throughout the modern era, see Marfleet (2007a, 2013).
5 Meanwhile, in North Africa, settler colonialism also produced mass movements of population. In Algeria, emplacement of settler communities – *colons* – displaced millions of people. French commander Marshal Soult had instructed: 'we cannot wait: it is absolutely imperative that we make colons and construct villages, summon all energies to sanction, consolidate and simplify the occupation we achieve by arms' (Clegg, 1971: 24). The army razed villages and expelled the indigenous population from urban centres.
6 In the form of the Balfour Declaration of November 1917, a message from the British Foreign Secretary Arthur Balfour to Baron Rothschild, to be communicated to the Zionist Federation. This noted that the British government viewed 'with favour', the establishment in Palestine of 'a national home for the Jewish people'.
7 Turner (1994: 34–5) comments on continuous discussions in the states of western Europe about problems of 'Oriental despotism' and the need for radical political change in the Middle East. These, he suggests, reflected concerns about the difficulty of maintaining social order in Europe, especially fear of the mass of the population among those who monopolised power.
8 Moreover, in a development often ignored in analyses of migration in the MENA region, large numbers of Jews also moved from Arab states to Israel. Some had experienced hostility and discrimination; others moved in response to sustained efforts by Israel to stimulate emigration by means of clandestine operations and by disseminating fear among Jewish citizens of Arab states. On the experiences of the Jews of Egypt during the 1940s and 1950s, see Beinin (1998).
9 When during the 1967 War, Israeli forces occupied the Golan area of Syria, they also expelled thousands of Circassians who in the nineteenth century had fled to the Ottoman regions of the Balkans and had later been resettled in Syria.
10 Iraq's large Jewish community had been greatly diminished by migrations to Israel in the early 1950s; of those who remained, most left in the late 1960s in response to campaigns of Ba'thist repression.
11 The influence of sectarianism in Iraq had been diminished during the mass political movements of the 1940s and 1950s, then reasserted when the Ba'th Party took power, see Batatu (1978). On the impact of invasion in 2003 and subsequent mass migrations, see Marfleet (2007b).
12 Figures from World Bank database, http://data.worldbank.org.
13 This study was undertaken for Save the Children (UK) by a team of Egyptian researchers for whom the present authors provided academic advice and guidance.

Focusing on agricultural communities in Beheira province, the team interviewed young people and their families about motivations for attempting migration to Europe. It also sought their views on the economic and socio-cultural impacts of migration upon family and community life. Some findings are recorded in Save the Children (SCUK, 2012).

14 Information from participants at a workshop convened by Save the Children (UK), Cairo, 24 September 2011.

15 Informal estimate of the Forced Migration and Refugee Studies Center at the American University in Cairo.

16 For an account of challenges faced by refugees in Egypt (including problems of legal recognition), see Marfleet (2006).

17 A term used in research on forced migration to refer to large refugee populations confined to camps or settlements and largely dependent upon humanitarian aid. See definitions offered by the US Committee for Refugees and Immigrants, available at: http://www.refugees.org/our-work/refugee-rights/warehousing-campaign/ (accessed 1 October 2013).

References

Abdalla, A. (1985) *The Student Movement and National Politics in Egypt, 1923–1973*. London: Saqi Books.

Abdelhamid, D. and El Baradei, L. (2009) *Reforming the Pay System for Government Employees in Egypt*. Working Paper 151. Cairo: Egyptian Centre for Economic Studies.

Abdul-Fadil, M. (1980) *The Political Economy of Nasserism: A Study in Employment and Income Distribution Policies in Urban Egypt, 1952–72*. Cambridge: Cambridge University Press.

Abu Jaber, T. (1997) 'Jordanian Labor Migration: Social, Political and Economic Effects', in M. Shtayyeh (ed.) *Labor Migration: Palestine, Jordan, Egypt and Israel*. Jerusalem: Palestinian Center for Regional Studies.

Abu-Lughod, J.L. (1991) *Before European Hegemony: The World System 1250–1350*. Oxford: Oxford University Press.

Achy, L. (2010) *The Uncertain Future of Egypt's Economic Reforms*. Beirut: Carnegie Endowment for International Peace.

Adams, R. (1989) 'Workers' Remittances and Inequality in Rural Egypt', *Economic Development and Cultural Change* 38(1): 48–71.

AfDB (African Development Bank) (2010) *Land Policy in Africa: North Africa Regional Assessment*. Addis Ababa, Ethiopia: AUC-ECA-AfDB Consortium.

Batatu, H. (1978) *The Old Social Classes and the Revolutionary Movements of Iraq*. Princeton, NJ: Princeton University Press.

Baumann, Z. (2004) *Wasted Lives: Modernity and its Outcasts*. Cambridge: Polity.

BBC News (2011a) 'Tunisia Migrants: Italy Puts Europe on Alert', 15 February.

——(2011b) 'Silvio Berlusconi Warns Milan Could Become "Gypsytown"', 23 May.

Beinin, J. (1990) *Was the Red Flag Flying There? Marxist Politics and the Arab-Israeli Conflict in Egypt and Israel, 1948–1965*. Berkeley, CA: University of California Press.

——(1998) *The Dispersion of Egyptian Jewry*. Cairo: The American University in Cairo Press.

Black, R. (2001) 'Fifty Years of Refugee Studies: From Theory to Policy', *International Migration Review* 35(1): 57–78.

Migration and 'crisis': Middle East, N Africa   43

Botman, S. (1988) *The Rise of Egyptian Communism, 1939–1970*. Syracuse, NY: Syracuse University Press.

Bush, R. (1999) *Economic Crisis and the Politics of Reform in Egypt*. Boulder, CO: Westview Press.

——(2004) 'Civil Society and the Uncivil State Land Tenure Reform in Egypt and the Crisis of Rural Livelihoods', United Nations Research Institute for Social Development Programme Paper No. 9. Geneva: United Nations Research Institute for Social Development.

Chatelard, G. (2004) 'Jordan: A Refugee Haven', *Migration Information Source*. Washington, DC: Migration Policy Institute, July 1. Available at: http://www.migrationinformation.org/feature/display.cfm?ID=794 (accessed 3 June 2012).

Chatty, D. (2010) *Displacement and Dispossession in the Modern Middle East*. Cambridge: Cambridge University Press.

Civic Pole (n.d.) 'Little Italy in Fayoum: Escaping Unemployment and Poverty in Fayoum'. Available at: http://www.civicpole.net/en/on-the-ground/egyptian-view/165-little-italy-in-fayoum-escaping-unemployment-and-poverty-in-fayoum (accessed 1 October 2013).

Clegg, A. (1971) *Workers' Self-Management in Algeria*. London: Allen Lane.

Collyer, M. (2004) 'The Development Impact of Temporary International Labour Migration on Southern Mediterranean Sending Countries: Contrasting Examples of Morocco and Egypt', Sussex Centre for Migration Research Working Paper No. 16. Brighton: University of Sussex.

Der Spiegel (2011) 'Thousands of Tunisians Arrive in Italy', *Der Spiegel*, 14 February.

Elmeshad, M. (2012) 'After the Revolutions: Egyptian Migrant Workers Struggle to Return to Libya', *Egypt Independent*, 13 February. Available at: http://www.egyptindependent.com/news/egyptian-migrants-find-it-difficult-return-libya.

FAO (2005) *Breaking Ground: Present and Future Perspectives for Women in Agriculture*. Rome: Food and Agriculture Organisation of the United Nations.

Farrag, M. (1999) 'Emigration Dynamics in Egypt', in R. Appleyard (ed.) *Emigration Dynamics in Developing Countries*. Vol. 4, *The Arab Region*. Geneva: IOM and UNFPA.

Forte, D. (1978) 'Egyptian Land Law: An Evaluation', *American Journal of Comparative Law* 26: 273–8.

Glain, S. (2012) 'Egyptian Farmers Make Themselves Heard', *New York Times*, June 27. Available at: http://www.nytimes.com/ (accessed 28 June 2012).

Goodwin, G. (2006) *The Janissaries*. London: Saqi Books.

Hanieh, A. (2011) 'Beyond Mubarak: The Politics and Economics of Egypt's Uprising', *Studies in Political Economy* 87.

——(2013) *Lineages of Revolt: Issues of Contemporary Capitalism in the Middle East*. Chicago: Haymarket Press.

Hourani, A. (1991) *A History of the Arab Peoples*. London: Faber and Faber.

Ibrahim, S. (1982) *The New Arab Social Order: A Study of the Social Impact of Oil Wealth*. Boulder, CO: Westview Press.

IMF (International Monetary Fund) (2006) 'Arab Republic of Egypt: 2005 Article IV Consultation Staff Report', Public Information Note. Washington, DC: IMF.

——(2011) 'Regional Economic Outlook: Middle East and Central Asia', World Economic and Financial Surveys, 11 April. Available at: http://www.imf.org/external/pubs/ft/reo/2011/mcd/eng/pdf/mreo0411.pdf (accessed 5 July 2012).

IOM (International Organisation for Migration) (2009) *Migration and Development in Egypt*. Available at: http://www.egypt.iom.int/.

44 Philip Marfleet and Adam Hanieh

——(2011) *Migrants Caught in Crisis*. Geneva: IOM.

——(2012) *IOM Egypt Newsletter, Spring 2012*. Available at: http://www.egypt.iom. int/Doc/IOM%20Egypt%20Newsletter_Spring%202012_ENG.pdf.

Joya, A. (2008) 'Egyptian Protests: Falling Wages, High Prices and the Failure of an Export-Oriented Economy', *The Bullet*, 2 June.

Kadri, A. (2011) 'A Period of Revolutionary Fervour', *New Politics*, 19 February. Available at: http://newpolitics.mayfirst.org/node/431.

Kundnani, A. (2001) 'In a Foreign Land: The New Popular Racism', *Race and Class* 43(2).

Lesch, A. (1990) 'Egyptian Labor Migration', in I.O. Oweiss (ed.) *The Political Economy of Contemporary Egypt*. Washington, DC: Center for Contemporary Arab Studies, Georgetown University.

Marfleet, P. (2006) *Refugees in a Global Era*. Basingstoke: Palgrave.

——(2007a) 'Refugees and History: Why We Must Address the Past', *Refugee Survey Quarterly* 26(3): 136–48.

——(2007b) 'Iraq's Refugees: War and the Strategy of Exit', *International Journal of Contemporary Iraqi Studies* 1(3): 397–419.

——(2013) 'Explorations in a Foreign Land: States, Refugees and the Problem of History', *Refugee Survey Quarterly* 32(2): 14–34.

Marfleet, P. and Cetti, F. (2013) 'Identity Politics: Europe, the EU and the Arab Spring', in T. Ismael and G. Parry (eds) *International Relations of the Contemporary Middle East*. London: Routledge.

Marrus, M.R. (1985) *The Unwanted: European Refugees in the Twentieth Century*. Oxford: Oxford University Press.

Mazower, M. (2004) *Salonica – City of Ghosts: Christians, Muslims and Jews, 1430–1950*. New York: Alfred A. Knopf.

Mitchell, T. (2002) *Rule of Experts: Egypt, Techno-Politics, Modernity*. Berkeley, CA: University of California Press.

Monroe, E. (1963) *Britain's Moment in the Middle East, 1914–1956*. London: Taylor & Francis.

Moore, K. (2012) 'Introduction to Migrations and the Media', in K. Moore, B. Gross and T. Threadgold (eds) *Migrations and the Media*. New York: Peter Lang.

Naufal, G. and Varga-Silva, C. (2012) 'Migrant Transfers in the MENA Region: A Two-Way Street in Which Traffic Is Changing', in I. Sirkeci, J.H. Cohen, and D. Rath (eds) *Migration and Remittances during the Global Financial Crisis and Beyond*. Washington, DC: World Bank Publications.

Ouda, M. (1974) 'Migration to Cairo', *National Sociological Journal* 12 (in Arabic).

Ramalho, R. (2007) 'Adding a Million Taxpayers', in World Bank *Celebrating Reform 2007: Doing Business Case Studies*. Washington, DC: World Bank.

Rashwan, H. (2010) 'Study: 16.3 Million Egyptians Now Live Below Poverty Line', *Egypt Independent*, 30 December. Available at: http://www.egyptindependent.com/news/study-163-million-egyptians-now-live-below-poverty-line.

RDI (2000) *Land Title Registry: Recommendations to Improve the Land Registration Process Towards a Formal Rural Land Market*. Available at: http://pdf.usaid.gov/pdf_docs/PNACS209.pdf. (accessed 9 May 2012).

Reimer, M. (1997) *Colonial Bridgehead: Government and Society in Alexandria, 1807–1882*. Cairo: The American University in Cairo Press.

Said, E. (1978) *Orientalism*. London: Penguin Books.

SCUK (Save the Children UK) (2012) 'Irregular Youth Migration and Smuggling from Egypt to Southern Europe', Draft Report, unpublished document, Save the Children UK, Cairo.

Soguk, N. (1999) *States and Strangers: Refugees and Displacements of Statecraft*. Minneapolis, MN: University of Minnesota Press.

Turner, B.S. (1994) *Orientalism, Postmodernism and Globalism*. London: Routledge.

USAID (2010) *Country Profile, Egypt, Property Rights and Resource Governance*. Available at: http:// http://usaidlandtenure.net/egypt (accessed 4 June 2012).

Vitalis, R. (1995) *When Capitalists Collide: Business Conflict and the End of Empire in Egypt*. Berkeley, CA: University of California Press.

World Bank (2010) *Global Economic Prospects: Crisis, Finance and Growth*. Washington, DC: World Bank.

Wurzel, U. (2009) 'The Political Economy of Authoritarianism in Egypt', in L. Guazzone and D. Pioppi (eds) *The Arab State and Neo-liberal Globalization: The Restructuring of State Power in the Middle East*. Reading: Ithaca Press.

Zohry, A. (2003) 'The Place of Egypt in the Regional Migration System as a Receiving Country', *Revue Européenne des Migrations Internationales* 19(3).

——(2005) *Interrelationships between Internal and International Migration in Egypt: A Pilot Study*. Forced Migration and Refugee Studies Program, Cairo: American University in Cairo.

——(2009) *The Impact of the Current Economic Crisis on Egyptian Migration and Egyptians Abroad*. Cairo: Egyptian Society for Migration Studies.

Zubaida, S. (1999) 'Cosmopolitanism and the Middle East', in R. Meijer (ed.) *Cosmopolitanism, Identity and Authenticity in the Middle East*. London: Curzon Press.

3 Histories and contemporary challenges of crisis and mobility in Somalia

Anna Lindley and Laura Hammond

Famine struck south-central Somalia in 2011, accompanied by massive, headline-hitting displacement. This was in many ways an archetypal crisis of migration: a complex political, economic and environmental crisis generating large-scale population movement and significant challenges in destination areas. Yet at the same time, it is typically seen as the latest episode in a longer-running crisis: since the collapse of the state, Somalia – and particularly its south-central regions – are generally viewed as chronically crisis-ridden and displacement-producing. The classic image of the people displaced is of impoverished victims of violence or drought, warehoused in regional refugee camps. With significant political consolidation in south-central Somalia in 2012 and 2013, many now view this long-running crisis as finally on the ebb, with displacement slowing and increasing discussion of prospects for return prompting fresh policy debates.

This chapter engages in a critical historical analysis of crisis and mobility in south-central Somalia since 1991. The first section outlines the key features of the political landscape and mobility patterns in three distinct periods, as well as making some observations about earlier historical antecedents and recent events. These are explored in some depth to establish the basis for the analytical points made in the second part of the chapter. First, we argue that the evidence often contradicts dominant narratives of crisis – pointing to crises not broadcast and normalities unnoticed – and then we highlight various political functions served by crisis narratives. Second, we show how the evidence on Somali mobilities challenges conventional images of conflict-related movements – pointing to its multi-causal and differentiated nature, strategic aspects and its centrality to social change in the Somali territories. Finally, in light of these considerations, we outline key contemporary challenges for policy-makers in relation to Somali mobility.

This chapter draws on and brings together insights from various research projects we carried out between 2003 and 2012, in the Somali territories and the wider region and diaspora, exploring aid, livelihoods, food security, migration, displacement, diasporas and remittances (e.g. Lindley, 2010a, 2010b, 2011, 2013; Hammond et al., 2011; Hammond and Vaughan-Lee, 2012; Hammond 2013a, 2013b, 2013c). It also draws on secondary sources, including quantitative data on displacement and commentaries by aid workers, journalists and other observers.

Three points should be made about our approach. First, we are not analysing a methodologically 'tidy' body of data, but rather drawing on multiple sources, combining conclusions of earlier research with secondary sources to construct a moving picture of crisis and mobility, and the socio-political landscapes in which they unfold. A major challenge is the lack of reliable longitudinal data on many issues in Somalia, including migration, a problem partly attributable to the 'emergency mentality' discussed later in the chapter (see also UNDP 2001).[1] Second, much of this chapter relates to the unfolding of events in south-central Somalia[2] which we have not witnessed first-hand; instead we use evidence gathered through research with displaced people and key informants (aid workers, businesspeople, politicians) in other Somali territories and abroad, collaborative work with local research teams, secondary data, and web-based discussions. Third, despite these challenges, we want to focus on south-central Somalia, as distinct from Puntland and Somaliland, because it represents an on-going and dramatic crisis situation, whereas the latter have followed distinct political and migration trajectories. At the same time, we acknowledge that there are diverse violence, governance and mobility experiences within south-central Somalia, and important parallels and links between the distinct Somali territories, some of which we draw out in our analysis.

Contextualising wartime mobility

In the wake of the ousting of President Mohamed Siyad Barre and the collapse of the state in 1991, south-central Somalia witnessed large internal and international movements of people, marking a reasonably distinct period both politically and in terms of mobility dynamics. It is here that we begin our account. However, it would be hard to understand what happened after 1991 without establishing some principal antecedents.

First, clan appears prominently in accounts of the causes and dynamics of civil war violence in Somalia. However, clan is not a 'natural category', but is constructed politically in ways that change over time and vary across space (Kapteijns, 2013). Clan constructs were shaped through colonial indirect rule and, following independence, became a key political resource for individuals to access state power (ibid.). After taking power by military coup in 1969, Barre banned overt expressions of clanship, but his increasingly neo-patrimonial regime relied on its covert manipulation, buoyed by aid from Cold War superpowers and other international donors (Samatar, 1988). As this financial base disintegrated and opposition mounted, the ensuing civil war in turn transformed what clanship meant to people. These 'national' processes unfolded in different ways for particular places and groups. A nuanced and contextual view of clanship is particularly important in relation to south-central Somalia, historically more socially mixed than other areas: alongside patrilineal descent, territorial connection and cross-cutting

48   *Anna Lindley and Laura Hammond*

patterns of alliance and affiliation have featured prominently in people's social identifications.

Another key piece of the backdrop is the deeply mobile nature of Somali society, even before the outbreak of war. Nomadic pastoralism, a widespread occupation, requires the seasonal concentration and dispersal of herders and their livestock in search of water and pasture, typically in areas where their clan is viewed as having customary rights to move, reside and graze. This mobility has arguably reduced somewhat over the years, with some groups developing permanent water resources and enclosing rangeland or adopting more of an agropastoral livelihood. In addition, rural people seek income and support from urban areas, sometimes dividing their time between rural and urban homes; there is some evidence to suggest that increasing (but unspecified) numbers of people have been moving into urban and peri-urban areas permanently in search of livelihood and physical security. Many people routinely circulate across colonially imposed and present-day international borders in pursuit of their livelihoods. Longer-distance international migration has been well established since at least the 1920s. People migrated particularly to the UK, where seamen from the British Somaliland Protectorate had settled, and to the Gulf states where there were historical trade links and later on jobs created by oil wealth. In the 1980s, Somalia was in the midst of an *incoming* refugee crisis, after the Somali-Ethiopian War of 1977–78 – indeed, for some years manipulation of the humanitarian aid for refugees helped to reinforce Barre's ailing regime. These migrations and transnational and translocal connections influenced subsequent wartime movements.

Third, Somalia was already a violent society in the 1980s, with increasingly widespread and displacement-inducing *state* violence, targeting civilians suspected of sympathising with emerging rebel fronts. Following the emergence of the Somali Salvation Democratic Front in 1978, the regime wreaked collective punishment on Majerteen civilians in the north-east. In the north-west, in the context of the emergence of the Somali National Movement (which drew on diaspora support), government repression of Isaaq clan members escalated into a brutal military campaign in 1988–89 which laid waste major urban centres and prompted massive displacement, with some 500,000 people fleeing to Ethiopia in one of the largest and fastest movements ever recorded in Africa (Bradbury, 2008). In the south, state-sanctioned appropriations of land for private gain triggered displacements and fomented grievance. Throughout the country, people designated 'counter-revolutionaries' were persecuted; many were forced into exile, while others, frustrated by the neo-patrimonial system and the economic and political constraints resulting from it, sought better opportunities abroad. These experiences later on coloured Somalis' attitudes to state reconstruction efforts.

It is important to note the different path taken by the northern territories, since the outbreak of civil war. In the north-west, Somaliland had declared independence in 1991, and begun to forge an alternative political system, triggering massive 'self-organised' repatriation from Ethiopian refugee camps

Challenges of crisis and mobility in Somalia   49

as well as relocation of people from south-central Somalia (Ambroso, 2002; Bradbury, 2008). An outbreak of internal civil strife in 1994–96 prompted fresh displacement into Ethiopia but was followed by the UNHCR-assisted repatriation of some 170,000 refugees by 2001 (Frushone, 2001). Meanwhile, in the north-east, Puntland was established as an autonomous regional administration in 1998, and also saw large-scale repatriations. After years in camps, many returnees who had been effectively urbanised through displacement were unable or unwilling to return to their former rural livelihoods, and congregated in informal settlements in major towns and cities. Both territories subsequently experienced intermittent outbreaks of violence and displacement, but none on the scale of earlier years. Fresh, post-conflict migration dynamics emerged. Rural-urban migration renewed, driven by recurrent drought, changing pastoral livelihoods and improving urban labour and education opportunities. *Tahrib* – the smuggling of people by sea and land seeking to obtain a better livelihood and secure status – became a thriving business. With time, Somaliland and Puntland became a key destination and onward transit point for southern Somalis and Ethiopians fleeing conflict, persecution and poverty.

In sum, the concept of clan has long been politicised and there were already high levels of mobility and violence in the 1980s. The year 1991, however, marked a key political turning point in south-central Somalia, with a dramatic surge in displacement. Lindley's (2012b) research participants generally distinguished three periods in the years that followed. This is broadly supported by the estimates of displacement in Figure 3.1, which suggest a sharp surge in the early 1990s, followed by relative stabilisation, and a later surge since 2007. While the first surge included significant displacement from the northern territories, the latter was primarily from south-central Somalia. The key features of each period are explored below.

1991–95: state collapse, factional violence, acute displacement

The combined efforts of the armed opposition, comprising of the Somali National Movement (SNM), the United Somali Congress (USC) and the Somali Patriotic Movement (SPM) resulted in the ousting of Barre from Mogadishu in January 1991. However, the rebels failed to agree on how to form a new national government, and devastating factional violence ensued in which all public institutions and services collapsed. In the 'clan cleansing' campaign of 1991–92, the USC's leadership, fighters and civilian supporters, emphasising their 'Hawiye' umbrella identity, 'adopted a politics that defined as mortal enemy all Somalis encompassed by the genealogical construct of Daarood' (Kapteijns, 2013: 2), who were equated with Barre's regime, foreignness to the area, and unjust domination. This was despite the fact that many so-called Daarood had also not done well under Barre, that some prominent Hawiye clan members had profited greatly from the regime, and that people from both sides had lived peacefully side by side in Mogadishu for

50   *Anna Lindley and Laura Hammond*

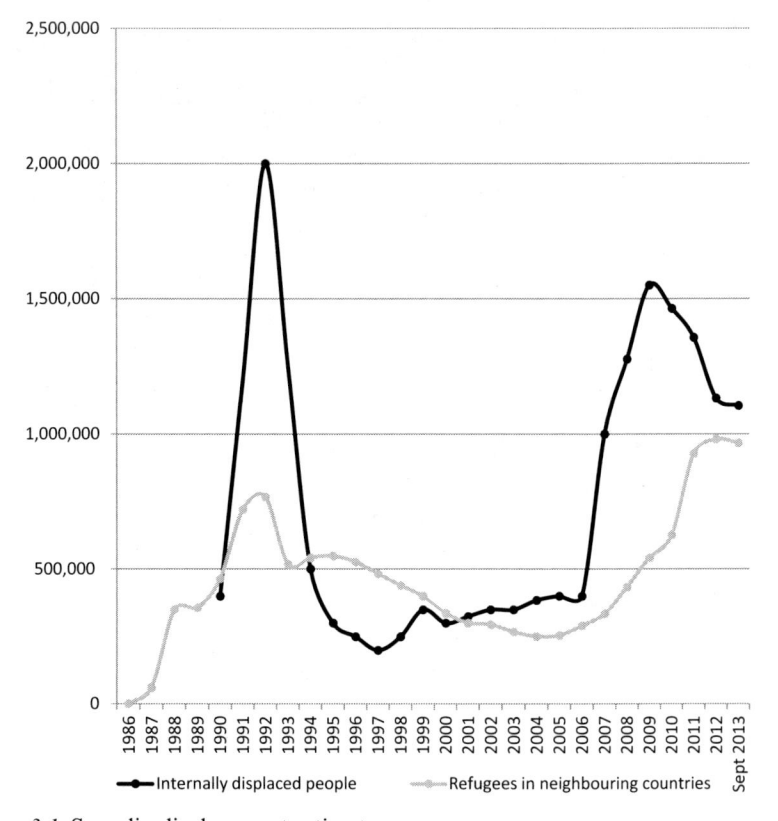

Figure 3.1 Somalia displacement estimates
Sources: a) Internal displacement estimates: 1990–2000 from NRC (2003: 27, 40);
2001–2004 from IDMC (2010); 2005–2012 from UNHCR Statistical Online Population
Database, 7 Oct. 2013, and UNHCR (2013). Where range given, mid-point used. Data
missing for 1991 and 1993. b) Figures for refugees living in neighbouring countries
(Djibouti, Ethiopia, Kenya and Yemen) taken from UNHCR Statistical Online Database,
1 February and 7 October 2013, and UNHCR (2013).
Note: These figures should be taken as broadly indicative of population trends; they
certainly do not represent a precise enumeration of displaced people. Since 2006,
UNHCR's population movement tracking system has improved the quality of data on
internal displacement, but systematic independent enumeration remains difficult in
many locations. While official figures for registered refugees capture a major part of the
refugee population in neighbouring countries, some do not register as refugees.

generations. Because of this early targeting and their historical predominance in
areas close to the southern border, people of Daarood lineages formed the bulk
of initial arrivals of refugees in Kenya (Horst, 2006). But Daarood militias also
mobilised against the Hawiye inside Somalia. While some covertly resisted this
polarisation, hiding neighbours and saving friends, public resistance became
dangerous.
    As time went on, however, the emphasis shifted as the armed movements
splintered and made cross-cutting alliances at sub-clan level. As rival militia

Challenges of crisis and mobility in Somalia   51

battled back and forth across south-central Somalia, they killed civilians as well as combatants, and undermined communities through rape and other physical abuse, by looting or destroying livelihood resources and forcing displacement. Some areas saw successive waves of scorched earth tactics by different groups contesting control. 'Warlords' mobilised clanspeople in pursuit of individual and collective wealth and power. Their militias contested control of key resources: markets, ports, water points, road blocks, state property, private property in urban centres, and the fertile agricultural lands between the Juba and Shabelle rivers. For some, therefore, crisis became a lucrative opportunity. Kapteijns (2013) argues that 1991 marked a critical political shift: the violence occurred outside the state institutions which had previously mediated social relations; it had a strong communal dimension, with civilians targeted *and* mobilised; and its axis shifted from government/opposition to pitting people against each other based on particular constructions of clan identity.

Prior to state collapse, south-central Somalia was a fairly socially mixed area, and there were many groups that were not identifiable as either Hawiye or Daarood living in urban centres or the agricultural areas between the Shabelle and Juba rivers (ibid.). Generally perceived as socially distinct from the 'prestigious' Somali clans of nomadic heritage (though some were historically allied to more powerful clans, and the nature of narratives of difference and levels of economic success varied considerably), they were subject to considerable discrimination. Now often referred to as 'minorities', these groups lacked weapons and militia at the outbreak of the civil war, and the dominant factions were able to kill, rape, and expropriate their property with impunity, often accompanied by a discourse that the group was 'non-Somali' or had collaborated with Barre's regime or an opposing civil war faction. For example, the Bravanese and the Benaadiri (people associated with the early historical settlement of coastal cities) were comprehensively 'othered', and victimised (ibid.). The rural farming peoples who came to be known collectively as the Somali Bantu or *Jareer* (tracing their descent to historical Bantu expansion and slave transportation from further down the East African coast), despite long-standing client relationships with prominent clans, found themselves largely unprotected after civil war broke out (Luling, 2002). Successive militia devastated their farms and communities, committing abuses against civilians, confiscating land and property, forcing displacement or subjecting them to intensely exploitative labour relationships. The Rahanweyn confederation of clans who historically had relied on agro-pastoral livelihood activities in the inter-riverine areas, maintaining a distinct (if not as heavily discriminated) identity, also found themselves highly vulnerable to more powerfully armed actors (Majid and McDowell, 2012). In this context, the 1991–92 famine was basically 'man-made' (De Waal, 1997; Hansch et al., 1994; Little, 2003). Drought combined with intense political violence which disrupted food production, water infrastructure, trade and transport, coping migration and remittance flows. Drastically reduced milk and meat yields left poorer pastoralists in a desperate situation, though some were able to shift their normal mobility patterns to weather the crisis. Worst affected were the Rahanweyn agro-pastoralists and Somali Bantu famers, whose food security plummeted because of their vulnerability to violence, and more sedentary livelihood practices. The global acute malnutrition rate reached 40–70 per cent of Somalia's population and an estimated 212,000–248,000 people perished in the emergency period of 1992–93 (Hansch et al., 1994; FSNAU, 2011).

The international community recognised these clear crisis conditions and, inspired by early post-Cold War optimism, mounted large-scale high-profile peace-keeping and humanitarian interventions between 1992 and 1995 (Hammond and Vaughan-Lee, 2012). Under the aegis of US and UN forces, vast amounts of food aid were distributed, saving many lives, while fuelling a mushrooming war economy. Initially emphasising humanitarian rationale, the international intervention became increasingly political as US peacekeepers became catastrophically embroiled in direct conflict with warlord General Mohamed Farah Aideed in June 1993, an episode which marked the turning of the tide in the international community's willingness to intervene in African conflicts. UN efforts to facilitate political reconciliation between factional leaders continued until the eventual withdrawal of the peacekeeping forces in March 1995.

These early years of the civil war in south-central Somalia were marked by high levels of displacement, as demonstrated in Figure 3.1. At the peak of the upheaval an estimated two million people throughout Somalia were internally displaced, and nearly 800,000 were seeking refuge in neighbouring countries. A significant proportion originated from south-central Somalia. Initially, there was dramatic flight from conflict-torn urban centres to rural areas and towns where people thought they would be safer. Then, in the context of the famine, there was an exodus of rural people from famine-hit rural areas towards towns and cities.

Where possible, people fleeing violence and hunger sought refuge wherever they had kin or contacts who could host or assist them. This represents the less visible component of displacement. Many (particularly those who historically came from more sedentary farming groups) lacked such connections but were drawn to major urban centres in the hope of finding sustenance, congregating in informal settlements. They found little by way of reliable employment, and humanitarian assistance did not really ramp up until 1993. Malnutrition, terrible living conditions and endemic infectious diseases meant that displaced people, along with children under 5, exhibited the highest mortality rates during the famine (Hansch et al., 1994). While some of the decrease in the estimated size of the internally displaced population by 1994 was probably due to people returning to their former places of residence, or moving abroad, many simply perished in the famine.

Many urbanites, and to a lesser extent rural people, embarked on longer journeys. The refugee population in neighbouring countries mushroomed, peaking in 1992 at 513,950 for Ethiopia (including a large proportion of refugees originating from the northern Somali territories) and at 285,619 for

Kenya (largely people from south-central Somalia). While wealthier individuals were able to fly into Kenya, most refugees' journeys were made on foot or vehicle; these difficult and dangerous treks, often unfolding in several stages, across territory ridden with political and criminal violence. Another movement northward saw people fleeing towards Yemen in overcrowded and unsafe ships. After initial attempts to prevent arrivals by closing its border, the Kenyan government's policy was to offer temporary protection, registering them as *prima facie* refugees, and delegating their care to UNHCR in several refugee camps. Initially donor funding flooded in to respond to the emergency conditions. But by 1993, as morbidity and mortality stabilised and the registered refugee population decreased somewhat, donor interest waned. UNHCR declared the humanitarian emergency over, embarking on a new operational strategy of 'care and maintenance' (Milner, 2009). The decreasing registered population was due not only to return (more on this below) but also probably to movement to urban areas in Kenya and Ethiopia, outside the structures of the official refugee regime, and secondary movement beyond the region.

Migration patterns were differentiated economically, with those who were better-off and more internationally networked able to travel further afield, seeking visas, family reunion, and asylum in western Europe and North America. These destinations increased in importance relative to the Gulf countries where labour migration opportunities offered less long-term security; moreover, the 1991–92 Gulf War saw the expulsion of many migrant workers, making the region a less attractive destination. Factions and family members both called on those abroad for money during this period, providing the impetus for the development of a Somali-run money transfer system (Lindley, 2010a).

UNHCR's records suggest significant return to south-central Somalia during this period, with 170,192 repatriations from Kenya, partly under the aegis of a 'Cross-Border Operation' launched in 1993 by UNHCR, under pressure from the Kenyan government, and within the framework of the UN/US intervention (Kirby *et al.*, 1997). It was not possible for all these people to return to their former places of residence within Somalia. It is well known that many people registered to obtain the repatriation package, subsequently reappearing in Kenya. Of those that remained, many will have been displaced again in subsequent violence.

Overall, then, the early 1990s were characterised by a situation of indisputable crisis (in the sense of marked discontinuity and widespread threats to life itself, as well as to life as people knew it), and associated with dramatic displacement.

1996–2006: relative stabilisation, protracted displacement

The period from 1996 to early 2006 was marked by selective patterns of stabilisation. Repeated internationally-sponsored efforts to re-establish a national government failed, but over time, from the all-out warfare of the early 1990s, conflict became sporadic, 'more localized and less bloody, and criminality

54   *Anna Lindley and Laura Hammond*

more constrained' (Menkhaus, 2003: 405). Some pockets of relative stability emerged, where majority clans or well-formed coalitions of clans held sway. Customary law and neighbourhood-based sharia courts to some extent constrained violence and criminality. Among the business class in Mogadishu, while some continued to have vested interests in the conflict, many sought a more predictable operating environment to facilitate commerce and service provision, mobilising their own security forces to this end. Economically, some segments of the economy thrived: pastoralism quickly adapted to the stateless setting, and money transfer, telecommunications and construction industries flourished (Little, 2003).

However, though preceded and followed by more dramatic and terrible events, this period was nevertheless one of great hardship. Heavy oppression of weaker groups became routinised: in Afgoye, just outside Mogadishu, a local described their town as 'colonised' by General Aideed's Habar Gedir forces (Luling, 2002: 198). Very high levels of malnutrition and infant and maternal mortality persisted (Bradbury, 1998). Households devastated by conflict were subjected to recurrent shocks – drought, flooding and renewed bouts of violence, and livestock trade bans by major importing countries. The most vulnerable found themselves stuck at or regularly slipping below sub-subsistence economic levels (LeSage and Majid, 2002).

Despite this on-going humanitarian need, in the context of a global reduction in aid, and an international community newly nervous of political engagement in Somalia, with a more minimalist agenda, donor funding shrank massively. Aid agencies talked of rehabilitation, reducing aid dependency, and moving from relief to development – even where there was recurrent violence and no stable political framework (Bradbury, 1998). Indeed, the Consolidated Inter-Agency Appeal which raised emergency response funds became a regular programming document, and had to be supplemented by 'flash appeals' to address sudden onset emergencies such as the 1997 floods.[3] Effectively, high levels of human distress became accepted as 'normal for Somalia'.

The period 1996 to 2006 was characterised by more moderate displacement levels. There were recurrent bouts of fresh, but relatively small-scale displacement. Interviewees who lived in Mogadishu at the time described the violence as more or less predictable and negotiable: they coped by restraining their habitual movements (avoiding going outside, and staying away from volatile areas) and temporary micro-displacements (within or between urban neighbourhoods, to city outskirts, or to stay with kin in the rural hinterland), among other strategies (see Lindley, 2010b). Indeed, many people suggested that their major security problem in this period was in fact the *mooryaan*, a derogatory term for criminal gangs of marginalised youths, which grew partly as a result of new migration to the capital (Marchal, 1997). However, experiences varied considerably depending on one's social situation: many people were still forced to migrate by situations of intense structural violence and frequent abuse by predatory actors. Meanwhile, more 'routine' internal, regional and global mobility patterns, organised around livelihood problems

Challenges of crisis and mobility in Somalia   55

and opportunities (mediated by but not immediately triggered by the political context) became more apparent: the circuits of nomadic pastoralists, rural-urban labour migration, and the movement of the dissatisfied better-off to locations overseas.

In these years, protracted displacement became an established feature of the Somali landscape, with estimates of internally displaced persons (IDP) varying between 200,000 and 400,000. Local social networks and economic resources substantially eased settlement, and their absence signalled major insecurity (Lindley, 2013). Many IDPs experienced dire conditions, living in settlements with very poor shelter, sanitation and water access, eking out a living through begging, casual work, and intermittent humanitarian assistance. Rape of IDP women by members of dominant local clans occurred with impunity. The cheap labour benefitted employers, and the international emergency assistance that the IDPs attracted was easily diverted by self-appointed camp 'gatekeepers'. Often, migration was part of the re-concentration of clan groups and power struggles that underlie (and undermine) current federal state-making processes; in other instances, migration led to the social diversification of urban centres, leading to new forms of interconnection, cooperation and contestation. In Somaliland and Puntland, displaced southerners found greater political stability, but their distinct socio-political identities often left them vulnerable.

The Somali refugee presence in the wider region persisted, though fresh movement decreased and the total remained fairly stable. Kenya's registered Somali refugee population remained in the region of 150,000 from 1999 to 2005. Kenya remained inclusive, recognising all Somalis *prima facie* as refugees without individual status determination, but as time went on, restrictions on their rights became more obviously problematic (Betts, 2013). In terms of 'durable solutions', there was no integration policy, the issue proving controversial in light of the historic turbulence of Kenya's predominantly Somali North Eastern Province. Donor funding dwindled. Refugees encamped close to Nairobi and Mombasa were relocated, primarily to the remote Dadaab camps in the North Eastern Province, and police harassed those remaining in urban centres (Milner, 2009). Regional refugees increasingly sought their own, informal solutions to the difficult situations they encountered. Camp inhabitants became adept at maximising access to meagre international assistance, developed mutual social support mechanisms, tapped diaspora and urban-based relatives for remittances, and engaged in informal trade and services (Horst, 2006). Despite the 'encampment policy', they also settled informally in urban areas, seeking employment, education and business opportunities, famously fuelling the development of the dynamic Eastleigh district of Nairobi (Lindley, 2010a).

Despite western states' preference for containing the refugees in the region of origin, the wider diaspora grew as Somalis drew on their social networks to organise migration through family reunion channels, student and work visas, as well as clandestine movements to work or claim asylum. Official resettlement

56   *Anna Lindley and Laura Hammond*

programmes targeted people deemed particularly vulnerable: according to UNHCR statistics, some 73,709 Somalis were resettled from the region in 1996–2006, the majority to the USA. As pressure on the resettlement system mounted, corruption and fraud by administrators and refugees also increased, and Somalis came to view official resettlement as something that required organised effort to achieve (Horst, 2006). Smuggling grew as immigration regimes tightened and new migration pathways were forged across Africa, and eastwards to Asia. Diasporic fortunes varied considerably: in some contexts, Somalis were viewed as a 'problem minority' with poor levels of integration and high unemployment; others pointed to entrepreneurial successes and strong family networks. There was some secondary movement within the diaspora as families and sub-clans strategically re-organised to access opportunities. Transnational engagement flourished. By 2002, the remittance economy provided an estimated 23 per cent of total household income, conveyed by an increasingly sophisticated and efficient money transfer system (Lindley, 2010a). Relatives overseas provided regular instalments of income and an important means of coping with intermittent health and livelihood crises for many families. Diaspora groups also raised funds collectively for a wide spectrum of activities in Somalia, from armed conflict to charitable relief; engaged in business; and supported numerous educational and health institutions with their skills and capital (Hammond *et al.*, 2011).

While repatriation to Somaliland and Puntland from Ethiopia proceeded apace, recorded repatriations from Kenya, where the majority of the refugee population originated from south-central Somalia, dwindled to an average of a few hundred each year. Obstacles included continued political insecurity uncertainty in home areas, difficulties reclaiming land and property or accessing social protection there because of changed balances of power, and lack of funds to re-establish livelihoods. Occasionally people returned from the wider diaspora, although most returning voluntarily had the security of permanent residence or citizenship in another country, often forming a 'part-time diaspora' rather than becoming permanent returnees (Hammond *et al.*, 2011).

An important political shift occurred towards the end of this period. The Transitional Federal Government (TFG), the latest in a long line of internationally-sponsored governments treated with scepticism by ordinary people, was established in Kenya in 2004; by 2006, it had barely a foothold in Somalia. Meanwhile, however, building on the successes of the local shar'ia courts, the Islamic Courts Union (ICU) emerged as a major social and political force. In 2006, it gained control of most of Mogadishu, despite opposition from militia leaders courted by the USA as counter-terror allies (Menkhaus, 2007). The ICU brought Mogadishu under a unified administration for the first time in 15 years and extended control across southern Somalia. They disarmed militia or brought them under its control, greatly increasing security. Nearly every displaced person interviewed by Lindley's team in Somaliland in 2008 commented positively on the short-lived rule of the ICU, emphasising how it became easier to move around the city, even at night (Lindley, 2010b).

Challenges of crisis and mobility in Somalia 57

Improved security, lifting of roadblocks and reopening of sea and airports opened up mobility within and between urban centres. There were even reports of returns from enthusiastic segments of the diaspora, though like earlier returnees, many held passports for other countries.

Thus, this somewhat ambiguous period saw relative stabilisation/localisation of conflict; moderation of new displacement and relative growth of more routine movements; and the entrenchment of protracted displacement and normalisation of dire humanitarian need. However, this situation was not to last: before 2006 was out, Somalia was plunged into a new kind of political crisis.

2007–11: a perfect storm: massive and complex mobility patterns

Both Western and regional hostility to the idea of a strong Islamist state in Somalia propelled foreign military intervention to oust the ICU. Ethiopian troops pushed into Somali territory and in late December 2006 installed themselves and the weak Transitional Federal Government (TFG) in Mogadishu. An African Union peace-keeping mission, AMISOM, was established to train Somali troops and protect government institutions within a very small section of Mogadishu. Ousted from the capital, the ICU fragmented politically. Its hardline militia wing, organising under the name Al Shabaab (meaning 'the Youth') mobilised and fought back against the TFG, Ethiopian and AMISOM forces. The movement became popular with many who did not necessarily share the movement's Wahabist extremism but felt incensed by the foreign interference. Thus, in the second half of the 2000s, the axis of the conflict shifted again, moving from one based on the machinations of political entre-preneurs and clan-based mobilisation, to a radical opposition movement clashing with a foreign-supported 'national' government, albeit still infused with clan-based influences.

Disappointment in the TFG's inability to deliver victory or garner popular support, combined with dismay at the abuses perpetrated by TFG militia and foreign troops prompted internal and international pressure for a more inclusive approach (HRW, 2007). Talks in Djibouti in 2008 led eventually to Ethiopian forces withdrawing from most parts of Somalia. Efforts to draw in some of the moderate former ICU leaders saw Sheikh Sharif Sheikh Ahmed appointed as TFG President, although the government still failed to win over the armed opposition. Al Shabaab took control of most parts of Somalia that had been vacated by Ethiopia, since AMISOM and the TFG lacked the personnel to pose a serious challenge to them outside the capital, and until late 2011 continued to control most parts of south-central Somalia. Initial goodwill towards Al Shabaab eroded over time, as the introduction of severe punishment, forced recruitment, rigid political decrees and taxation affected many aspects of people's lives (HRW, 2011).

The year 2007 heralded a dramatic transformation in the intensity, forms and consequences of violence (see HRW, 2007; Grubeck, 2011). In Mogadishu, both sides indiscriminately bombarded urban neighbourhoods, showing little regard for civilian life. Ethiopian troops became particularly infamous for abusing civilians, while Al Shabaab deployed suicide and roadside bombs and guerrilla tactics, using the civilian population as a shield. Alongside this combat-generated insecurity suffered by all those living in affected areas, was more targeted persecution: threats, punishment and assassinations of politically exposed people by both Al Shabaab and TFG associates – in the early phases particularly politicians, aid workers and journalists, but as time went on anyone associated with the enemy side came to be at risk. The violence also had economic dimensions. Mogadishu's economic infrastructure – largely controlled by the Hawiye, and especially the Ayr subclan, which had backed the ICU financially – was targeted by the TFG and Ethiopian forces. People who lived in Mogadishu at the time found it difficult to get on with their usual livelihoods because it was not safe to move around the city and the physical and financial assets and infrastructures that their livelihoods relied on were vulnerable to attack (Lindley, 2010b). This was compounded by wider economic problems of hyperinflation and a spike in global food and fuel prices. A wide socio-economic spectrum of people were forced to move, as earlier protection mechanisms and coping strategies disintegrated.

Displacement during this period rocketed, with estimates of the internally displaced population tripling. In 2007–8, whole neighbourhoods of Mogadishu emptied as two-thirds of the residents of the city fled. A sprawling IDP complex mushroomed in the Afgoye corridor, a stretch of road some 10–30 km from Mogadishu, UNHCR estimating that as many as 400,000 people had settled there by the end of 2010, which would have made it the third most populous urban concentration in the Somali territories, after Mogadishu and Hargeisa, and quite probably the largest IDP settlement in the world (UN News Centre, 2010).[4] Satellite imagery testified to the rapid urban intensification of the area, with more permanent structures emerging alongside makeshift shelters. As violence flared across south-central Somalia, both recent and long-term IDPs found themselves moving back and forth, or onwards again, between insecure locations, displaced multiple times in search of safety. This was not a particularly new phenomenon, but became more pronounced due to the intensification of the conflict and its rapidly shifting frontlines.

International aid agencies struggled to respond as the violence made it even more dangerous to work in many areas and political actors sought to co-opt or block their work (Hammond and Vaughan-Lee, 2012). TFG officials and allies repeatedly imposed restrictions on aid delivery and tried to manipulate aid distributions to their benefit. From 2009 onwards Al Shabaab banned the majority of UN and Western aid agencies (including the World Food Pro-gramme), citing political bias. At the same time, agencies drew back from areas controlled by Al Shabaab, now designated a terrorist organisation, for fear of falling foul of counter-terror legislation in donor countries, particularly the USA, which suspended $50 million of humanitarian assistance. 'Mainstream' aid activity became restricted to the relatively small portion of south-central Somalia controlled by the TFG and its allies, and some minimal, low-profile activities

Challenges of crisis and mobility in Somalia 59

via local NGO partners in Al Shabaab areas. In this context, the role of 'alternative' aid providers, mainly Muslim humanitarian organisations and diaspora groups, gained increasing recognition.

As this new phase of conflict continued, the situation was compounded by environmental factors. In 2010, the worst drought for decades hit East Africa, with parts of the region experiencing their driest years since 1950/51. Consecutive seasons of low rainfall led to poor local harvests and difficulties for pastoralists finding water and pasture. The rural people of the riverine areas were once again particularly badly affected (Majid and McDowell, 2012). Since 2007, political restrictions, conflict and insecurity had limited opportunities for labour migration to urban areas (an established income diversification and coping strategy), and these communities had more limited diaspora networks. Thus, they faced high levels of covariate risk, i.e. their food, income and coping sources were focused on local farming, and extremely vulnerable to any production shock (Majid and McDowell, 2012). In July 2011, the UN declared that 3.7 million people in Somalia were at risk of starvation and the situation in southern Bakool and Lower Shabelle had reached famine proportions.[5] Famine was later declared in other areas of southern Somalia as well. The global acute malnutrition rate reached 20–45 per cent of the population. Some 258,000 people are thought to have perished in the period of most severe food insecurity and famine (October 2010 – April 2012); around half were children under 5 years old (Checchi and Robinson, 2013; FSNAU, 2011).

Unfolding over several months, this was clearly a slow-onset situation – indeed from August 2010 to June 2011, no less than 78 communications were issued by the FAO's Food Security and Nutrition Analysis Unit for Somalia highlighting the deteriorating situation (Lautze *et al.,* 2012). But in the six months prior to the declaration of famine, the World Food Programme called only two meetings of the food security cluster that it was tasked with coordinating (Nicholson *et al.*, 2012: 17). It is the height of tragic irony that the Integrated Food Security Phase Classification (IPC) system, a global tool to help avert crisis by classifying food security and triggering appropriate preventative action, was first developed in Somalia in the first half of the 2000s. The extremely polarised conflict situation and climate of inertia among major political and aid actors allowed famine to take hold in what are usually Somalia's most fertile agricultural areas.

In the absence of local assistance, mobility was vital for survival, but became acutely politicised. During 2011, Al Shabaab (which in fact tried to position itself as a voice for marginalised southerners) tried to contain people inside the areas it controlled, forcing back those who tried to flee, beheading the drivers of vehicles found to be smuggling people out, and forbidding people to leave, in an attempt to hold onto population and power (Lindley, 2013). After the famine declaration, spokesmen claimed that the situation was exaggerated by Western agencies for reasons of political propaganda, that large amounts of food aid would undermine local livelihoods, and promised

60   *Anna Lindley and Laura Hammond*

assistance to people staying at home or in Al Shabaab-run displacement camps (BBC, 2011). Difficulties moving and accessing humanitarian assistance undoubtedly increased famine mortality (Majid and McDowell, 2012). At the same time, the TFG also politicised movement and immobility by trying to lure people into – or keep them inside – areas under its control with offers of famine relief and other aid, citing this as evidence of increasing support and legitimacy of the government, even if their movement often had less to do with political loyalties than desperation and lack of other options.

In response to the UN declaration of famine and the ensuing 'CNN effect', an outpouring of aid was mobilised, and provisions blocking aid to Al Shabaab-controlled areas were relaxed (Lautze *et al.,* 2012). It is not the first time that an environmental crisis has contributed to opening up new horizons in a political conflict. Natural 'blameless' disasters often manage to (re)engage an uninterested, fatigued or cynical donor community (Hyndman, 2011). The largest-scale cash transfer programme recorded in any humanitarian emergency was initiated, and 'alternative' aid actors, including diaspora charitable networks, were increasingly recognised as critical to the aid response.

Thus, echoing the situation in the early 1990s, initial urban flight was followed by a rural exodus in the context of drought. In the context of prolonged drought, and no external assistance to help them remain in rural areas, many headed for urban centres and refugee camps. They often had to leave some family members behind, because they were too weak to make the journey, or to look after household assets. In fact, IDP estimates did not rise in 2011. While this may have been in part because of forced immobility referred to above, the figure may also mask a sort of replacement effect by which those who perished as a result of the famine or who fled as refugees were 'replaced' by newly displaced persons. In the context of the drought, global acute malnutrition worsened, reaching 46 per cent among IDPs in Mogadishu and Afgoye by August 2011 (IDMC, 2011).

In 2007–11, the parameters of the regional refugee situation shifted dramatically, from protracted and relatively stable displacement to a situation of mass influxes. The registered refugee population tripled, increasing markedly year on year, and spiking in 2011. Official figures likely underestimate the scale of regional movement, as the system could not keep up with the rapidly growing population, and many people who had the wherewithal or contacts preferred to move to urban areas and remain outside the structures of the official refugee regime. Originally established for 90,000 people, the Dadaab complex of camps in Kenya was believed to house around half a million people by the end of 2011 – one of the largest population centres in Kenya, after Nairobi and Mombasa. Against the background of the long-awaited Refugees Act of 2006, which finally formalised Kenya's relatively inclusive refugee policy in national legislation, and planned for greater government involvement in refugee affairs, refugee politics hardened. The sense in which refugees were spoken of and dealt with as a 'burden' increased, with talk of 'paying the Somali tax' – despite evidence pointing to real (albeit unevenly

Challenges of crisis and mobility in Somalia 61

socially distributed) economic gains resulting from their presence (Enghoff *et al.*, 2010; Betts, 2013). Security concerns escalated, with fears of synergies between Al Shabaab and creeping indigenous radical Islamism or the grievances of ethnic Somali Kenyans. There were worries that border violence could jeopardise Kenya's investment in a major new transport corridor and oil pipeline linking a deep water port at Lamu to South Sudan and Ethiopia. This was compounded by the kidnappings of foreign tourists and aid workers in 2011. Any discussion of 'local integration' as a durable solution was off the agenda and the focus moved to securing repatriation. In October, the Kenyan government launched Operation Linda Nchi ('Protect the Country'), sending troops into Somalia for the first time, aiming to oust Al Shabaab, establish a friendly buffer zone, and enable refugees to return.

In this period, immigration restrictions continued to make it difficult for Somalis to lodge asylum claims outside the region. Despite this, new asylum claims by Somalis in Europe reached a record high of more than 21,000 in 2008 and 2009, reflecting the dire situation at home. The turning of Somalia into a stage for the 'war on terror' has overshadowed host state responses to Somalis and prompted much debate within the diaspora. The diaspora continue to play a vital role in Somali affairs: with all parties to the conflict garnering financial support and marshalling finance, foot soldiers and leaders from abroad. Many parliamentarians in the Mogadishu, Puntland and Somaliland assemblies are from the wider region, the Middle East, Europe and North America. There is some resentment about diaspora returnees taking government and NGO jobs, and it has been important – and sometimes a challenge – for them to demonstrate to local communities that they are in touch with ordinary Somalis' problems (Hammond, 2013a). Remittances, by now estimated at US$1.3–2 billion per year, continue to be a major element in the economy, and large amounts of humanitarian and development assistance is raised by diaspora groups to the tune of US$130–200 million annually, benefitting displaced people, as well as communities of origin, and becoming a key component of the famine response (Hammond *et al.*, 2011; Hammond, 2013a).

In sum, the period since 2007 has indeed marked a distinct crisis in several respects for south-central Somalia: the macro-political battles for control of the state, combining powerfully with economic challenges and severe drought, disrupted the precarious normalities established in previous years, posing widespread and severe threats to lives and livelihoods, and generating a sharp and massive increase in displacement, alongside a greatly intensified politicisation of mobility. The famine of 2011 may not have caused a turning point all by itself, but it certainly marked one, and provided public impetus for renewed political and military intervention on behalf of the TFG.

Somalia rising?

The fortunes of the Somalia government began to change significantly in September 2011 when Al Shabaab announced a 'tactical withdrawal' from

Mogadishu. By September 2012, government forces, backed by AMISOM and Kenyan and Ethiopian military, had succeeded in gaining control of all major urban centres in south-central Somalia. In August 2012, the transitional government that had been in place in various forms since 2004 made way for the new Somali Federal Government (SFG). The SFG was significant not only for the fact that it was selected by a Parliament sitting in Mogadishu for the first time in two decades, but also for the fact that it held control of sufficient territory to embark on a meaningful governance programme (Hammond, 2013a). There followed a flurry of optimism in international media coverage, staple images including people enjoying the beach in Mogadishu, and diaspora returnees setting up businesses in newly rehabilitated premises.

The SFG faces enormous challenges in translating this optimism into reality (ibid.). As of late 2013, much of rural Somalia remains in the hands of Al Shabaab, which is poised to take advantage of any weakness and continues to mount devastating suicide attacks on key targets in urban centres. SFG control still depends in large part on delicate relationships with regional militaries deployed in Somalia, where foreign intervention is far from popular with the people. The promise of federalism and decentralised power is keeping many powerful domestic forces on side, for now, but the devil is in the detail, and how power and resources are used remains highly contentious. History cautions us against taking the present government's aspirations for achievements.

Meanwhile, though the famine was declared over in February 2012, large numbers of displaced and non-displaced people are still living in really dire conditions. Médecins Sans Frontières (MSF) recently withdrew from Somalia, citing the failure of the various Somali authorities to ensure safe humanitarian access. Internally displaced people suffer on-going abuses and aid diversion by gatekeepers over whom the SFG appears to exert little effective control. A process of government-led eviction from IDP centres in Mogadishu to contested areas on the outskirts of the city was instigated to make way for economic investment and political consolidation; these relocations were carried out with little recognition of the rights of the displaced (Yarnell, 2012). Meanwhile, Western regulatory concerns threaten to lead to a restructuring of the money transfer market which may disrupt remittance flows to IDPs, refugees, and others.

Despite these reasons for caution regarding the situation within Somalia, political pressure is mounting for repatriation to begin. Security concerns and xenophobic sentiments in Kenya have escalated as the incidence of terrorist attacks, some launched as a protest against that country's military intervention in Somalia, has increased. Police abuse of urban refugees has escalated as the authorities do what they can to pressurise them to move to the Dadaab camps (HRW, 2013). Meanwhile, the access of foreign humanitarian workers to Dadaab has been heavily restricted, and the camps are increasingly managed remotely by mobilising the refugee community. The Kenyan military has focused on 'liberating' areas close to the border from Al Shabaab, and supporting the establishment of Jubaland state as a friendly buffer. Reported modest declines

Challenges of crisis and mobility in Somalia 63

in the Dadaab population suggest that some refugees are opting to return (though whether because they see return as desirable or because of the shrinking asylum space remains unclear) have given further impetus to return preparations. In 2013, UNHCR and the Kenya and Somalia governments initiated formal dialogue on repatriation issues, and in November they signed a tripartite agreement paving the way for initiation of voluntary return to areas deemed safe enough. To its credit, though, UNHCR has been proactive in trying to think creatively about what alternative solutions there might be, convening a High Level Panel in November 2013 tasked with recommending measures for the short and medium term that go beyond the 'repatriation as best possible option' premise.

This brief and necessarily somewhat general history of developments in south-central Somalia over the past two decades points to the need to rethink the use of the term 'crisis' in this context. It also highlights several aspects of mobility in this context that defy conventional images of displacement. The next sections develop these points, and the chapter concludes by exploring contemporary policy challenges.

Rethinking 'the Somali crisis'

As outlined in the introduction, there are several ways that the term crisis is commonly used in relation to Somalia. Commentators often talk about 'the Somali crisis', referring sweepingly to the two and a half decades of civil war, and to the whole geography of the long fragmented Somali Republic. This shades quickly into exceptionalist conceptions of Somalia, portrayed as 'a black hole into which a failed polity has fallen' (Rotberg, 2002: 90), an ungoverned space, a zone of death and disaster undergoing a process of 'development in reverse' (Collier *et al.*, 2003: 13), convulsed with violence and haemorrhaging displaced people. The crisis narrative is often extended geographically to the wider region, such that the Horn of Africa 'over the last forty years … has been virtually synonymous with crisis' (Kendie, 2003: 67). Sometimes, as this shows, the time frame is extended, or the emphasis is on endemically recurrent rather than permanent crisis: as also illustrated by the title of a recent book: *Politics of Cain: One Hundred Years of Crises in Somali Politics and Society* (Bulhan, 2008).

The empirical evidence about the situation 'on the ground' which we have reviewed above – from displaced people's own accounts, as well as from statistical sources and political economy analyses – undermines these narratives in several important respects.

First, our account points to the need to dissect crisis, to separate distinct, if interacting problems and issues – the prolonged crisis of state political institutions, political conflict in its various permutations, lawlessness and criminality, economic and environmental conditions, and humanitarian indicators of basic welfare of the population – rather than lumping them into a 'single syndrome' (Menkhaus, 2003: 406) or 'Somali crisis'. The common assumption that Somalia

64   *Anna Lindley and Laura Hammond*

since the collapse of the state has been in comprehensive social crisis seems to misread the role of state institutions in this setting historically, and underestimate the role of other factors in shaping people's lives (Little, 2003; Hagmann and Hoehne, 2009). The severity of the situation in 2007–11 was not just about the rise of Al Shabaab, it involved a 'perfect storm' of factors, domestic governance shifts blending with global and regional geopolitics, drought and globalised economics.

Our account also debunks the notion of *constant* crisis, pointing to a dynamic history, with times of intense instability and rapid transformation, easily viewed as moments of crisis, but other times, of relative calm, stagnation and more incremental processes of change. There have been ebbs and flows of displacement, forced immobility, and more routine migration patterns. As people got on with everyday life in this extraordinary political setting, new senses of normality emerged, new crises erupted. Facing up to what has constituted normality from the point of view of many people in Somalia may be more shocking than seeing it as a crisis condition. The 'constant crisis' narrative robs south-central Somalia of much of the history of the last two and a half decades.

Finally, the evidence points to important *socio-spatial variations* in the experience of crisis (see also Díaz-Leal and Albuja, Chapter 4 in this volume). 'The Somali situation' is in fact many situations. Most obviously, the northern Somali territories forged an autonomous political trajectory, and generated somewhat distinct mobility patterns. But even within south-central Somalia there are pronounced localised elements to the drivers of mobility. There are also socially differentiated patterns of threat, vulnerability and opportunity. While some groups indeed experienced a situation of chronic livelihood crisis, living on the edge of survival throughout the period examined, explaining how the 2010–11 drought so easily translated into famine, others managed to achieve a significant level of material security.

So why, then, has the image of 'constant crisis' proven so persistent and so popular? We argue this narrative has several political functions. For foreign states, the image of Somalia as endemically crisis-ridden is politically malleable: a rationale for action or a justification for failure or inaction. It can be used both to construct Somalia as in need of radical intervention of a particular kind (as in 1992–95 and since 2007) or as an intractably challenging situation justifying minimal political intervention or disengagement (as in 1996–2006). Moreover, the notion of endemic crisis tends to gel with internalist explanations of the onset and perpetuation of conflict, providing implicit cover for the disruptive role of external political actors in *generating* crisis and mediating mobility at key points (examples include the impact of Cold War finance on the development and disintegration of Barre's regime; the international convening of repeated peace conferences privileging warlords with doubtful interests in peace; Western insistence on making Somalia another theatre for the war on terror; the focus on supporting central leadership often without sufficient attention to governance and legitimacy at local level). In 2012 and 2013, however, with foreign states investing heavily and publicly in supporting the SFG against Al Shabaab, there is a growing political pressure to foresee an 'end' to 'the Somali crisis'.

Challenges of crisis and mobility in Somalia 65

A sense of crisis is central to the work of international humanitarian aid agencies, which focus on meeting very basic human needs: it is their *raison d'être* and their institutional bread and butter, and they deploy crisis narratives strongly to galvanise funding. However, there can be problems with the resulting 'emergency mentality', particularly in situations where severe human distress and unmet basic needs persist over long periods of time. The overwhelming conception of the Somali situation in terms of an emergency/crisis, even its relatively more stable phases and places, has often been misused as a justification for not effectively monitoring aid distributions and diversions which have famously fuelled the war economy; not critically reflecting on the long-term consequences of compromising humanitarian principles to secure access to beneficiaries; and often for not engaging in the admittedly challenging livelihoods and protection work which might better serve beneficiaries, including internally displaced and refugees, in the long term (Abild, 2009; Hammond and Vaughan-Lee, 2012). UNHCR became heavily institutionally mired in regional camp management, which may have weakened its work pushing governments for durable solutions during the more protracted and stable phase of the refugee situation. At the same time, however, there is also a now well-recognised history of 'normalising the crisis' in the absence of political interest and resources: basically accepting sustained malnutrition and recurrent insecurity and only listening to really 'loud' humanitarian emergencies coming from Somalia (Bradbury, 1998; LeSage and Majid, 2002; Menkhaus, 2010). Thus one aid worker felt it necessary to remind the aid community that IDP displacement in 2007 was in fact an 'emergency within an emergency', highlighting the prior existence of extreme levels of deprivation (Noor, 2007). Despite urgent warnings of rapidly rising food insecurity, aid levels in the first half of 2011 were similar to a 'normal' year – and by July, surveys suggested that the excess death rate in some parts of southern Somalia had already reached *three times* the famine threshold (Checchi and Robinson, 2013).

Different narratives of crisis also serve domestic political actors in varied ways. An emphasis on crisis, and the pivotal moment of state collapse as the 'beginning' of 'the Somali crisis', tends to divert attention from closer historical analysis which reveals the importance of decisions taken by domestic political actors at particular junctures since that point. For example, the way that the USC leaders, combatants and civilian supporters turned on Daarood civilians in the wake of the state collapse and the bouts of 'clan cleansing' which followed, and the response, are very painful aspects of Somali history about which there is a studied public silence (Kapteijns, 2013). In 2005–12, the intransigent strategies adopted by south-central Somali politico-military actors in pursuit of state control imposed great suffering on the civilian population (Menkhaus, 2007). Over the last two decades, an emphasis on crisis and the extremity of the political situation has worked to privilege the voices of dominant political actors, who are perceived to have the power to resolve things, marginalising those of ordinary people, particularly vulnerable

66 *Anna Lindley and Laura Hammond*

groups, from the political debate, relegating their experiences to a special interest human rights or humanitarian issue rather than central to the political future of Somalia. Meanwhile, domestic political actors have also 'normalised crisis' at certain junctures. In the 1990s, aid disbursements helped vest warlords' interests in on-going conflict, contributing to a formidable 'war economy'. In 2011, Al Shabaab strenuously denied that there was a famine, insisting that they were capable of managing the situation. The SFG also sometimes adopts a 'business as usual' discourse, needing to show signs of delivering security to shore up its political legitimacy and international support.

Rethinking Somali mobility

Reflecting the generally disastrous narratives about 'the Somali situation' outlined above, the dominant image of Somali mobility is that of acute displacement: people forcefully propelled out of their place of residence by conflict or drought. Media images convey the proverbial 'sea of humanity' amassing in regional refugee camps (Malkki, 1996: 377). Displaced people are typically depicted as stripped down to their bare humanity: malnourished, abused, bereft of specific attributes, identities and preferences. 'By crossing the border, we became a UNHCR statistic', as one Somali refugee put it (Farah, 2000: 16, cited in Horst, 2006). Somali refugees are often cast as either vulnerable victims depending on aid and welfare handouts, or as cunning crooks ferociously manipulating aid and immigration systems to get ahead (Horst, 2006). The evidence reviewed above nuances these images in several ways, highlighting the often multi-causal, differentiated, strategic and transforming elements of Somali mobility in the shadows of crisis.

First, the causality of Somali mobility is routinely over-simplified, boiled down to single causes: 'these people fled civil war' or 'these people fled drought'. Forced migration research, with its applied orientation, tends to focus on destination situations. The policy-driven data collection and mapping of so-called 'mixed migration' also largely focus on host state responses. There has been little systematic analysis of the interplay of political, economic and environmental drivers of migration. Regional governments were quick to characterise the 2011 movements as 'drought displacement', implicitly circumscribing their responsibilities (see, for example, Government of Kenya, 2011) while also laying blame on Al Shabaab for misgovernance. In fact, such simple epithets grossly misrepresent the situation. The majority of people are displaced by a combination – and quite often also a culmination – of forces, rather than a single identifiable factor (see also Lindley, 2014). For example, a structural factor could be the long-term marginalisation of a particular group; a proximate cause the progressive impoverishment of a particular village at the hands of predatory actors; an immediate trigger an episode of flooding, drought or escalation of violence; and an intervening factor the absence of local humanitarian and livelihoods support (see also Van Hear, 1998). To develop appropriate policy responses to displacement, these combinations and

Challenges of crisis and mobility in Somalia   67

layers of causality must be recognised. One cannot presume that once the more immediate causes of movement are eliminated – for example, once the drought is over, or Al Shabaab is booted out – migration can easily be reversed. Deeper-lying factors may still be at play. An individual's personal situation, and conditions at home or potential areas of return, may have changed beyond recognition. It is more appropriate, in many cases, to consider return as new migration.

Second, Somalis on the move are too often reduced to a sea – or boatloads – of humanity, whereas in fact they constitute a rather differentiated population in several respects. Migrants have moved to different locations, and find themselves in widely varying situations. Refugee camp residents appear most often in the international media; the even larger numbers of people who are internally displaced and the people who 'self-settle' in regional towns and cities constitute a hugely important, if less visible and accessible component of displacement (see also Polzer and Hammond, 2008). Length of stay may vary significantly: in many locations displaced people who arrived yesterday live alongside those who arrived 20 years ago, and a second and even a third generation have been raised in exile. There is also a wide range of economic and socio-political vulnerabilities among displaced people.

Third, dominant images of Somalis on the move are of vulnerability and victimhood – but the evidence points to strong strategic elements to migration. This is not only the case for more routine migration, oriented around improving livelihoods and accessing opportunities, rather than in response to particular push factors. Even in highly constrained circumstances, people may exert their agency in critical ways. In particular, they make careful decisions about how to deploy their family members most effectively, in terms of mini-mising risks of different kinds, and accessing opportunities (see also Kaiser, Chapter 9, this volume). Migration in these contexts is certainly often a source of great suffering, but it is also a vital means to negotiate crisis. Indeed, the perils of forced immobility are an often under-recognised dimension of the crisis in south-central Somalia, with many stuck where they are as a result of disability, poverty, the insecure environment, or the strategies of political actors. Among communities where diverse forms of mobility were well established before the war, some wartime migration may not be such a 'destructuring' experience as often imagined, and certainly may be preferable to the alternatives (Monsutti, 2005; Lubkemann, 2008). However, an emphasis on agency and the strategic elements of migration should not lead to mirror stereotypes, that Somalis are inevitable nomads (justifying complacency in relation to movements often driven by major distress, danger and rights deprivations), or cunning crooks, but rather highlight how they respond, given their capacities, to the predicaments and opportunity structures they find themselves in (Horst, 2006).

Finally, migration and displacement are often seen as a side effect of conflict and other social processes, whereas here they are shown to be a central social force in Somalia. (Im)mobility is simultaneously an inadvertent consequence

68   *Anna Lindley and Laura Hammond*

of generalised crisis environments; and a ground-level strategy through which people negotiate the impact of crisis. Mobility is highly political and central to how the conflict has unfolded. With an estimated quarter of Somalia's population displaced at home and abroad, migration has major consequences in its own right, transforming troubled places of origin, crowded places of destination, through people's departures, arrivals, and transnational connections (UNHCR, 2011). Mobility is far from being a marginal phenomenon: it is central to any understanding of social, political and economic dynamics in the Somali territories. This account has attempted 'to place forced migration back in the flow of social history' rather than treat it only as a crisis-induced humanitarian emergency (Ranger, 1994: 279; Malkki, 1996).

Looking forward

The 2011 famine engaged the international community in no small part because it was a highly mobile crisis – with aid restricted inside Somalia, refugees poured out. They were viewed not only as people in need of protection and assistance, but also as potential vectors of destabilisation and the spread of Islamist militancy. Foreign states' policy approaches and debates have once again focused on containment – in the region of origin, in border zone refugee camps, and through repatriation to 'safe havens' within the country of origin.

There should be less haste to 'put Somalia back in its box'. Making Somalia safe is a long-term project: there are no quick fixes. Premature or forced returns might well destabilise a still precarious political situation. Current circumstances are still a considerable way from being conducive to the orchestration of large-scale legal, voluntary repatriation, in safety and dignity; even more dim are the immediate prospects for sustainable reintegration. Refugees know this. If the government continues to make advances, much work needs to be done on ensuring protection for civilians by the various security forces, establishing a framework to address land issues, and comprehensive livelihood regeneration and expansion, in order to facilitate for the current displaced population a somewhat humane level of existence, let alone to reintegrate any repatriating refugees.

By developing a nuanced understanding of who the displaced are, what their experiences of migration have been, and what the conditions are in areas where they might potentially settle (whether in south-central Somalia or elsewhere), the problems of both refugees and policy-makers may be more appropriately addressed. This will need to include providing some routes to local integration in host countries, or at least providing opportunities for employment and mobility for some of those longest-displaced and those born as refugees. Resettlement will probably continue to be appropriate for those with acute socio-political vulnerabilities.

Constructive responses might also focus on how policy might work in harmony with, rather than against, the strategic self-help capacities of people on the move. Ensuring that displaced people are able to access their full range of rights

Challenges of crisis and mobility in Somalia 69

is key. Other examples include ensuring the flow of remittances in a hostile regulatory climate; facilitating refugees' local and international mobility as students and workers; including refugees in peace-building processes and repatriation discussions; and partnering with diaspora organisations to deliver assistance in hard-to-reach locations. In this way, mobility and transnationalism may be part of the raft of processes by which the Somali territories may forge a more stable future.

Notes

1 Refugee figures in this chapter are taken from the UNHCR's Statistical Online Population Database, unless otherwise noted.
2 That is, the regions of Gedo, Middle and Lower Juba, Middle and Lower Shabelle, Bay, Bakool, Hiraan and Galgaduud and the city of Mogadishu.
3 Email correspondence with Mark Bradbury, 30 August 2013.
4 Given the difficulties of enumeration in this setting, this estimate remains controversial.
5 The UN uses the term famine to describe situations where more than 30 per cent of children are acutely malnourished, more than two people in every 10,000 die each day and people have no food or other basic necessities. This definition was adopted only in 2006. No standard definition of famine was used prior to that time. See FAO (2008).

References

Abild, E. (2009) 'Creating Humanitarian Space in Somalia', *New Issues in Refugee Research*, No. 184. Geneva: UNHCR.
Ambroso, G. (2002) 'Pastoral Society and Transnational Refugees: Population Movements in Somaliland and Eastern Ethiopia, 1988–2000', *New Issues in Refugee Research*, No. 65. Geneva: UNHCR.
BBC (2011) 'Somali Islamists Maintain Aid Ban and Deny Famine', 22 July. Available at: http://www.bbc.co.uk/news/world-africa-14246764.
Betts, A. (2013) *Survival Migration: Failed Governance and the Crisis of Displacement.* Ithaca, NY: Cornell University Press.
Bradbury, M. (1998) 'Normalising the Crisis in Africa', *Disasters* 22(4): 328–38.
——(2008) *Becoming Somaliland.* Oxford: James Currey
Bulhan, H.A. (2008) *Politics of Cain: One Hundred Years of Crisis in Somali Politics and Society.* Bethesda, MD: Tayosan International Publishing.
Checchi, F. and Robinson, C. (2013) *Mortality Among Populations of Southern and Central Somalia Affected by Severe Food Insecurity and Famine During 2010–12.* Nairobi: FAO/FSNAU.
Collier, P., Elliot, V.L., Hegre, H., Hoeffler, A., Reynal-Querol, M. and Sambanis, N. (2003) *Breaking the Conflict Trap: Civil War and Development Policy.* Washington, DC: World Bank and Oxford University Press.
De Waal, A. (1997) *Famine Crimes.* Oxford: James Currey.
Enghoff, M., Hansen, B., Umar, A., Gildestad, B., Owen, M. and Obara, A. (2010) 'In Search of Protection and Livelihoods: Socio-economic and Environmental Impacts of Dadaab Refugee Camps on Host Communities', Report for the Royal Danish Embassy, the Republic of Kenya and the Norwegian Embassy.

70   Anna Lindley and Laura Hammond

FAO (2008) *Integrated Food Security Phase Classification: Technical Manual Version 1.1.* Rome: FAO. Available at: http://www.fao.org/docrep/010/i0275e/i0275e.pdf.

Frushone, J. (2001) *Welcome Home to Nothing: Refugees Repatriate to a Forgotten Somaliland.* Washington, DC: US Committee for Refugees.

FSNAU (2011) 'Food Security and Nutrition Analysis Post Gu 2011', FSNAU Technical Series Report VI 42. Nairobi: Food Security and Nutrition Analysis Unit – Somalia.

Government of Kenya (2011) 'Briefing on the Refugee and Drought Situation in the Country'. Available at: http://reliefweb.int/node/435254 (accessed 25 August 2011).

Grubeck, N. (2011) *Civilian Harm in Somalia: Creating an Appropriate Response.* Washington, DC: Campaign for Innocent Victims in Conflict.

Hagmann, T. and Hoehne, M.V. (2009) 'Failures of the State Failure Debate: Evidence from the Somali Territories', *Journal of International Development* 21: 42–57.

Hammond, L. (2013a) 'Somalia Rising: Things Are Starting to Change for the World's Longest Failed State', *Journal of Eastern African Studies* 7(1): 183–93.

——(2013b) 'Somali Transnational Activism and Integration in the UK: Mutually Supporting Strategies', *Journal of Ethnic and Migration Studies* 7: 1–17.

——(2013c) *Family Ties: Remittances and Social Support to Puntland and Somaliland.* Nairobi: FAO/FSNAU.

Hammond, L., Awad, M., Ibrahim Dagane, A., Hansen, P., Horst, C., Menkhaus, K. and Obare, L. (2011) 'Cash and Compassion: The Somali Diaspora's Role in Relief, Development and Peacebuilding', unpublished report, United Nations Development Programme – Somalia.

Hammond, L. and Vaughan-Lee, H. (2012) 'Humanitarian Space in Somalia: A Scarce Commodity', Humanitarian Policy Group Working Paper. London: Overseas Development Institute.

Hansch, S., Lillibridge, S., Egeland, G., Teller, C. and Toole, M. (1994) *Lives Lost, Lives Saved: Excess Mortality and the Impact of Health Interventions in the Somalia Emergency.* Washington, DC: Refugee Policy Group.

Horst, C. (2006) *Transnational Nomads: How Somalis Cope with Life in the Dadaab Camps of Kenya.* Oxford: Berghahn Books.

HRW (2007) *Shell-Shocked: Civilians Under Siege in Mogadishu.* Washington, DC: Human Rights Watch.

——(2011) *You Don't Know Who to Blame: War Crimes in Somalia.* New York: Human Rights Watch.

——(2013) *'You Are All Terrorists': Kenyan Police Abuse of Refugees in Nairobi.* Washington, DC: Human Rights Watch.

Hyndman, J. (2011) *Dual Disasters: Humanitarian Aid after the 2004 Tsunami.* Boulder, CO: Kumarian Press.

IDMC (2010) *Internal Displacement Caused by Conflict and Violence.* Geneva: Internal Displacement Monitoring Centre. Available at: http://www.internal-displacement.org/IDMC_IDP-figures_2001–10.pdf.

Kapteijns, L. (2013) *Clan Cleansing in Somalia: The Ruinous Legacy of 1991.* Philadelphia, PA: University of Pennsylvania Press.

Kendie, D. (2003) 'Toward Northeast African Cooperation: Resolving the Ethiopia-Somalia Disputes', *Northeast African Studies* 10(2): 67–109.

Kirby, J., Kleist, T., Frerks, G., Flikkkema, W. and O'Keefe, P. (1997) 'UNHCR's Cross-border Operation in Somalia: The Value of Quick Impact Projects for Refugee Resettlement', *Journal of Refugee Studies* 10(2): 181–98.

Challenges of crisis and mobility in Somalia   71

Lautze, S., Bell, W., Alinovi, L. and Russo, L. (2012) 'Early Warning, Late Response (Again): The 2011 Famine in Somalia', *Global Food Security* 1: 43–9.

LeSage, A. and Majid, N. (2002) 'The Livelihoods Gap: Responding to the Economic Dynamics of Vulnerability in Somalia', *Disasters* 26(1): 10–27.

Lindley, A. (2010a) *The Early Morning Phone Call.* New York: Berghahn Books.

——(2010b) 'Leaving Mogadishu: Towards a Sociology of Conflict-Related Mobility', *Journal of Refugee Studies* 23(1): 2–22.

——(2011) 'Between a Protracted and a Crisis Situation: Policy Responses to Somali Refugees in Kenya', *Refugee Survey Quarterly* 30(4): 14–49.

——(2013) 'Displacement in Contested Places: Governance, Movement and Settlement in the Somali Territories', *Journal of Eastern African Studies* 7(2).

——(2014) 'Environmental Processes, Political Conflict and Migration: A Somali Case Study', in S. Martin, S. Weerasinghe and A. Taylor (eds) *Humanitarian Crises and Migration: Causes, Consequences and Responses.* London: Routledge.

Little, P. (2003) *Somalia: Economy Without a State.* Oxford: James Currey.

Lubkemann, S. (2008) *Culture in Chaos: An Anthropology of the Social Condition in War.* Chicago: University of Chicago Press.

Luling, V. (2002) *The Somali Sultanate: The Geledi City-State Over 150 Years.* London: HAAN/Transaction Publishers.

Majid, N. and McDowell, S. (2012) 'Hidden Dimensions of the Somalia Famine', *Global Food Security* 1: 36–42.

Malkki, L. (1996) 'Speechless Emissaries: Refugees, Humanitarianism, and Dehistoricization', *Cultural Anthropology* 11(3): 377–404.

Marchal, R. (1997) 'Forms of Violence and Ways to Control it in an Urban War Zone: The Mooryaan in Mogadishu', in H.M. Adam and R. Ford (eds) *Mending Rips in the Sky: Options for Somali Communities in the 21st Century.* Lawrenceville, NJ, and Asmara: Red Sea Press, pp. 193–208.

Menkhaus, K. (2003) 'State Collapse in Somalia: Second Thoughts', *Review of African Political Economy* 30(97): 405–22.

——(2007) 'The Crisis in Somalia: Tragedy in Five Acts', *African Affairs* 106(204): 357–90.

——(2010) 'Stabilisation and Humanitarian Access in a Collapsed State: The Somali Case', *Disasters* 34(3): 320–41.

Milner, J. (2009) *Refugees, the State and the Politics of Asylum in Africa.* Basingstoke: Palgrave Macmillan.

Monsutti, A. (2005) *War and Migration: Social Networks and Economic Strategies of the Hazaras of Afghanistan.* London: Routledge.

MSF (2013) *Hear My Voice: Somalis on Living in a Humanitarian Crisis.* New York: Médecins Sans Frontières.

Nicholson, N., Longley, K., Fisher, M. and Walters, T. (2012) *Somalia: An Evaluation of WFP's Portfolio. Vol. I, Full Report.* Rome: World Food Programme. Available at: http://documents.wfp.org/stellent/groups/public/documents/reports/wfp251694.pdf.

Noor, H. (2007) 'Emergency Within an Emergency: Somali IDPs', *Forced Migration Review* 28: 29–31.

NRC (2003) *Profile of Internal Displacement: Somalia.* Norwegian Refugee Council/Global IDP Project. Available at: http://www.madhibaan.org/in-depth/Somalia+-June+2003.pdf.

Polzer, T. and Hammond, L. (2008) 'Invisible Displacement', *Journal of Refugee Studies* 21(4): 417–31.

Ranger, R. (1994) 'Studying Repatriation as Part of African Social History', in T. Allen and H. Morsink (eds) *When Refugees Go Home*. Trenton: NJ: Africa World Press.

Rotberg, R.I. (2002) 'The New Nature of Nation-State Failure', *Washington Quarterly* 25(3): 85–96.

Samatar, A. (1988) *Socialist Somalia: Rhetoric or Reality?* London: Zed Books.

UN News Centre (2010) 'Violence in Mogadishu Swells Number of Displaced Somalis: UN Survey'. Available at: http://www.un.org/apps/news/story.asp?NewsID=36311&Cr= somali&Cr1= (accessed 13 April 2011).

UNDP (2001) *Human Development Report: Somalia*. Nairobi: UNDP.

UNHCR (2011) *Donor Update: Somalia Situation Response*. Available at: http://www. unhcr.org/4e157f499.pdf.

——(2013) *Somali Refugees in the Region as of 10th Sept 2013*. Nairobi: UNHCR. Available at: https://data.unhcr.org/horn-of-africa/regional.php.

Van Hear, N. (1998) *New Diasporas*. London: UCL Press.

Yarnell, M. (2012) *Gatekeepers and Evictions: Somalia's Displaced Population at Risk*. Refugees International Field Report. Washington, DC: Refugees International.

4 Criminal violence and displacement in Mexico

Evidence, perceptions and politics

Laura Rubio Díaz-Leal and Sebastián Albuja

> You get used to anything, except seeing bleeding and dead people at your doorstep; or receiving phone calls to threaten you; or the raping of your children ... you never get used to that. That's why we left. Even though we're worse off here, without a home, and living in a crowded house with relatives, we live with less fear.[1]

Since 2007, Mexico has experienced a dramatic surge in violence, as the government adopted a confrontational military strategy aimed at bringing down drug cartels, and as the cartels fragmented and fought over distribution routes and zones of influence for new criminal activities (Guerrero, 2013). As a result, the number of homicides, threats, disappearances, extortions, and attacks on civilians, journalists, public officials, and human rights advocates, and deaths of bystanders increased exponentially. The explosion of violence by drug cartels has been accompanied by human rights abuses perpetrated by state security forces (Human Rights Watch, 2011, 2013). Yet impunity and corruption reign to an extent unprecedented in living memory, compounding fear among ordinary Mexicans and fomenting frustration and mistrust of the government. Both direct violence and threats and generalised fear and insecurity have prompted significant internal displacement, and increasing international movement of refugees.

However, whether this situation constitutes a crisis has been subject to debate. This chapter presents statistical data in terms of the impact of violence and associated displacement, as well as narratives from ordinary Mexicans, which suggest that the recent situation is significantly discontinuous with earlier patterns of violence, and poses a major threat to the lives and well-being of a large proportion of the population. However, by contrast, the government persists in denying that there is a crisis, let alone that hundreds of thousands of Mexicans have been displaced, for various reasons relating to its own political legitimacy domestically, for international credibility, and due to the lack of institutional structures to deal with displacement. In other words, depending on how the question of whether Mexico is in crisis is interpreted or

74   *Laura Rubio Díaz-Leal and Sebastián Albuja*

constructed, by whom, and at what level politically and geographically, different answers come into focus.

This chapter first outlines the changing political economy of crime in Mexico and the statistical data on violence, then explores the narratives of crisis among ordinary people, and in the media and the arts. Then we turn to the issue of displacement, showing statistically that there is a significant link between violence and internal migration, and examining the triggers for movement and the scale of displacement. Finally, we discuss how and why the crisis has been largely denied by the government and ignored by international actors, and with what consequences.

This chapter draws upon a wide range of sources, including: the 2010 population census, the Citizenship, Democracy and Narco-Violence survey (CASADE, 2011), the National Survey of Victimisation and Perceptions of Public Security (INEGI, 2011), national security reports, artistic representations, official press releases, media items, and policy papers.

In addition, the authors conducted a survey of 277 Mexicans, which elicited perceptions of the general social situation and personal everyday experiences of the violence, including its impact on work routines, leisure habits, mobility, security measures and communication with other people in their community. Respondents were selected through the researchers' social networks, and snowball sampling, and they included Mexicans from a range of backgrounds, including some currently living abroad.[2] This was not intended to be a representative sample of any population or of any segment of the population but, rather, to provide exploratory insights into how different people in different locations are experiencing violence.

Finally, we carried out qualitative research in 2011–13 with people affected by the violence. In 2011, we worked with the Movement for Peace with Justice and Dignity (MPJD) headed by the poet Javier Sicilia (whose son was killed in the crossfire of organised crime in the state of Morelos), which carried out two major caravans, to the North and the South of Mexico, travelling through some 21 states to gather testimonials from victims. In total, testimonials were collected from some 29 families, involving approximately 190 displaced people. We have since carried out additional interviews in other locations.

Our aim here is to combine analysis of 'hard data' with people's own narratives of their experiences of social change. Narrative as a central tool for qualitative research is grounded in the assumption that meaning is ascribed to phenomena through being experienced and, furthermore, that we can only know something about other people's experiences from the expressions they give to them. Therefore, an individual's life story should be looked at various levels: as how it is *lived*, by looking at the flow of events that touch on a person's life; as how it is *experienced*, by looking at how the person perceives and ascribes meaning to what happens; and as how it is *told*, by looking at how experience is framed and articulated in a particular context (Eastmond, 2007: 258). These different aspects were included in our analysis.

Political economy of drug-related violence

> Mexico is a battlefield, an extremely dangerous battlefield affecting innocent people like us. In this battlefield petty criminals, drug lords and government forces are all guilty of inflicting pain … No one is safe here; there is no guarantee of life here, especially if your only crime was to have been born in one of the 'cursed' states like Michoacán, Veracruz or Guerrero. Because of the lack of protection, most people prefer to keep quiet and flee if they can.[3]

Drug cartels and drug-cartel violence in Mexico are not a new phenomenon. Drug cartels, whose purpose is to profit by producing, distributing and selling drugs that are illegal in many jurisdictions, have been operating in Mexico since the nineteenth century and have expanded rapidly in the mid- and late twentieth centuries (Osorno, 2009). They flourished thanks to the corruption networks they developed with the 70-year-long administration of the Institutional Revolutionary Party (PRI), resulting in lucrative tacit agreements of co-existence, and to the increased popularity of Mexico as a shipping route for Colombian drugs in the early 1980s, when crackdowns from US authorities on shipments through the Caribbean and Florida became more common (Collins et al., 1997).

Drug cartels, like many other criminal structures, normally prefer to hide and bribe rather than fight, which is usually a costly and inefficient means to their ends, and generally deployed only as a last resort (Lessing, 2011). Motivated by profit rather than quest for political change, they generally have little interest in directly confronting state actors. Cartels in Mexico have typically resorted to overt violence or 'predatory crime' as reprisal for arrests or killings of kingpins, or to assert their position vis-à-vis other cartels in specific locations (Guerrero, 2013). Thus, during the 1990s, while there were occasional outbreaks of communal violence in various states, and kidnapping was on the increase across Mexico, the overall situation did not result in a generalised perception of insecurity that altered in fundamental ways the lives of ordinary Mexicans in most of the country.

However, the state inertia and impunity that accompanied the different escalations of violence in the northern states of Chihuahua and Baja California, and the southern state of Chiapas during the 1990s foreshadowed the current situation in significant ways. Violent crime increasingly flourished unchecked in the northern states of Chihuahua and Baja California, a stark example being the 'femicides' of the Valley of Juárez. From 1993 to 1998, at least 162 homicides of young women (between 15 and 25 years old) were reported in Ciudad Juárez alone, of which 110 were categorised as serial killings by the local police (Monárrez, 2000). Most of these women were from poor backgrounds, started working at an early age to help their families, were mostly employed in the maquiladora industry, and were abducted as they were commuting to work. These spates of killings are thought to be related to a combination of increasing male economic insecurity, growing drug gang activity, as well as high levels of impunity associated with the corruption of

76   *Laura Rubio Díaz-Leal and Sebastián Albuja*

the municipal police, and connections between the state's political elite and the big drug lords (González, 2002). Although these crimes prompted widespread public outrage and condemnation by the press, civil society and opposition leaders, they continued to occur throughout the 2000s (Gaceta Parlamentaria, 2012). Meanwhile, Chiapas was the scene of violent clashes between the government and the Zapatista movement (campaigning for the eradication of poverty, for justice and respect for the rights of indigenous communities), officially recognised as a local conflict requiring military intervention by the state in 1994. According to federal and local authorities the conflict subsided after the signing of the San Andrés Agreements (February 1996), but Chiapas remained a highly insecure environment. Key issues included the emergence of paramilitary groups, responsible for the massacre of 45 people in the village of Acteal in 1997; the lack of appropriate responses to victims of violence in the aftermath of the military intervention; the displacement of hundreds of indigenous people by development projects; conflicts over land tenure; and religious intolerance. Thus, government inaction in relation to violence and insecurity was evident in these states even prior to the 2000s.

In 2000, there was a significant break with the past when the main opposition party – the National Action Party (PAN) – won the presidential elections. With this political change came an upheaval in the traditional political and social order, which included the reassessment of the former government's co-existence 'pacts' with the main drug cartels. This was partly due to the new president's goal of working toward the amelioration of public security and the rule of law to improve the quality of life of Mexicans and enhance the government's credibility worldwide. Following a second general election victory in 2006, the government embarked on a new security strategy, aiming to bring down the cartels by confronting and attacking them through military operations and joint operations with police in the most crime-affected areas of the country.

This resulted in the fragmentation of the drugs sector. While in the 1990s, there were large cartels run by drug lords with established control of certain territories and zones of influence, the recent government offensive that has killed or imprisoned many cartel leaders has resulted in more atomised and horizontal structures, fleeting alliances, and internal divisions (Loyola, 2009). A myriad of smaller groups emerged, clashing in their quest for territory and influence. While larger drugs lords still maintain control of transnational drugs trafficking networks, the smaller criminal actors turned to domestic criminal activity, especially extortion, protection rackets, kidnapping, and drug dealing (Escalante, 2011; Guerrero, 2013). These smaller kingpins embarked on a fierce and often violent competition for the local drug market, establishing a presence in everyday community venues including high schools, shopping malls, so-called *narco-tienditas* (little drug outlets within small grocery stores everywhere in the country), and food stalls in markets. They also run protection rackets threatening ordinary Mexicans with violence if they do not pay monthly or weekly fees; failure to comply results in torture, the killing of a relative, and the like. This phenomenon, previously limited to particular

Criminal violence and displacement in Mexico 77

areas, now occurs throughout the country and targets people from all walks of life, from the wealthy, to school principals, doctors, small business owners and peasant farmers.

The consequences of this shifting political economy of crime were dramatic. As part of the MPJD caravan process, human rights lawyers, victims and activists together developed a typology of violence documented, consisting of nine main crimes: human rights violations, homicides, lack of due legal process, unjust imprisonment, rape and sexual violence, forced disappearances, forced displacement, threats and extortion. Daily homicide rates shot up from 8 to 18 for every 100,000 inhabitants in the course of 2008 (INEGI, 2010). According to official information, in total, some 47,000 people died and 26,000 disappeared between 2007 and September 2011 (PGR, 2011). Other sources estimate that at least 70,000 died during Calderón's six-year term (Sicilia, 2012). Approximately 13,000 died in the first year of the Enrique Peña Nieto's administration (Sistema Nacional de Seguridad Pública, 2013). According to Human Rights Watch, Mexico is experiencing the worst forced disappearances crisis ever in Latin America, with evidence of involvement of the security forces (army, navy, federal, state and municipal polices) as well as criminal organisations (HRW, 2013). Reported cases of extortion have increased sharply, from 2,979 in 2005 to 4,582 in 2011, and further to 7,272 in 2012; reported kidnappings rocketed from 278 in 2005 to 1,344 in 2011 (Sistema Nacional de Seguridad Pública, 2013). In 2011, the commonest reported violent crime was extortion (Guerrero, 2011). However, due to fear, lack of trust in the government and the penal and justice systems, many Mexicans do not report crimes they are victims of.[4]

The violence has caused people to change the way they live significantly. In 2011, 61 per cent of Mexicans at the national level had stopped going out at night because of fear of being victims of crime; 45 per cent of parents stopped allowing their children to go out at night (73 per cent in Chihuahua); 27 per cent stopped going out altogether at night for leisure (53 per cent in Chihuahua and Nuevo León); 42 per cent stopped travelling to certain areas of the country out of fear of violence (53 per cent in Chihuahua and 54 per cent in Nuevo León); and 51 per cent had tightened security measures at home (CASADE, 2011). All our survey respondents reported that violence and insecurity affect at what time they go out and when they return home (avoiding leaving home before dawn and at night on their own, particularly if they have to walk a long way to the bus stop or subway station); what type of public transport they use and when; where they go on holidays;[5] who they go out with; and what they do for fun or for leisure. Most women respondents mentioned they stopped wearing jewellery and wear more conservative and simple clothing when they use public transportation to avoid being noticed (particularly in Chihuahua with its history of 'femicides'). All businessmen and women surveyed claim they have chosen to either drive cheaper cars to avoid being targeted by organised crime, or hired a driver or drive bullet-proof cars.

78   *Laura Rubio Díaz-Leal and Sebastián Albuja*

Into this picture enter other actors. There is a long tradition of communal forces mobilising violently to counteract social injustice and circumstances leading to misery in various parts of the country, particularly in the northern states and the poorer regions of the south. Their aims have generally been to tackle petty crimes, and abuses from the government and private enterprises that threatened the interests of communities (for example, the construction of dams that would displace indigenous communities, and the exploitation of natural resources traditionally in the hands of local ethnic groups, such as wood) and to stop criminals from entering towns. Nonetheless, since 2008, as insecurity became more acute and the absence of the state was felt in many areas, community police and self-defence forces have sprouted in 22 munici-palities (across nine states). These aim to protect local communities from pillage, extortion, and the presence of paramilitaries, gangs, drug cartels and gen-eralised violence, and also often take justice into their own hands. Even some female squads (formed of mothers, grandmothers and sisters of homicide victims, or who have been victims themselves of some kind of crime) have emerged in the most violent cities of Guerrero (Orlinsky, 2013). Often criminals have retaliated by cutting the communities in question off from basic commodities, such as petrol and food, further undermining already vulnerable communities. The picture is reportedly sometimes complicated when criminal gangs and members of the state security forces infiltrate some of these community polices, exacerbating the problems of instability, insecurity, and governability. Weapons exclusively used by the army have been found among these forces. As a result, federal authorities have detained members of some community self-defence forces (Agencias de Noticias, 2013). This demonstrates the limited ability of the government to maintain law and order and protect its citizens.

Perceptions and narratives of crisis

In the survey conducted by the authors, the term 'crisis' was avoided, to prompt respondents to use their own words to describe the current situation in Mexico. Although only 36 per cent spontaneously used the term 'crisis' explicitly, the remaining 64 per cent used other terms that also evoke a sense of crisis: describing the situation as 'a climate of violence', 'a helpless situation', 'social degeneration', 'misery', 'loss of human values', 'an environment of criminality', 'social alienation', 'economic deprivation', 'social and economic polarisation', 'corruption, corruption, corruption', 'impunity,' and 'an environment where no one respects the law, least of all our government officials, and no one does any-thing about it'. No wonder opinion polls suggest that 80 per cent of Mexicans at the national level are 'very worried' about the violent situation the country is experiencing (CASADE, 2011). Some 53 per cent do not believe the so-called war against the cartels is being won. And half the population report a sense of helplessness vis-à-vis organised crime and the government's ability to bring peace.

All our respondents perceive the current wave of violence and insecurity as the worst the country has ever experienced in living memory, and as entirely

Criminal violence and displacement in Mexico   79

different from previous situations of instability. The two main historical reference points, situations that were perceived as critical by respondents, were the 1994 economic crisis when the PRI was still in power, and the more recent democratic transition in 2000. During the economic crisis in 1994, the major challenges were the widespread poverty, lack of accountability and good governance practices, major corruption, and sporadic bursts of violence. Nevertheless, the current wave of violence is perceived as a distinct type of situation, even among the respondents 65 years old or older who have experienced several economic, political and social crises during their lives.

Another break with the past commonly narrated is that earlier economic crises and other crises such as environmental catastrophes had the effect of mobilising civil society, stimulating a sense of community, and prompting a quick response to assist and protect their victims.[6] The current situation of violence, by contrast, is perceived to alienate, divide society, silence and frighten people. Some surveys reveal that Mexicans perceive that they tend to help each other less nowadays as a result of insecurity. This is particularly acute in Mexico City, the State of Mexico and Chihuahua (CASADE, 2011). Thus, silence seems to be the dominant feature in this crisis; people are afraid to speak out because they feel unsafe, frustrated, and helpless. A representative statement of this situation was given as follows:

> Journalists reporting crimes in the violent states are silenced by narcos; victims denouncing crimes are silenced by criminals or corrupt officials; you cannot count on your neighbours any more as before, because you never know what they are up to. So your safest option is to mind your own business, and if you see something bad, you look the other way and pretend you didn't see it.[7]

Many journalists whose work addresses violence and injustice are concerned about the effects of such silencing on society, since many people do not know what is really happening, particularly since 2010, when threats and attacks on journalists increased (Turati, 2011). Eighty-three persons who work for newspapers and radio-telecommunications have been killed since 2000, and there is constant harassment of journalists, bloggers, and editors, making Mexico the most dangerous country in the world to practise journalism (IDMC, 2011; Ríos, 2012). Discussions about violence, reports on deaths, confrontations involving criminal organisations, the consequences of these, and so on, are reported in print and online newspapers, blogs, and some key reviews and journals. For example, the magazine *Nexos* and the weekly publication *Proceso* have covered violence and corruption in rigorous detail, with some reporters killed in the process (Carrasco, 2012; Word Press, 2012). The online versions of the newspapers *La Jornada*, *Milenio*, and *El Universal*, as well as other sources such as *Animal Político* and *El blog del narco*, have been systematic in covering all aspects of violence, including forced displacement. However, victims of

80   *Laura Rubio Díaz-Leal and Sebastián Albuja*

violence interviewed claim that very little of what really happens in their communities is ever reported, leaving the rest of the country in complete ignorance of the situation in the most violence-stricken states, particularly in small isolated towns.[8]

Other isolated voices have gradually been breaking the silence. Some NGOs such as Asociación Alto al Secuestro (Stop Kidnapping Association, founded in 2005) and Mexico SOS (founded in 2008), as well as less institutionalised movements such as the Movement for Peace with Justice and Dignity (founded in 2011), work to demand justice, the rule of law, and an end to violence, while providing legal advice and support to families of kidnap victims. All three of these organisations were founded by parents who had lost a son to kidnapping or in the crossfire between criminal organisations, because the cases were not resolved properly by the authorities or were full of irregularities.[9] Although their impact is still very limited, they have given some voice to otherwise helpless and hopeless victims of crime and violence, and they were instrumental in the drafting of the recent Anti-Kidnapping Law (2012) and the General Law for Victims of Crime (2013).

Interviewees highlight the climate of corruption and impunity which has fostered the escalation of violence (see also Osorno, 2012). Corruption has always been rampant in the police forces and at various levels of government, but is now perceived to involve a higher degree of shamelessness and cynicism than ever before, involving public servants at all levels of government, congressmen and congresswomen, union leaders and their families. Respondents mentioned their outrage about particular cases of corruption. For example, the former leader of the Teachers' Union (SNTE), Elba Esther Gordillo, was imprisoned in February 2013 on charges of money laundering, organised crime, tax evasion and misappropriation of public funds. Two '*narco alcades*' (narco mayors) in Guerrero have caused particular public outrage, the *corridos* singer Eleuterio Aranda Salgado and Ignasio de Jesús Valladares Salgado, both thought to be in the payroll of la Familia Michoacana (one of the most sadistic and violent drug cartels). Similar cases exist in other states such as Tabasco and Tamaulipas. Corruption is also perceived to have penetrated local government and the security forces at various levels, leading to questions about their legitimacy and damaging their credibility. These facts have increased the general sense of insecurity, helplessness and indignation among ordinary taxpayers. According to opinion polls, 52 per cent of Mexicans at the national level believe the army and police have been corrupted by narcos (CASADE, 2011).

Respondents also allude to the presence and visibility of cartels in many states of the country, giving rise to a widespread 'narco culture'. This culture includes a language and vocabulary of drug-related violence;[10] a music genre (*narco corridos*) praising the exploits and virtues of the big drug lords;[11] and a pop culture built on narco religious paraphernalia and imagery (common images are *La Santa Muerte, La Virgen de los Olvidados, La Niña Blanca*, and *Santo Malverde*). The lives of drug lords have been fictionalised and sensationalised, and become prime subjects in soap operas, films and novels.[12]

Criminal violence and displacement in Mexico 81

Meanwhile, during 2010, the celebrations of the bicentennial of Mexican independence and the centennial of the Revolution prompted a serious probing of the accomplishments and defects of Mexican society among scholars, artists, journalists, writers and politicians. The result was a proliferation of events, seminars, art and photography exhibitions, films, a series of books revisiting Mexican history from various perspectives, novels – extolling, questioning, examining, blaming, berating ... What most of these had in common was a need to make sense of today's situation by looking to the past, trying to give a sense of direction to a wounded society. In the visual arts, crises leading to displacement are portrayed as 'fearful' and 'dark'. A prime example is the film *El Infierno*, by director Luis Estrada. This film portrays life at a border town; the return of the main character from the United States after years of hard work there; the intricacies, discrepancies, and degradation of a society corrupted by drugs, drug trafficking and violence, and his immersion into such a world. It emotively portrays ghost towns, poverty, political apathy, and the impotence of local authorities, as well as the displacement, frustration and lack of choices of ordinary individuals. Luis Estrada – an acute social critic – managed to pinpoint the woes and foes of today's economic, social and political environment in Mexico. It was a box office hit, and won the 2011 Ariel Award for best film, best director, best actor and best actor in a secondary role.[13]

Another example is the work of Teresa Margolles, a world-renowned artist from the violence-stricken state of Sinaloa. Her work exhibits controversially, using material from crime scenes, and mostly focuses on death, the socio-cultural context of corpses, and violence. Her most recent work is an installation, *La Promesa* (The Promise), exhibited at the end of 2012 and early 2013 at the University Museum of Contemporary Art, which is made of the debris of a dismantled, abandoned, and vandalised house in Ciudad Juárez. An hour a day, for six months, a volunteer went to move the remains of the house until it covered the entire surface of the exhibit space. *La Promesa* expresses the irreversible ways in which violence and the fight against the drug cartels shatter the dreams of ordinary people in cities like Ciudad Juárez. Juárez (represented by the debris of the house), once a promised land of opportunities, became a metaphor for what is happening elsewhere in the country, leaving many people frightened, homeless and hopeless. The daily movement of the debris conveys a permanent sense of loss, and a fearful atmosphere.

Such artistic expressions interpret and reflect the perceptions of ordinary citizens and to some extent articulate a counter-discourse to officials' denial that the country is in crisis. Many traits of the current situation have been experienced in the past, such as economic deprivation, rampant corruption and lack of government accountability. However, the scale of the violence, and the cynicism and impunity that currently accompany it are unprecedented. This has generated an environment of fear and distrust of the Mexican legal and justice systems, as well as of the government in general (Magaloni *et al.*, 2012). It is a situation that has prompted significant displacement.

82   *Laura Rubio Díaz-Leal and Sebastián Albuja*

Links between violence and internal displacement

México, ¡ Agarra a tus hijos ... Vienen por nosotros! (Mexico, grab your children, they are coming to get us!)[14]

Dominant views of migration in Mexico have not tended to construe it as a problem, in contrast with other contexts where more sedentary notions tend to predominate (Lindley, Chapter 1, this volume). On the contrary, migration (both within Mexico to rapidly expanding urban centres and to the neighbouring United States) has been widely recognised as a decisive, defining, and long-lasting aspect of the country's history, development, and social context. While the structural inequalities underlying migration and its social downsides are acknowledged, so are its significant benefits. Perhaps as a result of the salience of both international and internal labour migration, there has been very little research on the link between political crisis and migration in Mexico: indeed, one key study sees this as a future challenge (Sobrino, 2011). Studies of the role of crime and insecurity in prompting migration (e.g. Morrison, 2011) have not focused on the contexts affected by severe drug cartel-related violence since 2007, and perhaps unsurprisingly, therefore, find that more general socio-economic and cultural factors are stronger drivers of who migrates within Mexico.

So how has the recent upsurge in criminal violence affected the internal and international migration patterns of Mexican nationals? There is no reliable data on the national scale of forced internal displacement. In 2010, a survey conducted at the Universidad Autónoma de Ciudad Juárez gave estimates of 230,000 displaced persons from Ciudad Juárez alone, of which at least 115,000 had fled to the United States and the other 115,000 stayed in Mexico as internally displaced persons (IDPs) (CIS-UACJ, 2010). A repeat survey in 2011 found that in that year alone, 24,426 people were forcefully displaced from Ciudad Juárez, fleeing to other municipalities within Chihuahua, or to Coahuila, Durango and Veracruz. Much-cited national-level estimates of IDPs during Calderon's tenure range from 700,000 to 1,648,387 IDPs (Emeequis, 2011; Parametría, 2011), but their margin of error is very high due to the probability that many of the surveyed families referred to the same known cases of displaced persons. Our systematic review of estimates cited in the electronic and print media of forced internal displacement since 2011 shows that generally these relate to mass displacements of whole communities (in the wake of major bouts of criminal violence), as in the latter situations, local government is drawn into co-ordinating some sort of response.[15] But even in these more visible cases, quantification methods around the country have not been systematic or consistent,[16] and reporters do not use any specific bureaucratic or legal category (such as 'internally displaced persons') when referring to violence-induced patterns of migration. These kinds of estimates also tend not to include families who have moved one-by-one in response to specific personal threats or the generalised insecure environment, but who do not form part of a 'mass influx'.

Criminal violence and displacement in Mexico 83

However, we have been able to establish a clear relationship between violence and population movement, by comparing homicide rates with population census data (results reported in detail in Albuja, Gutiérrez, Rubio and Rivero, forthcoming). This reveals that states and localities hit by intense violence in recent years have experienced markedly increased levels of out-migration (both internal and international). The 12 states most affected by criminal violence in recent years have been Baja California, Chihuahua, Coahuila, Durango, Guerrero, Michoacán, Nuevo León, San Luis Potosí, Sinaloa, Sonora, Tamaulipas and Veracruz, all with homicide rates of over 20 deaths per 100,000 inhabitants, accounting for only 38 per cent of Mexico's population, but for 68 per cent of homicides. Eight of these states have had a net migration rate of zero or a negative figure, which indicates that the population is in decline as emigration outstrips immigration. The four states losing the most population in the country – Guerrero, Sinaloa, Chihuahua and Durango – are among the most violent states. Considered together, the 12 most violent states had a negative net migration rate of 55,700 people, and the correlation coefficient between homicides and net migration rate is negative (–0.27), which was evidence that they were experiencing a significant loss of population which may be linked to drug cartel violence.

The association between violence and outmigration at the state level indicated that analysis at a more local level was required to find evidence of forced displacement. Within those states, comparing localities with average crime conditions with highly violent ones provided an even clearer picture. Overall, in the 104 municipalities with the highest levels of violence – i.e. those with proportions of homicides that account for 75 per cent of all homicides and other crimes in the 12 states – the rate of outmigration was 15 times higher than in municipalities without such high levels of violence. Controlling for the effects of other drivers of migration, including economic and demographic conditions and urbanisation, the number of people leaving violent municipalities was 4.5 times higher than those leaving non-violent municipalities.

This association between crime, violence and migration is corroborated by analysis of other sources as well. According to the Latin American Public Opinion Project (LAPOP, 2012), conducted by Vanderbilt University, USA, 13 per cent of its Mexican sample (approximately 228 people) changed residence because of fear of crime. According to the CASADE survey, in the last four years (2007–11), 3 per cent claimed they had abandoned their traditional areas of residence due to violence (4 per cent in Chihuahua, 5 per cent in Mexico City, 5 per cent in the State of Mexico, and 3 per cent in Guerrero) (CASADE, 2011).

Precise triggers for movement vary. Some are directly victimised, with financially crippling demands for 'quota' payments by cartel groups, extortion, disappearances and killing of family members. Other families suffer the killings of members and damage to property and assets during violent disputes between criminal groups over distribution routes, and between criminal groups and the government. This has left many with little choice but to move to safer parts of the country, leading in some instances to the abandonment of whole towns.

Others move because of generalised fear and perceptions of crisis and instability. For example, all 17 students surveyed from the states of Sinaloa, Nuevo Léon, Michoacán, and Chihuahua, who were among the more comfortably off segment of society, claimed they had chosen to study in Mexico City to escape from violence in their hometowns. These students claim they could not go out to party in their hometowns and they were tired of feeling afraid all the time. For all 20 graduate students surveyed living abroad, except for one who had been a kidnap victim in 2008, security was not their prime concern when choosing to go abroad, though they did report feeling relieved that they do not have to worry about insecurity now that they live abroad.

This displacement has significant consequences. Many towns and villages have been largely deserted in the wake of violent events, and others are severely undermined by the exodus of those with the means to leave, including many of their most principled citizens. Through displacement, the present crisis is also transmitting pressures to more and more parts of Mexico not directly affected by severe criminal violence. Thus, short-, medium- and long-term protection and relief measures targeting vulnerable and displaced people are required in a much broader area of the national territory, requiring federal leadership, which has not been forthcoming.

Due to the lack of a more in-depth qualitative research, it is hard to know the extent to which these crisis-related patterns intersect with or build on more routine labour-oriented migration patterns, though clearly in some cases internal labour migrants have been forced to return or move onwards to new destinations as a result of violence. Central American migrants in transit through Mexico have been acutely vulnerable because they lack both support networks and information about the threats in the areas they travel through (Albuja, forthcoming). In the Pacific states, criminal violence was overlaid in 2013 by the environmental crisis caused by Hurricanes Raymond, Ingrid and Manuel and the resulting flooding, which saw newly flood-displaced people congregating alongside violence-displaced people in refuges provided by the state authorities and the local churches. The flooding also re-displaced many people who had already been forced to move once because of criminal violence.

Meanwhile, the international image of Mexico as primarily a labour migration country may be changing. At the international level, according to the United Nations High Commissioner for Refugees (UNHCR), 35 Mexicans apply for asylum in the United States and Canada every day (Hernández, 2013). In 2011, there were 6,816 Mexican refugees worldwide, the vast majority in the USA and Canada. This represents an increase of 94 per cent compared with the previous year. The US government received 12,806 applications for asylum in 2011, and 14,610 in the first half of 2013, making it the biggest source of asylum applications in the United States (Aristegui Noticias, 2013).

Politics of crisis: why the silence?

The evidence presented here suggests that drug-related violence constitutes a major crisis for many Mexicans, in terms of a marked discontinuity with previous patterns of violence and the severe threats they experience, and in terms of forcing significant displacement. Despite the fact that national media and civil society organisations have decried the scale and impact of this violence over the last few years as a serious crisis, the dominant political construction and interpretation of this situation by the Mexican government have been to deny that there is any kind of crisis, downplaying the severity and the human impact of violence (Freemantle and Misago, Chapter 7 in this volume, present another example of a government, in very different setting, taking a 'non-crisis'/ 'just crime' stance).[17] The government has done this in two ways. First, it has focused on gains made against the drug cartels such as the killing or capture of some 20 drug lords, along with the confiscation of hundreds of tons of cocaine and other illegal drugs, as evidence that the security strategy is working. Second, the government has persistently refused to acknowledge crisis realities, instead referring to 'unstable areas', and refusing to recognise the scale of collateral damage, or that internal displacement is taking place in any significant way. It emphasises that the bulk of the violence occurs in 'only' around 12 of Mexico's 32 states, claiming that this does not amount to a national-level crisis.[18]

Local authorities are left to deal with the situation on the ground, with very limited funds and human resources. As a result, thousands of victims of crime and displacement have been left unprotected. Combined with the fear generated by the drug cartels, this lack of state protection has a powerful silencing effect on the victims of violence and displacement. This denial of crisis has arisen because government legitimacy (particularly of Felipe Calderón's administration) at domestic and international levels is so bound up in its present security strategy. At the domestic level, the Calderón administration was elected with a mandate to improve public security and the rule of law, and acknowledging the severity and human impact of the on-going violence would be to acknowledge its failure in this key goal. Not only this, the government security forces and public officials have themselves been implicated in abuses and deaths of civilian bystanders. Another major problem is that there is simply no normative or institutional framework within the Mexican state to deal with internal displacement. At the federal level there is no law that provides for a mechanism to assist victims of forced internal displacement; there is no legal definition or category within the existing legal framework of such a phenomenon; and finally, there is no institution with the specific mandate to assist and protect its victims. Only in Chiapas – a state struggling with violence and forced internal displacement since 1994 – was a local law for the prevention and protection of the internally displaced passed in 2012, though it has not come into force with a defined programme, enough funds, and institutions to provide assistance to its victims.

86 *Laura Rubio Díaz-Leal and Sebastián Albuja*

There are also issues of international credibility, with the government concerned to sustain foreign investment and confidence. Mexico is in good internationalstanding: it is the second largest economy in Latin America and a member (and chair in 2012) of the G-20, and an OECD member. The common assumption is that if such a country experiences violence, it must be a minor issue of localised insecurity, not one posing a serious threat to the country as a whole. Mexico has a strong interest in maintaining this image, as the government's security intervention received substantial support from the USA through the Merida Initiative to combat drug trafficking, the USA's most highly publicized intervention in Mexico in recent years (Albuja, 2013). Hence, references to the situation in Mexico as an insurgency, including US Secretary of State Hillary Clinton's remarks in 2010 prompted an angry response from the Mexican government, as have claims that Mexico is becoming a failed state or is undergoing 'Colombianisation' (Samper Pizano, 2010; Beittel, 2011).

A key unresolved issue in this context is whether the current situation represents an internal armed conflict as defined in international humanitarian law (IHL), because this would trigger International Committee of the Red Cross (ICRC) intervention and imply specific legal obligations for armed groups and the state (this is the subject of extended debate in Albuja, forthcoming). In brief, the criteria for this are set out in Article I of the Additional Protocol II to the Geneva Conventions and in case law, particularly decisions by the International Criminal Tribunal for the Former Yugoslavia (ICTY), and relate to the intensity of the violence (when it produces casualties every day over a long period of time, as opposed to isolated and sporadic acts of violence), the cohorts of armed actors (when they are relatively well organised with a clear structure and command base) as well as the types of weapons used, use of military rather than police to confront the armed group, and the displacement of civilians.

Some of these criteria are easily met by the Mexican situation. In terms of intensity, violence in Mexico since its outbreak in 2007 is hardly sporadic – it has been going on for five years and it includes frequent, cruel, and heinous acts of violence, including assassinations, beheadings, use of bombs, and destruction of public and private property. The weapons used by both criminals and the security forces are advanced, sophisticated, and high calibre – financed (in the case of criminal organisations) with the dividends of the illegal drug trade, and brought illegally from the United States. The Mexican military was sent in early 2007 to combat the cartels in various states. The Calderón administration continued to use the military throughout its term of office while going out of its way to assert that despite the military presence, Mexico was not undergoing a war. Large joint operations involving the intervention of the army, navy, local, and federal police have taken place in at least nine states: Michoacán, Baja California, Guerrero, Nuevo León, Tamaulipas, Chihuahua, Durango, Sinaloa and Veracruz (Escalante, 2011). While the displacement of civilians has been hard to measure, as outlined above, it is clearly highly significant.

Criminal violence and displacement in Mexico 87

The evidence regarding the organisations and intentions of the groups taking part in the hostilities is more ambiguous. On the one hand, Mexican drug cartels have historically operated as organisations with well-defined leadership and a hierarchy – often based on family links guaranteeing extreme loyalty – and have had functional and well-defined structures, including firepower, transportation, money laundering, and intelligence cells (Alvarez, 2006). These groups are classified as 'formally organized groups' in the Uppsala University Conflict Data Programme. However, since 2007, when the violence broke out, cartels have increasingly become devoid of leadership and have been led by thugs with few allegiances (Celaya Pacheco, 2009). Regarding the armed groups' intentions, this has been primarily non-political in the sense of motivated by profit rather than capturing state power (although the ICTY determined in the *Limaj* case that the motives of armed groups were irrelevant in determining whether there is a formal internal armed conflict which triggers the application of IHL).

In legal terms, the applicability of the law of non-international armed conflict would mean that armed groups must protect and respect those who are not or are no longer taking part in fighting and must not cause superfluous injury or unnecessary suffering. Furthermore, the state would have an obligation to teach these rules to its armed forces, and to prevent and punish violations.

But independently of whether Mexico's situation constitutes an internal armed conflict in a strict legal analysis, seeing Mexico's violence from the perspective of IHL is important in terms of the politics of crisis, as the presence of significant aspects of armed conflict in Mexico calls for more serious treatment of the consequences of violence by the Mexican authorities and international actors – in other words, it is a serious argument for the government to stop denying that Mexico is facing a crisis.

Conclusion

This chapter has critically examined the extent to which Mexico's recent situation of violence can be construed as a crisis. Starting from the premise that the construction of crisis is a highly mediated and political process, we gathered first-hand data about the way in which people in different social and geographic positions experience the on-going violence, in an attempt to describe the effect of the situation shaped both by criminals and the state. The analysis based on all sources used, qualitative and quantitative, showed that the violence taking place in Mexico since 2007 signals a marked discontinuity with the past and represents a severe threat to ordinary people.

Criminal violence in Mexico became a crisis the moment it affected not only politicians, human rights advocates, journalists, and members of the security forces, but also ordinary citizens. The sea change occurred in 2007 when homicide rates escalated, when extortion, disappearances, kidnappings, among other crimes, generated an environment of fear, altering the way most Mexicans live. The existence of self-defence forces and community police – clearly a

88 *Laura Rubio Díaz-Leal and Sebastián Albuja*

manifestation of institutional weaknesses and lack of state presence in various parts of the country – in a context of impunity, corruption and the lack of rule of law nationwide is, without doubt, the key marker of this crisis, affecting all Mexicans.

The narratives of ordinary citizens show the sometimes subtle, sometimes overt ways in which the dramatic upsurge of violence and insecurity have driven them to adapt their lifestyles and behaviour to cope with crisis, leading some to flee within the boundaries of the state or beyond them. These changes ranged from behavioural and social changes, including adapting their work routines and the times and places chosen for leisure, to deeper, long-lasting changes such as relocating elsewhere. Analysis of selected media and the arts also eloquently testify to how a sense of crisis is entrenched in people's lives. Additionally, the evidence reviewed here points to a strong link between violence and internal population movements, with significant displacement occurring in states most affected by violence, and particularly from the most violent municipalities.

The chapter also discussed the politics and institutional conditions that have shaped the official discourse, construction, and response to the violence and ensuing displacement. The official position over the years has been to downplay the violence as a geographically contained and limited side-effect of a solution to the issue of organised crime. This drove the government to adopt a narrow focus on 'the problem', emphasizing gains made against drug cartels and disrupting the drug trade. It has ignored, meanwhile, the enormous social costs, and the evidence presented herein – that, if one examines the situation with a more powerful magnifying lens, Mexicans from all walks of life have experienced abrupt and drastic changes in their lives and have to coexist with persistent and unbearable threats – or leave. Such a deliberate narrow construction of the situation has resulted in an inadequate response for people affected by the violence even if its intensity and features require a protection-based intervention.

Notes

1 Excerpt from a testimonial of a displaced person from Ciudad Juárez now living in the state of Veracruz, 2012.
2 Respondents included 65 university students between ages 19–23; 27 university faculty members and personnel; 62 women in Jalisco, Chihuahua, Tabasco, Mexico City, Chiapas, Querétaro, Michoacán, Nuevo León, Hidalgo, Quintana Roo, Estado de México, and Morelos; 23 entrepreneurs/businessmen and women; 25 young professionals; 35 domestic workers; 9 taxi drivers; 21 postgraduate students studying abroad; and 10 professionals working abroad.
3 Excerpt from a testimonial of a displaced person from Michoacán collected by the authors in Mexico City in September 2013. Four of his brothers had 'disappeared'; to date, the local authorities and federal police have not been able to ascertain their whereabouts, or recover their bodies.
4 According to the survey referred to above (INEGI, 2011), 92 per cent of the crimes do not lead to a preliminary investigation and hearing, which leads to a generalised

Criminal violence and displacement in Mexico   89

lack of trust in the penal and justice systems, which in turns leads to a reluctance to denounce and report crimes, from car and home break-ins to more serious crimes.

5 For example, the top holiday destination Acapulco, only four hours away from Mexico City, significantly declined in popularity, particularly during 2011–13 when violence hit the port harshly and even foreign tourists were targeted.

6 Natural disasters mentioned in the survey were: the 1985 earthquake, Hurricanes Gilberto in 1988, Wilma and Paulina in 2005, the floods in Tabasco in 2007, and the 2011–12 droughts.

7 Interview with a displaced person from Chihuahua, May 2013. Moreover, five students studying in Mexico City, originally from various parts of the country, who worked as research assistants in their home towns for the internal displacement project were asked by their parents to stop asking questions of neighbours and family members, arguing that it was too risky to do so.

8 In six interviews (carried out in 2011–13) with displaced victims of crime from Michoacán, they made the claim that in violent small towns controlled by criminal organisations, most of the disappearances, for instance, are never reported. They argue that this is due to the fact that the majority of the families of the abducted do not file a complaint, and because narcos and the municipal police threaten reporters who dare to speak out.

9 Organisations like this also appeared throughout the 1970s–1990s but were more limited in scope, though some still remain active today. One example is the NGO Mexicanos Unidos contra la Delicuencia (Mexicans United against Crime, founded in 1997 by Josefina Ricaño, after his son was kidnapped and killed), still active today. This organisation was the first to organise a massive silent march against violence and impunity (120,000 people participated in Mexico City alone, and many thousands more in other cities around the country).

10 For instance, *levantado* (to be taken in the streets – kidnapped), *encajuelado* (victim is alive or dead body carried in the boot of a car), *encobijado* (body wrapped in a blanket), *narco mensajes* (messages left at crime scenes to the rival gang, or to the security forces).

11 Famous *narco-corridos* bands are Los Tigres del Norte and Los Tucanes de Tijuana, among others. It can be considered a musical sub-genre that developed from traditional northern *corridos*.

12 For example, *Reina del Sur* (Queen of the South), a novel written by Arturo Pérez-Reverte, supposedly based on the life of Teresa Mendoza, initially a victim of drug trafficking and displaced from her native state, Sinaloa, who later became one of the most powerful drug baronesses of the 1990s. The book became a best-seller and was made into a soap opera on national television.

13 The Ariel Award is the highest award granted by the Mexican Academy of Arts and Cinematographic Sciences to films produced in Mexico.

14 This was the cry associated with women of a small peasant and farming community in Ixtayotla (Guerrero) persecuted and forced to flee by narcos in July 2012 for failing to show up at a meeting where narcos announced every member of the community had to pay *derecho de piso* (illegal protection fee).

15 This was the case, for example, of Ciudad Mier (Tamaulipas in 2010), Tierra Caliente (Michoacán in 2011), of La Laguna (Guerrero, 2012, 2013), the so-called Juarocho community of Ciudad Juárez who fled to their native state of Veracruz in 2010, and various communities in different parts of Sinaloa in 2012 and 2013.

16 Among the most serious methodological difficulties we found is that many media reports refer to 'displaced families,' but it is unclear if they refer to nuclear or extended families, or if they assume the INEGI standard of 4.3 members per (nuclear) family.

17 The government adopted a similar political attitude in relation to widespread femicides in the 1990s.

90 Laura Rubio Díaz-Leal and Sebastián Albuja

18 Authorities have consistently emphasised that the only state which has experienced an armed conflict leading to massive internal displacement has been Chiapas (interview with Katia Somohano, former Director of Comisión Mexicana de Ayuda para Refugiados (COMAR), May 2011). At the 149 period of sessions at the Inter American Commission for Human Rights in Washington, DC, in November 2013, representatives of the Mexican state did not recognise the phenomenon.

References

Agencias de Noticias (2013) 'Autodefensa michoacana va a penal de Villa Aldama, Imagen de Veracruz'. Available at: http://www.imagendeveracruz.com.mx/Noticias principales/tabid/92/ID/5685/Autodefensa-michoacana-va-a-penal-de-Villa-Aldama. aspx (accessed 4 November 2013).

Albuja, S. (2013) 'Stabilization Next Door: Mexico's U.S-Backed Security Intervention', in R. Muggah (ed.) *Stabilization Operations, Security, and Development*. London: Routledge.

——(forthcoming) 'Criminal Violence, Displacement, and Migration in Mexico and Central America', in S. Martin (ed.) *Movement in Humanitarian Crises: Causes, Processes, Consequences.* London: Routledge.

Albuja, S., Gutiérrez, E., Rubio, L. and Rivero, E. (forthcoming) 'Forced Displacement Linked to Transnational Organized Crime in Mexico.'

Alvarez, V. (2006) 'The History, Structure, and Organization of Mexican Drug Cartels', doctoral dissertation, El Paso: University of Texas. Available at: http://digitalcommons. utep.edu/dissertations/AAI1441328/ (accessed 30 August 2012).

Aristegui Noticias (2013) 'EU recibe 14,610 solicitudes de asilo de mexicanos por violencia', August 27. Available at: http://aristeguinoticias.com/2708/mexico/eu-recibe-14610-solicitudes-de-asilo-de-mexicanos-por-violencia/ (accessed 4 November 2013).

Beittel, J.S. (2011) 'Mexico's Drug Trafficking Organizations: Source and Scope of the Rising Violence'. Washington, DC: Congressional Research Papers.

Carrasco, J. (2012) 'Asesina a la corresponsal de Proceso en Veracruz, Regina Martínez', *Proceso*, 28 April. Available at: http://www.proceso.com.mx/?p=305816 (accessed 4 November 2013).

CASADE (2011) 'Encuesta Ciudadanía, Democracia y Narcoviolencia (CIDENA 2011)', Mexico City. Available at: http://www.seguridadcondemocracia.org/encuestas/ encuestas/encuesta-de-ciudadania-democracia-y-narcoviolencia-cidena-2011.html.

Celaya Pacheco, F. (2009) 'How Has Narcoterrorism Settled in Mexico?' *Studies in Conflict and Terrorism* 32(12): 1021–48.

CIS-UACJ (2010) 'Encuesta de percepción ciudadana de inseguridad en Ciudad Juárez 2010', Universidad Autónoma de Ciudad Juárez. Available at http://www. observatoriodeJuárez.org/dnn/Portals/0/encuestas/Encuesta%20de%20Percepcion%20 Ciudadana%20sobre%20Inseguridad%20en%20Ciudad%20Juárez%20II-2010%20v6 mayo2011.pdf (accessed 7 April 2013).

Collins, S.M., Lustig, N. and Bosworth, B. (1997) *Coming Together? Mexico-U.S. Relations*. Washington, DC: Brookings Institution.

Eastmond, M. (2007) 'Stories as Lived Experience: Narratives in Forced Migration Research', *Journal of Refugee Studies* 20(2): 248–64.

Emeequis (2011) *Emeequis*. Available at: http://www.m-x.com.mx/xml/pdf/261/18.pdf (accessed 2 May 2012).

Escalante, F. (2011) 'Homicidios 2008–9, la muerte tiene permiso', *Revista Nexos*, January 3.

Escalante, F. *et al.* (2011) 'Nuestra Guerra: una conversación', *Revista Nexos*, 1 November.

Gaceta Parlamentaria (2012) 'Las Muertas de Juárez, (3630) (III)', 23 October. Available at: http://gaceta.diputados.gob.mx/Black/Gaceta/Anteriores/62/2012/oct/20121023-III/Proposicion-13.html (accessed 10 July 2013).

González, S. (2002) 'Las Muertas de Juárez', *Letras Libres*, December: 48–52.

Guerrero, E. (2011) 'La Raiz de la Violencia', *Revista Nexos*, 402 (June): 30–46.

——(2013) 'Security Policy and Crisis of Violence in Mexico', in D. Villiers Negroponte (ed.) *The End of Nostalgia: Mexico Confronts the Challenges of Global Competition.* Washington, DC: Brookings Institution Press, pp. 112–51.

Hernández, A.L. (2013) '35 Mexicanos por Día Piden Asilo en el Extranjero; La Cifra Aumentó 94 Por Ciento con Calderón', ACNUR. Available at: http://www.sinembargo.mx/20-06-2013/660305?utm_source=Monitoreo+de+Medios&utm_campaign=178410 3119-Monitoreo_del_19_de_junio_de_20136_19_2013&utm_medium=email&utm_term=0_7ae0297426-1784103119-28054841 (accessed 4 November 2013).

Human Rights Watch (2011) *Ni Seguridad, Ni Derechos: Ejecuciones, Desapariciones y Tortura en la 'Guerra contraEl Narcotráfico' en México*. Available at: http://www.hrw.org/sites/default/files/reports/mexico1111spwebwcover.pdf (accessed November 2012).

——(2013) *Los Desaparecidos de México: El Persistente Costo de una Crisis Ignorada.* Available at: www.hrw.org/es (accessed 20 March 2013).

IDMC (2011) *México: Desplazamiento Debido a la Violencia Comunal y Criminal.* Oslo: Norwegian Refugee Council.

INEGI (2011) 'Encuesta Nacional de Victimización y Percepción de Seguridad Pública (ENVIPE)'. Mexico City: INEGI. Available at: http://www.inegi.org.mx/inegi/contenidos/espanol/prensa/comunicados/envipe.asp (accessed 1 September 2013).

——(2012) *Censo de Población y Vivienda 2010.* Available at: http://www.inegi.org.mx/sistemas/consulta_resultados/scince2010.aspx (accessed 30 September 2013).

LAPOP (Latin American Public Opinion Project) (2012). Available at: http://www.vanderbilt.edu/lapop/ (accessed 22 September 2013).

Lessing, B. (2011) 'The Logic of Violence in Criminal War: Cartel-State Conflict in Mexico, Colombia, and Brazil'. Paper presented at Violence, Drugs and Governance: Mexican Security in Comparative Perspective Conference, Stanford University, Palo Alto, CA, 3 October. Available at: http://iis-db.stanford.edu/evnts/6716/LessingThe_Logic_of_Violence_in_Criminal_War.pdf.

Loyola, M. (2009) 'Mexico's Cartel Wars', *National Review* 61(11): 36–8.

Magaloni, B., Díaz Calleros, A. and Romero, V. (2012) 'La Raiz del Miedo: ¿Por qué es la Percepción de Riesgo Más Grande que la Tasa de Victimización?' in J.A. Aguilar (ed.) *Las Bases sociales del Crimen Organizado y de la Violencia en México.* Mexico City: Secretaría de Seguridad Pública.

Monárrez, J. (2000) 'La Cultura del Feminicidio en Ciudad Juárez, 1993–99', *Frontera Norte* 12(23): 97.

Morrison, A.R. (2011) 'Violence and Migration on the Arizona/Sonora Border'. Available at: http://works.bepress.com/scott_whiteford/3.

Orlinsky, K. (2013) 'Mexico's Vigilante Squads', *Women in the World.* Available at: http://www.thedailybeast.com/witw/articles/2013/10/05/mexico-s-female-vigilantes-take-justice-and-safety-into-their-own-hands.html (accessed 13 October 2013).

Osorno, D. (2009) *El Cartel de Sinaloa: Una Historia del Uso Político del Narco.* Mexico City: Grijalbo.

92   Laura Rubio Díaz-Leal and Sebastián Albuja

——(2012) 'Las Causas Estructurales de la Violencia', in J.A. Aguilar (ed.) *Las Bases Sociales del Crimen Organizado y la Violencia en México*. Mexico City: Secretaría de Seguridad Pública.

Parametría (2011) *Parametría*. Available at: http://www.parametria.com.mx/DetalleEstudio.php?E=4288 (accessed 12 February 2012).

Procuraduría General de la República (2011) 'Homicidios Relacionados con Rivalidad Delicuencial'. Available at: http://www.pgr.gob.mx/temas%20relevantes/estadistica/estadisticas.asp (accessed 2 July 2013).

Ríos, V. (2012) 'Tendencias y Explicaciones al Asesinato de Periodistas y Alcaldes en México: El Crimen Organizado y la Violencia de Alto Perfil', in J.A. Aguilar (ed.) *Las Bases Sociales del Crimen Organizado y la Violencia en México*. México, D.F.: Secretaría de Seguridad Pública.

Samper Pizano, E. (2010) 'La "Colombianización" de México', *El País,* 5 October. Available at: http://elpais.com/diario/2010/10/05/opinion/1286229605_850215.html.

Sicilia, J. (2012) 'Entrevista con Javier Sicilia: Caravana por la Paz en Estados Unidos', *CNN*. Available at: http://mexico.cnn.com/nacional/2012/08/09/el-poeta-javier-sicilia-encabeza-caravana-por-la-paz-a-estados-unidos (accessed 4 November 2013).

Sistema Nacional de Seguridad Pública (2013) *Informe Federal en Materia de Seguridad: Cifras de la Incidencia Delictiva*. Available at: http://www.secretariadoejecutivosnsp.gob.mx/es/SecretariadoEjecutivo/09082013 (accessed 11 September 2013).

Sobrino, J. (2011) *La Urbanización en el México Contemporáneo*. Mexico City: CEPAL.

Turati, M. (2011) *Fuego Cruzado: Las Víctimas Atrapadas en la Guerra del Narco*. Mexico City: Grijalbo.

Word Press (2012) 'Asesinan a la periodista Regina Martínez de la revista *Proceso* en Veracruz', *Reporte Político*, Word Press. Available at: http://reportepolitico.wordpress.com/2012/04/28/asesinan-a-la-periodista-regina-martinez-corresponsal-de-la-revista-proceso-en-veracruz/ (accessed 4 November 2013).

5 The global economic crisis and East Asian labour migration

A crisis of migration or struggles of labour?

Dae-oup Chang

This chapter aims to identify the impact of the on-going global recession on migrant workers in East Asia whose movement and mobility are deeply embedded in East Asia's regional development today. The current global crisis of neoliberalism has overshadowed the East Asian region as stagnating economic growth in its major export destinations has slowed its growth. The severe downturn between 2008 and 2009 precipitated a tightening of international migration controls as well as interruptions to rural–urban movements in various countries. It was widely anticipated that the further development of the recession would generate a full-blown crisis of migration in East Asia. On initial examination, this would seem to fit the common assumption by policy-makers that labour migration is a temporary feature which in the event of an economic crisis can be simply 'turned off', mitigating the effect on the national population and institutions.

However, drawing on secondary sources as well as the author's extensive primary research on labour issues in East Asia, spanning two economic crises, this chapter shows that migration is an essential aspect of the regional integration of East Asia and its emergence as a centre of global capitalism. While the global economic crisis has indeed been met with nationalistic government rhetoric and migration restrictions, there is on-going demand for migrant labour among East Asian employers, indeed migrant labour is key to the intensification of labour and wage cuts deemed necessary to survive the recession. As a result, migration indicators have not been as deeply affected as the initial warnings anticipated.

Meanwhile, the tighter integration of migrant labour since the Asian economic crisis has created a new context through which migrants' political subjectivity has been formed. In China, Hong Kong, South Korea and Thailand, both stricter migration controls (whether genuine and effective or not) and employers' attempts to squeeze migrant workers have faced a wave of protests from politically maturing migrants who have been increasingly developing their bargaining power within the expanding circuit of capital in integrating East Asia. Rather than leading to a crisis of migration, then, the current global economic crisis has intensified the struggles of labour which are a key feature of contemporary East Asian development.

94   *Dae-oup Chang*

This chapter first discusses how the global economic crisis has affected East Asia, and triggered warnings of an impending crisis of migration. The second section puts this situation in historical context, highlighting the central role of migration in East Asian development over the last century, across a range of sectors and national economies. The third section demonstrates the impact of the global economic crisis on migration, showing that it is less significant or prolonged than one might expect, or government rhetoric suggests. The final section outlines the role of the global economic crisis in the development of migrant workers' activism.

Economic crisis leading to a crisis of migration in East Asia?

In light of the hopes for East Asia's gradual 'decoupling' from advanced economies, the fact that the region has been engulfed by the recession in the USA and Europe may seem surprising. The rise of East Asia as an important centre of global capitalism has relied on increasing intra-region investment and trade. The majority of foreign direct investment (FDI) inflow to the 15 East Asian economies (ASEAN+3, Hong Kong and Taiwan) has come from within the sub-region. The impressive FDI-driven development of China in recent years, which was the driving force of the region's export-led growth and vertical integration, also confirms this trend as a large portion of FDI to China is from East Asia itself.[1] East Asian economic development is driven also by increasing intra-regional trade. The intra-regional share of East Asian trade doubled during the decade between 1995 and 2004, reaching US$1,296 million (Asian Development Bank, 2007: 87). In 2011, about 55 per cent of Asia-Pacific exports of merchandised goods went to economies within the region (Asian Development Bank, 2012: 212). At first glance, it seemed true that the dynamic economic development of East Asia in the past few decades had transformed the continent into an independent centre of global capitalist development.

However, this seemingly East Asian-driven growth of the region is not insulated from the ups and downs of advanced capitalist economies. 'Decoupling' has in fact been slower than expected. Rather, the increasing intra-regional trade is marked by the increasing flow of components and parts that are produced and supplied to make final products to meet the demands in advanced capitalist economies outside East Asia. The China-driven growth of intraregional trade through vertically integrated production networks did not reduce East Asia's dependence on advanced capitalist economies as China's reliance on them had been consistently increasing at least till the mid-2000s. In a nutshell, East Asian manufacturers export their products not as much 'to' China as 'through' China to the traditional consumer markets of the global North. Reflecting this, as of 2001, about 73 per cent of intra-East Asian trade consists of intermediate goods used in and processed for production of final goods (Asian Development Bank, 2007: 69). Again about half of this intermediate goods trade was driven by final demand outside Asia, leaving

Crisis of migration or struggles of labour? 95

only 21.2 per cent of East Asian export finally consumed in East Asia (ibid.: 69). More recent trade data reveal that this trend continues. In 2008, about 71 per cent of the total exports' value from Asia as a whole went to external markets, including the USA and the EU which accounted for about 23.9 per cent and 22.5 per cent of total Asian exports respectively (Asian Development Bank, 2010: 52). In sum, tighter regional integration has gone hand-in-hand with heavy reliance on export sectors targeting advanced economies, thus explaining why East Asia has been significantly affected by the global recession.

The 1997–98 East Asian economic crisis forms an important historical backdrop to both East Asia's export boom and the current global economic crisis. Basically, the debt-driven and credit-ridden growth in the USA played a key role in rebuilding East Asia as a centre of global capitalism by contributing to the recovery of East Asia after the East Asian economic crisis of 1997 and 1998. The East Asian economic crisis of 1997 and 1998 is often mistaken as a regional financial crisis, but was in fact a predecessor of the current neoliberal crisis of global capitalism (McNally, 2011). While the USA is the epicentre of the present global crisis, East Asia was the epicentre in the second half of the 1990s.

The 1997–98 crisis began with the massively increasing inflow of capital into East Asia's developing countries triggered by the liberalisation of the financial and investment markets of East Asia in the 1980s. East Asia, with the almost endless supply of a cheap and disciplined workforce, has become the world's production site with large-scale productive capacity built in the region. After a decade or so of neoliberal policies, East Asia began to show signs of capital over-accumulation, with excess capacity established in almost all branches of industries, which then led to the steady decrease in the rate of profit for products competitively produced by both the first and second generation of developing countries targeting the same export markets since the mid-1990s.[2] To survive the heated competition pulling down the rate of profit, corporations began to rely on the 'hot money' that flew into East Asian markets for short-term profits (Chang, 2009: 121–6). Poorly regulated financial and investment markets allowed the fast inflow and outflow of hot money. Speculation for short-term profit drove already-overheated markets to the limit. Once the boom finally began to show clear signs of exhaustion in 1996, foreign money retreated massively, shaking financial markets and slicing the value of East Asia's local currencies. Banks and financial institutions either stopped rolling-back their loans or collapsed under loan defaults. Finally thousands of debt-ridden corporations went bankrupt as they could no longer find financial resources to sustain their unprofitable businesses.

It was only after large-scale liquidation of capital that East Asia began to finally recover. China has been at the centre of this recovery by attracting a tremendous amount of FDI from all the major players in East Asia. They tried to build a more cost-effective and integrated production networks of export industries centred on China where cheap and disciplined labour (mostly of migrant workers) offers cost advantages and the large local

96   Dae-oup Chang

population offered a supplementary market vis-à-vis traditional export markets. Hopes for recovery based on a resumed export boom finally resurfaced.

While transnational corporations from East Asian economies were rebuilding their productive capacity in China, it was the US market that absorbed many of their products. Underlying the sustained purchasing power of the US consumers was the debt-driven housing boom in the US. Throughout the boom, loans were zealously offered at low interest rates to the poor population through sub-prime mortgages, securitised and sold by financial institutions for profits. By 2005, the US housing market boom had reached its peak with US$625 billion sub-prime loans, of which about US$500 billion were securitised and sold (McNally, 2011: 103). Meanwhile, American working-class consumers could afford to keep buying cheaply made consumer goods imported from East Asia, particularly China, creating a 'win–win scenario' for East Asian capital and American consumers.

The boom did not last long, however. The sub-prime mortgage crisis in 2007 and the US recession hit East Asian exports hard, slowing down growth in East Asia since 2007. The series of the fiscal crises – particularly of those governments in the EU – also cast a shadow over East Asian economies. Most export-driven East Asian economies experienced difficulties. Malaysia, Thailand, Taiwan and Singapore experienced minus growth in 2009 with –1.6 per cent, –2.3 per cent, –1.8 per cent, –1 per cent GDP growth rate in 2009 respectively, while South Korea managed a mere 0.3 per cent growth in 2009 (Asian Development Bank, 2012). In China, manufacturing contracted (–4.2 per cent) in 2007 for the first time since China's opening, and the remarkable export-drive started slowing down from 2007 and hit the bottom in 2009 with –16 per cent export growth. This sharp downturn in many labour 'importing' countries was expected to eventually create a crisis of migration in East Asia, with a mass retrenchment of migrant workers and a reversal of migration flows (Abella and Ducanes, 2009; Macabuag, 2009). It was anticipated that about 5 million international migrant workers in East Asia could lose their jobs due to the recession (Macabuag, 2009).

Initial government policy responses in 2009 seemed to bear out the expectation of a crisis of migration. Most labour-importing countries in East Asia that experienced negative growth and acute downturn began to review their migration policy. The Singaporean as well as the Malaysian government urged employers to lay off foreign workers first in case of economic difficulties (Abella and Ducanes, 2009: 9). In 2009, the Malaysian authorities announced their plan to cut the number of migrant workers by doubling the levy imposed upon employers hiring migrant workers (Kanapathy, 2010: 7). South Korea followed by offering subsidies to employers hiring Korean nationals instead of migrant workers (Abella and Ducanes, 2009: 9). Furthermore, in early 2009, the government pledged to introduce harsher migration control to reduce the annual average number of newly arriving migrant workers to one-third of the pre-crisis level (Jeong, 2009: 56). South Korea, Malaysia and Thailand also

Crisis of migration or struggles of labour? 97

announced a temporary suspension of the issuance of new work permits and intensified the crackdown on undocumented workers (Abella and Ducanes, 2009: 9). The South Korean government encouraged undocumented migrant workers to voluntarily leave the country by waiving fines for overstay. The government of Thailand also announced in 2009 that a half million foreign workers would not be allowed to renew their work permits for 2010 (Gibb, 2009: 6).

These restrictive policy stances echoed the situation during the Asian economic crisis of 1997–98, when the governments of destination countries such as Malaysia, Thailand and South Korea competed in cranking up the anti-immigration rhetoric and policies in an attempt to blame migrants for sky-rocketing unemployment and to stabilise emerging discontent among the deprived local population. Over a million migrant workers lost their jobs in those hosting countries in the aftermath of the Asian economic crisis (Macabuag, 2009). Those who survived also had to tolerate deteriorating working conditions, lower wages and disappearing benefits. This partially supported the assumed correlation between capitalist economic crises and crises of migration. However, it is important to note that the decrease in the number of migrant workers in those hosting countries was far from permanent. Indeed, as soon as some signs of economic recovery surfaced, the number of migrant workers in East Asian economies began to increase and soon exceeded the pre-crisis figure. Even in the middle of the crisis, the seemingly bold approach of governments to migration control was used as a rhetoric rather than actually being implemented because both governments and employers were well aware of the fact that migrant workers had become an integral part of the industries and were no longer replaceable, highlighting 'the structural nature of the demands for migrant labour' (Wickramasekera, 2002: 27).

This 'structural nature' of demand for migrant labour has been a central feature of development throughout East Asia's history, in line with global trends, and understanding this is necessary to make sense of the response to the global economic crisis since 2007 (Castles and Vezzoli, 2009; Castles, 2012; Koser, 2009).

Miracles built upon mobile labour

Every phase of the rise of East Asia, from the industrialisation of Japan and the so-called tiger economies of North-east and South-east Asia to the emergence of China as a global factory, has been accompanied by a large-scale movement of labour within and beyond the region. In fact, it is no exaggeration to state that migrants built the 'miracle' of East Asian economic development from the very beginning.

The initiation of capitalist development, or 'primitive accumulation', relied upon the creation and utilisation of a mobile labour population deprived of land and other means of production and subsistence. People moved in search of opportunities and to avoid devastating conditions at home. The large-scale

98   Dae-oup Chang

international migration of labour contributed to the early capitalist development of East Asia by establishing the 'old' division of labour between the West and East for primary commodities production. Throughout the late nineteenth century and early twentieth century, millions of Chinese (as well as Indian) workers migrated to South-east Asia through their overseas networks to work in private plantations and mines (Kaur, 2004). The colonial authorities also actively supported the import of foreign workers, which was then a useful tool for divide-and-rule of the working population in the colonies (ibid.: 52). These labourers were characterised by both extreme mobility and immobility of labour as the jobs they found after a long journey shared more features with slaves than with waged workers. Workers were not 'free' in the sense that their workplaces were located often 'in remote areas and although the labourers were voluntary migrants, the use of the indenture contract in reality restricted mobility and prevented the free operation of market forces' (ibid.: 53). Indeed, they were subjected to private punishment including public executions that were often staged by planters as a means to tame the workers (Breman, 1989).

The earlier industrialisation of the first generation of East Asia's industrialised countries had to rely again on labour inflow from rural villages to cities. Many young women workers migrated to urban areas from rural villages where self-subsistence production, though declining, continued to dominate local economies. They became the first generation of workers carrying out semi-skilled or unskilled tasks in factories producing light goods such as garments and textiles for export, predominantly to the US market (Tsurumi, 1990; Gills, 1999; Kim, 2001; Macnaughtan, 2005; Faison, 2007). In the city-states of Hong Kong and Singapore, continuous large inflows of migrants provided cheap labour for the emerging industrial capitalists.

The dynamic economic globalisation of East Asian economies in the past few decades that transformed the continent into a new centre of global capital accumulation has also relied heavily on mobile labour. The increasingly *regionalising circuit of capital* has brought tighter but very uneven integration between East Asian economies at the same time as bringing about the deeper incorporation of East Asia as a whole into the global market. The resulting division of labour within East Asia is new not only in the sense that it is a bigger and wider division of labour and involves multiple players from all different East Asian countries. More importantly, it is new in the sense that it relies almost entirely on free market schemes and the increasing mobility of capital pursued by the states of more advanced economies in the region and powerful TNCs from Japan, Korea, Singapore, Hong Kong, Taiwan and increasingly China. It became particularly so after the economic crisis of 1997 and 1998, for the remedy to this crisis, pushed by the IMF and other international financial institutions as well as East Asian states, was further liberalisation of markets which accelerated the integration of the East Asian market centred on China. Consequently, the integration of East Asia is marked not by regionally balanced or harmonious development for all but by highly uneven development among regional states.

Crisis of migration or struggles of labour? 99

Tighter integration combined with increasing uneven development inevitably generated significant labour migration. Labour required by and necessary for the expanding circuit of capital is not fixed within local and national boundaries but exists as mobile labour who are in motion between jobs and occupations, between rural communities and global cities, and between poorer and richer nation-states. On the one hand, the expansion of capital into less advanced parts of the region to build factories, offices, plantations, roads, railways and power plants involves 'accumulation by dispossession' through which the labouring population is released from their land and communities. Subsequently vertically integrated production networks of corporations take advantage of this cheap and disposable floating labour force in producing and realising profits. In addition to creating a vast pool of mobile labour within less developed countries, regional integration also allows capital in advanced economies to take advantage of the newly emerging regional market of migrant labour. There are more than 13 million international migrants residing in East Asia, the vast majority of whom came from East Asia and other parts of Asia. The long-term tendency of the migrant population to increase within and beyond East Asia supports the theory that the movement of people is not separable from but embedded in wider social transformation precipitated by the regionalising circuit of capital (Castles, 2010).

A consequence of this integration process and the emerging regional labour market is the deepening 'structural dependence of key economic sectors in export-oriented Asian economies on migrant workers' (Gibb, 2009: 7). The structural dependence is not a feature of a few exceptional economic sectors but can be found in many different sites of the expanding circuit of capital, from the core of the manufacturing sector to the reproductive sphere, from primary commodity production to high-tech industries.

The increasingly pivotal role played by China as the assembly hub for exporting final products to markets in the global North is based on the most dramatic human migration ever from Chinese rural areas to coastal cities. According to official statistics, the number of migrant workers employed outside their hometowns reached 153 million by 2010. They are no longer the supplementary workforce but became a 'major component of the new Chinese working class', as they now account for more than half of the urban workforce (Leung and Pun, 2009: 552). The creation of new mobile labour was an integral part of China's capitalist transformation in which socialist production units became capitalist firms through, on the one hand, the relaxation of control over private firms and the massive growth of TNCs in coastal cities, on the other hand, the privatisation of state-owned enterprises (SOEs) and mass lay-offs of SOE workers. These simultaneous processes prompted a huge influx of young internal migrant workers to China's coastal cities. The *hokou* system, originally introduced to control rural-to-urban migration during the socialist era, has been loosened, in order to allow capital to take advantage of mobile labour, while still ensuring that migrants are not entitled to permanent residency or to social benefits in the cities where they work, and thus excessive

100 Dae-oup Chang

mobility is contained. By offering their disciplined labour power without burdening employers with the additional costs of social benefits, migrant workers allowed higher profits.

For many sectors in the NIEs such as Malaysia and Thailand, cost-cutting has been a key competitive strategy, and labour cost remains the easiest target. International labour migration has played an important role in keeping labour costs low and continuing to attract foreign investment in a range of economic sectors from primary commodities production such as mining, agricultural plantations and fishery, to food processing, to light manufacturing such as garments and textiles, to relatively high value-added production of automobile parts, general machinery and consumer electronics. Labour supply to these industries relies heavily on the circular migratory flow of cheaper labour from poorer neighbouring countries including Cambodia, Myanmar, Indonesia and Lao PDR. Industries in Malaysia employ a large number of migrant labourers from Indonesia and other South-east or South Asian origins, across industrial sectors. Estimates suggest that migrant workers with work permits exceeded 1.8 million by 2006 (IOM, 2008) and that there are over a million irregular migrant workers working for construction, electronics, agricultural plantations and fisheries. In electronics, a strategic export industry, more than 20 per cent of workers are migrants employed through recruitment agencies (SOMO, 2013: 19). As these agencies have been allowed to act as the actual employers of those migrant workers since 2012, transnational employers in electronics industries do not have legal obligations for workers' welfare and labour contracts (ibid.: 22). In Thailand, an estimated 2–3 million migrants (the majority being Burmese) work in agriculture, fishery, construction, food processing, light manufacturing and domestic work (Pearson and Kusakabe, 2012: 47). Migrant workers have played a key role in allowing made-in-Thailand agri-products to remain competitive in the international market, while migrant workers working for below the minimum wage in manufacturing sustain the price competitiveness of firms along the subcontracting chains of larger-scale manufacturing firms (Arnold and Hewison, 2005).

This circular migratory flow also contributes greatly to the survival of small and medium-sized enterprises in the first generation NIEs by reducing competitive pressure from East Asia's emerging economies. The so-called 'guest workers' are key to this. The South Korean government introduced the 'Foreign Trainees Programme for Overseas Firms' in 1991 to import guest workers from Korean TNCs' foreign subsidiaries to the mother companies of the subsidiaries in South Korea. Later this programme was expanded to benefit all small and medium-sized enterprises under the title of the 'Foreign Industrial Trainee Programme' in 1993. The introduction of these schemes coincided with the increasing labour costs in South Korea following 1987, with a massive wave of unionisation making it difficult for South Korean employers to simply rely on exploiting cheap local labour to make profits in an increasingly competitive environment in export markets (Chang, 2009: 118–21). One strategy was for South Korean corporations to invest substantially in operations in countries

Crisis of migration or struggles of labour? 101

where labour was cheaper. Another strategy was to import cheaper migrant workers, which proved particularly important for small and medium-sized enterprises whose capacity to relocate was limited.

Migrants working under these schemes had no freedom to change workplaces, suffered extremely short contract periods and extreme forms of workplace exploitation, including verbal abuse, physical punishment, forced overtime and wage arrears. Criticised as a modern form of slavery, the industrial trainee programme was partially replaced by the employment permit programme in 2004. In 2007, a renewed version of the programme was introduced. The new programme allowed migrant workers to change employers but only with their employers' consent, and extended the maximum contract period from three to five years (Kong *et al.*, 2010). The South Korean government signed an MOU for this programme with Bangladesh, Cambodia, China, East Timor, Indonesia, Kyrgyzstan, Mongolia, Myanmar, Nepal, Pakistan, the Philippines, Sri Lanka, Thailand, Uzbekistan and Vietnam. Between 1993 and 2010, the number of migrant workers increased ten-fold, reaching approximately 720,000 by 2010 (about 24 per cent of them being undocumented). These migrant workers form a significant part of, if not the majority of, the workforce in small-scale manufacturing, construction, agriculture and fishery.

Migrant labour is also becoming an integral part of not only the productive sphere but also the reproductive sphere in relation to the regionalising circuit of capital. The best example of this is the 'imported housewives' of Hong Kong, involving some 301,000 women migrants in 2011. They account for 16.7 per cent of the total female workforce in Hong Kong in 2011 (Law, 2012), about 4.2 per cent of the 7 million residents in Hong Kong and more than half of total foreign workers in the city. Hong Kong's high demand for migrant domestic workers is related to the increasing feminisation of labour in Hong Kong and the gender division of labour. The initial integration of women of Hong Kong into the labour market took place in its booming light industries which relied on a 'feminised off-shore proletariat' to participate in the internationalisation of manufacturing during the post-war period (Sassen, 2000). The feminisation of labour did not end the traditional gender division of labour but rather reformulated it. Women's jobs in the formal industries involved women's traditional domestic tasks, such as weaving and caring, and they were regarded as secondary and cheaper labour. The second wave of feminisation occurred with Hong Kong's transition to a service and finance-led economy in the 1980s, during which middle-class 'housewives' who 'had worked in their own homes for no income and would not have dreamed of doing factory work' (Constable, 2007: 26) entered the labour mass market. By 1986, women's labour force participation exceeded 50 per cent. Many women became employees in the service sector, but the gender pay gap persisted, with these women working for less than a 'family wage'. As in other global cities, the entry of middle-class women into the workforce created a demand for care and domestic labour, which was filled by female workers from poorer countries, creating a 'global care chain' (Perrons, 2004: 106).

102   Dae-oup Chang

Mostly from the Philippines, Indonesia and Thailand, these migrant domestic workers typically worked in isolation and often experienced extreme forms of exploitation, including slave-like contracts with work agencies, non-payment of wages, verbal abuse, physical punishment, controlled food provision and sexual harassment.

The persistence of migration in the context of economic crisis

Thus, ever since East Asian countries began the march toward industrial development, mobile labour has been embedded in the economic development of the region. It became particularly so with the regionalising circuit of capital that tied East Asian economies to one another. Many jobs in industrial sectors relying on cutting labour costs to remain competitive are unattractive to local workers as they often pay below-subsistence wages. This may explain why, despite the steep downturn that all labour-importing countries experienced in 2008 and 2009, deportation of migrant workers was limited.

Despite the anti-migration rhetoric of the South Korean government, the number of migrant workers did not decrease much during the current recession. The total number of migrant workers decreased slightly from 680,425 in 2008 to 675,096 and 668,381 in 2009 and 2010 respectively (Kim, 2012: 684; Seol, 2012: 122). By 2011, the number exceeded the pre-crisis figure, reaching 716,000, according to official statistics. This is a much less dramatic decrease and faster recovery in comparison to the 1997–98 Asian economic crisis, when the number of migrant workers decreased from 245,399 in 1997 to 157,689 in 1998 and did not exceed pre-crisis levels until 2000 (Kim, 2012: 684). Indeed, neither crisis stopped the long-term tendency of migrant labour to increase.

The embeddedness of migrant labour in economic development is even more obvious in East Asia's richer economies like Singapore and Hong Kong. The number of migrants in Hong Kong increased rather than decreased during the recession from 2,721,139 in 2005 to 2,741,800 in 2010, according to the World Bank. Hong Kong did not experience a decrease in the number of migrants during the East Asian economic crisis in the 1990s either. In Singapore, the migrant worker population continued to grow through both the 1997–98 Asian economic crisis and the current crisis. The number of foreign workers increased from 300,000 to 530,000 between 1996 and 1998 despite increasing unemployment rates. The proportion of foreign workers vis-à-vis the total labour force continued to grow throughout the past two decades from 16.1 per cent in 1990, to 28.1 per cent in 2000 and to 34.7 per cent in 2010 (Yeoh and Lin, 2012). The number of work permits issued by the government continued to increase except for a short period between December 2008 and December 2009. The total foreign workforce exceeded pre-crisis levels by December 2010, reaching 1,113,200, according to the Ministry of Manpower.

Although it is difficult to know the exact number of migrant workers in Thailand due to a wide variety of statistical estimates from different sources,

Crisis of migration or struggles of labour? 103

overall trends seem similar to other East Asian destinations. In the aftermath of the advent of the 1997–98 economic crisis, more than 300,000 (mostly Burmese) workers were deported from Thailand after a large-scale man-hunt for irregular migrants, reducing the estimated total number of migrant workers from 987,000 in 1998 to 652,000 in 1999 (Manning, 2002: 374). However, during the current economic recession, no such large-scale crackdown has been reported, and estimates of migrant workers decreased only slightly over the recession (Chalamwong *et al.*, 2012). The estimated number of migrant workers in 2010 was between 2 and 3.1 million (Huguet *et al.*, 2011; Chalamwong *et al.*, 2012).

Malaysia shows more fluctuating figures of migrant workers largely due to more aggressive methods deployed by the government to save jobs for local workers vis-à-vis migrant workers. Although definite figures have never been released, the Asian economic crisis of 1997 seems to have had a severe impact on migrant jobs, reducing the number of foreign workers in Malaysia from 1,127,652 to 799,685 between 1998 and 2000 (Green and Winters, 2010: 14). A similar result was expected in the current crisis (Koser, 2009). However, over the long term, migration continues to increase, from 2,029,208 migrants in 2005 to 2,357,603 in 2010. Again, despite two economic crises, the long-term trend for migrants to increase was clearly evidenced over the last decade.

While the on-going structural demand for immigration in destination countries is one part of this story, the other is the impact of the recession in poorer East Asian countries of origin, which further increased emigration pressure. As shown in Table 5.1, the global recession also did not buck the overall long-term trend in recorded remittances flows to major countries of origin, which increased between 2005 and 2010.[3]

Thus, the overall regional picture is one where migration continues to be a key element. This does not mean that migrant workers have not been affected by the crisis. The recession prompted mass lay-offs of domestic rural migrant workers, for example. Cambodia, for instance, experienced close-to-zero growth in 2009 after hyper-growth during the 2000s. The garment industry, the largest employer in the 'formal economy' was hit hardest by decreasing exports to the US market, reducing Cambodia's merchandise exports growth to –14.2 per cent in 2009 (Asian Development Bank, 2012). Within a year

Table 5.1 Remittance inflow to major labour sending countries in East Asia (US$ million)

Country	2005	2010
China	23478	52269
Indonesia	5420	6916
The Philippines	13561	21369
Thailand	1187	3580
Vietnam	3150	8260

Source: World Bank migration and remittance data.

104   *Dae-oup Chang*

from August 2008, 42 garment factories had closed down and 49,000 garment workers, about 14 per cent of the total workforce in the sector, had lost their jobs (Khin and Kato, 2010). Reduced orders from advanced capitalist economies also decreased overtime work and therefore workers' income, resulting in reduced remittance flow back to their rural homes (Kang *et al.*, 2009: 25–6). China also experienced mass lay-off of internal migrant workers during the recession. By the end of 2008, about 50 per cent of rural migrant workers had returned to their hometowns (Chan, 2010: 666). Although this was part of the routine movement of migrant population before the Spring Festival, according to Chan (ibid.), the rate of return was higher than usual largely due to disappearing jobs in Chinese cities. It is estimated that about 23 million migrant workers could not find jobs until March 2009, either in their rural home towns or cities (ibid.: 667). However, these mass lay-offs did not reverse the flow of migrant workers from rural to urban areas in those countries. Rather rural-urban migration flow resumed as soon as the economy in both countries began to recover.

The effect of tighter migrant control during the recession is also rather very short-term and more dubious than is often expected. To begin with, East Asian employers do not always welcome government policies encouraging more local employment as there is no guarantee that employing local workers will help their desperate attempt to overcome the crisis. For instance, the Malaysian government had to withdraw the decision to double the levy on foreign workers in 2009 in face of protests from employers (Kanapathy, 2010: 7). However, tighter migrant control can make migrant workers' jobs more insecure and in doing so force migrant workers to accept worse working conditions and lower wages. There is no doubt migrant workers face harsh realities during recessions. Nonetheless, migrant workers are so socially embedded in the societies of hosting economies that such anti-migration policies would produce much more discontent. Whereas migrant labour perhaps became an economically integral part of East Asia through earlier integration, the tighter integration of migrant labour since the Asian economic crisis has created a new context through which migrants' political subjectivity has been formed. This, as we will see in what follows, has contributed to the unfolding of clearly different relations between migrant labour, capital and the states within the region during the current global recession.

From a crisis of migration to the struggles of migrant workers

In this context, tensions have been rising between the politically maturing migrant workforce and employers who have been dealing with the crisis by squeezing migrant labour. There is evidence that from this tension a newly assertive political subjectivity is emerging among East Asian migrants. This is a consequence of regional integration and development and the integral role of migration in these processes. Migrant workers are becoming more aware of their vital role and their bargaining power. This trend has manifested itself in

Crisis of migration or struggles of labour? 105

the unfolding of the global recession in different economies in East Asia from China, to Hong Kong, South Korea and Thailand, signalling that the victimisation of migrant labour will not be as easy as before (Chang, 2012).

Although Chinese migrant workers are known for their willingness to work under harsh conditions with low wages, they have shown themselves increasingly willing to challenge employers and the government in the context of the conditions they have experienced since 2007. A new migrant subjectivity is embodied in the new generation of migrant workers who successfully presented themselves not as mere objects of exploitation but as active political subjects in their protests in the aftermath of mass lay-offs during the recession. It is believed that more than 60 per cent of Chinese migrant workers were born after 1980 (*China Labour Bulletin*, 2011: 13). Compared to the first generation, this new generation of migrant workers is more deeply embedded in urban China where claims of social rights are no longer unknown. These workers consider themselves not peasant workers but as city residents. They are relatively well educated and often aware of media debates about the pernicious corruption, inequality and environmental problems arising from China's rapid capitalist development.

Unlike the Asian economic crisis between 1997 and 1998, the severe economic downturn since 2007 was followed by more organised forms of protests by migrant workers. The *China Labour Bulletin* (2011) estimates that there were about 90,000 'mass incidents' in 2009, about one-third of them being labour disputes. These protests build on accumulated discontents. Even before these disputes, the struggles of migrant workers had been increasing in number and 'radicalising' in form (Leung and Pun, 2009). Between 1993 and 2005, the number of 'officially recognised' mass protests increased from 10,000 to 75,000, showing 20 per cent annual increase (ibid.: 553). Approximately 70 per cent of these disputes have been organised by peasants and workers (ibid.: 553).[4] Moreover, workers in the automobile industry even managed to enhance their bargaining power by organising effective strike action as soon as the economy showed signs of recovery (Wong, 2010; *Globalisation Monitor*, 2010; *China Labour Bulletin*, 2011). Although large numbers of migrant workers have been retrenched from collapsing or downsizing firms, the large-scale restructuring of labour relations at the expense of migrant labour could not be pushed.

In Hong Kong, migrant domestic workers responded to the global recession rather offensively than defensively. They had a bitter experience with the Asian economic crisis which the Hong Kong administration used to justify its decision to cut their wages by up to 20 per cent in 1998. Since the Asian economic crisis, the migrant workers movement in Hong Kong has developed significantly both in size and organisational strength. Most of all, migrant organisations have developed from loosely organised mutual-help organisations to trade unions. Starting with the transformation of the Indonesian Group of Hong Kong into the Indonesian Migrant Workers Union (IMWU) in the aftermath of the Asian economic crisis, many migrant workers' unions have

106   Dae-oup Chang

been subsequently established, including the Filipino Migrant Workers Union (1998), the Filipino Domestic Helpers General Union (2003), the Union of Nepalese Domestic Workers (2005) and the Thai Migrant Workers Union (2009). There have also been sustained efforts to build strong solidarity between migrants of different nationalities as well as between migrant and local domestic workers. The Federation of Asian Domestic Workers Union in Hong Kong (FADWU) was finally established in November 2010, which is affiliated to the Hong Kong Confederation of Trade Union and recruits Thai, Indonesian, Hong Kong, Filipino and Nepalese domestic workers under one umbrella (Choi, 2011).

As the migrant movement developed, their activism also began to engage with a wider range of issues such as democracy, international solidarity against neoliberal globalisation, and the right to residency. Migrant workers and their organisations were in the frontline of anti-WTO protests organised during the 6th WTO ministerial conference in Hong Kong in 2005, despite the risk of arrest and deportation. Since the 2000s, strong and mutually supportive links have developed between Hong Kong's democratisation movement and the migrant movement. In 2010, migrant workers in Hong Kong, with support from various advocacy groups of migrants, finally initiated a legal challenge to the fundamental basis of the full-scale discrimination against women migrant workers – the fact that of many 'types' of migrants, they are the only ones not entitled to right to residency. Although as yet unsuccessful, this campaign has put the issues of migrant workers' rights at the centre of political debates in Hong Kong.

A strong migrant workers' movement is also emerging in South Korea. The long history of the hyper-exploitation of migrant workers through the industrial trainee programme, a flawed employment permit programme encouraging migrant workers to go undocumented, and the border agency's infamous manhunt-style seasonal campaigns to arrest and deport undocumented workers have created a fairly militant migrant movement. This has emerged in close cooperation with local social movement organisations and Korean trade unions. The movement was initiated in a desperate attempt by the industrial trainees to secure basic human rights for migrant workers. In 1994, victims of industrial accidents and employer abuse organised a protest action accusing the industrial trainee programme of being modern slavery and calling for respect for the human rights of those recruited (Jung, 2012: 67). In 1995, the migrant workers' movement began to earn more public attention with a sit-in strike of 13 Nepalese industrial trainees in the Myundong Cathedral in downtown Seoul that is well known as the birthplace of the 1987 democratisation movement (Kim, 2012: 682). Many demands of the striking migrant workers, such as 'We are not slaves', 'Don't hit us please' (ibid.: 683) echoed the slogans of the great workers' struggle of 1987 and reminded the Korean labour movement that these problems were still not things of the past, and attracted the solidarity of social movements in a nation-wide support network called the Joint Committee for Migrants in Korea (JCMK). This was formed

Crisis of migration or struggles of labour? 107

by as many as 38 Korean civil, religious and labour organisations in the aftermath of the first sit-in strike of migrant workers (ibid.: 682).[5]

In following years, the migrant workers' movement in South Korea gained confidence through well-organised struggles against the industrial trainee programme, such as 69 days of a sit-in strike in 2002 and the 380 days of a sit-in strike between 2003 and 2004 at the Myungdong Cathedral. Increasingly confident actions taken by migrant workers themselves have made it clear that migrant workers were not poor foreigners in desperate need of protection from Korean citizens but an integral part of *the working class in Korea* if not part of *the Korean working class*. These struggles have contributed to the eventual abolition of the notorious industrial trainee programme. The migrant workers' movement diversified into two main strands, one emphasising class-based struggle, and the other focusing on service provision and humanitarian approaches. Migrant workers as well as Korean activists aligned with the class-based approach succeeded in establishing the migrant workers' branch in the Seoul-Gyeongi Equal Trade Union in 2001 and then the Migrant Trade Union (MTU) in 2005. In doing so, they attracted attention not only from religious and philanthropic organisations but also from major trade unions such as the Korean Confederation of Trade Unions. The Korean unions' view of migrant labour has changed over the years since the early 1990s. During the earlier period, the Korean Confederation of Trade Unions (KCTU) focused on protection and support rather than organising or integrating migrant workers as active participants in the Korean labour movement despite the rhetoric of international working-class unity (Jung, 2012: 69–71). It was the sit-in strikes of migrant workers between 2002 and 2004 that made the KCTU more involved in the migrant workers' movement. Since then, the KCTU has shown more genuine interest in working with and representing migrant workers.

From 2005, the MTU has been affiliated to the KCTU's Seoul office. In 2010, migrant workers began to be represented on the General Congress of the KCTU. The KCTU also began to employ a full-time migrant activist in its headquarters. In recent years, despite anti-migrant nationalist sentiment among Korean workers, more enterprise, regional and industrial unions began to invite migrant workers to join. The Metal Workers Federation has allowed migrant workers to be members since 2005 while enterprises unions under this federation such as the Samwoo Precision Industry Union, the Korea BorgWarner Changwon Union, and theYoungjin Industry Union organised migrant workers and represented them in collective bargaining (*Kyunghyang Shinmun*, 2 February 2010). The migrant workers' movement in Korea faces many challenges. Apart from the institutionalised discrimination that the work permit programme imposes upon migrant workers, the Korean state continues to criminalise undocumented migrant workers and the migrant workers' movement. The MTU has been outlawed from its establishment in 2005. Most of the MTU leaders have been arrested and deported by the border agency without regard to their legal status. Nevertheless, the migrant workers'

108　Dae-oup Chang

movement in Korea continues to advance and has become an integral part of the Korean labour movement. In so doing, migrants are not only becoming an integral part of the South Korean economy as cheap labour but also are turning increasingly into political subjects embedded in Korean society.

This growing assertiveness is not only apparent in places like Korea and Hong Kong where migrants can find solidarity from the well-established local labour movement, but also in very unexpected places where such support is hardly available. A good example is the Burmese migrant workers' movement in Mae Sot, a small industrial town located on the Thai side of the Thailand–Burma border. All over Thailand, there are more than a million Burmese migrant workers from different ethnic groups in Burma, such as Shan, Karen, Barma and Mon. The Thailand–Burma border is 2,532 km long, and thousands of Burmese manage to cross the border every day. The Burmese 'exodus' began seriously after the uprising of 1988, when the military government killed thousands of pro-democracy protesters. Many Burmese chose to go abroad rather than live under the draconian dictatorship. Subsequent civil wars between the military and armed ethnic groups also accelerated the migrant flow from Burma to Thailand in search of peace. On the other side of the border, Thailand's incorporation into the vertically integrated production networks in the region and the subsequent economic boom meant that there was a high demand for cheap labour, and foreign capital as well as Thai capital rushed to Mae Sot and other towns close to the Thailand–Burma border where cheap labour power was provided by Burmese migrant workers.

At the time, the Thai government had little incentive to implement strict border controls as the inflow of migrant workers from Burma to Thailand not only provided cheap labour to Thai industries but also contributed to imposing downward pressure on the wages of Thai workers. Consequently, the existence of a large number of 'illegal' migrant workers was tolerated by the Thai authorities. A rather generous resolution in 1996 allowed migrant workers to be legally employed as unskilled workers in the 11 industrial sectors avoided by local Thai workers. A total of 263,782 Burmese migrant workers registered for two-year labour contracts, representing more than 87 per cent of the total registered migrant workers in Thailand (Arnold and Hewison, 2005: 321). However, after the onset of the economic crisis in 1997, faced with soaring unemployment, the Thai government began to accuse illegal migrant workers of worsening the living conditions of Thai workers, and ramped up border controls and initiated a hunt for Burmese undocumented workers, which ended with the massive deportation of more than 290,000 Burmese workers in 1999. It was not until 2001 that the Thai government announced a new policy that again allowed migrant workers to be employed in ten industrial sectors.

The situation of Burmese workers in Thailand is very precarious.[6] It is estimated that about 120,000 Burmese migrant workers worked and lived in Mae Sot as of 2009 (*The Economist*, 19 March 2009). Most of them pass into Thailand through the official checkpoints, where they are given a day visa and then never go back. In spite of the relaunched registration policy of the

Crisis of migration or struggles of labour? 109

Thai government from 2001, many of those migrant workers choose to remain unregistered largely because employers deduct the registration fees from the workers' salary and registration is tied to a particular employer. Unregistered workers are often subjected to police crackdowns, arrested, and quickly deported to Burma. Any subversive action against employers can cause dismissal, making migrants vulnerable to arrest and deportation. For unregistered workers, it is even harder to complain as employers can get workers deported by simply making a phone call to the police. Migrant workers earn less than local workers because they are not paid the legal minimum wage though registered workers are entitled to the legal minimum wage in the Tak province. The average net income of each migrant worker is as little as US$2 per day. Workers often work more than 10 hours a day and 6 days a week in Mae Sot.

This inhumane treatment of Burmese workers went largely unnoticed for many years, due to the town's remote location, the turmoil of the 1997–98 Asian economic crisis, and the deteriorating living conditions in Burma throughout the 1990s. It was the workers themselves and local labour groups such as Yaung Chi Oo Workers Association who initiated actions against the employers in Mae Sot (Arnold and Hewison, 2005; Pearson and Kusakabe, 2012). In the 2000s, the migrant workers' movement in Mae Sot organised several collective actions aimed at addressing the various problems that the workers faced. These attempts to organise were met with heavy-handed suppression by the employers. Workers in the Nut Knitting Partnership Co., for example, were attacked by local gangsters armed with iron pipes when they took collective action to protest against the arrest of their 'unregistered' colleagues in the factory in 2002. Two workers were seriously injured and had to be hospitalised. Far from being cowed, the workers organised more concerted actions against the employer – they filed their first legal action against the crude discrimination and exploitation. Workers succeeded in pushing the labour court in Tak province to order the employer to pay 4.5 million Baht to the migrant workers to compensate for the serious violation of the minimum wage in Thai labour law. Although the final compensation for the workers was smaller after the employer's appeal, it showed workers could win (Arnold and Hewison, 2005). Certainly, not every labour dispute is as successful as the Nut Knitting Workers' case. More often than not, labour disputes in Mae Sot end up with massive deportation and dismissal. Nevertheless, migrant workers continue the struggle to improve their situation.

Importantly, this was the case even after the global recession severely hit Thailand's garment and textile industry in which most of the migrant workers in Mae Sot are employed. The increasing retrenchment of workers in bankrupt factories was followed by deteriorating working conditions and wage cuts and arrears. Rather than just tolerating worsening conditions, migrant workers responded with collective actions, building on earlier experiences. They walked out, organised representative committees, brought the case to the Labour Protection Office, and occupied workplaces (Pearson and Kusakabe,

110   *Dae-oup Chang*

2012: 139–50). As Pearson and Kusakabe state, this indicates that the migrant workers are not as submissive as they used to be.

Conclusion

The increasing flow of migrants within East Asia is tightly embedded in the process of East Asian integration through the regionalising circuit of capital, which creates highly uneven development within the region. The increasingly pivotal role played by China as the assembly hub for exporting final products to markets in the global North is based on the most dramatic human migration ever, from Chinese rural areas to coastal cities. Continuing foreign investment in industrial zones in newly industrialising countries in South-east Asia desperately needs the circular migratory flow of cheaper labour from poorer neighbouring countries including Cambodia, Burma, Indonesia and Lao PDR. Industries in first generation NIEs suffering from the increasing competitive pressure from East Asia's emerging economies need 'guest workers' to survive, while the highly dynamic circuit of capital in global cities like Hong Kong can only be sustained by 'imported housewives'. This growing intra-regional flow of migrant workers is, in short, an essential and integral part of the making of contemporary East Asia.

Due to this embedded structural demand, in the context of the current global economic crisis, it has not been possible to dispose of migrant labour as commonly envisaged. This does not mean that the crisis, and the states' increasingly restrictionist policy stances, and the employers' attempts to squeeze labour, have not affected migrants badly in some places. But this in turn has further fuelled an increasingly assertive political subjectivity and intensified activism on the part of migrants, who are connecting with local social and labour movements in the places where they live and work. Therefore, the global recession and crisis of neoliberal capitalist development are not leading to a crisis of migration but creating more struggles of migrant workers.

Acknowledgment

This work is a part of the research organised by the Institute for Social Sciences at Gyeongsang National University, which is supported by a National Research Foundation of Korea Grant (NRF-2010-413-B00027).

Notes

1 In 2010, according to the Chinese Ministry of Commerce, China received in total US$105.735 billion, of which investment from 10 East Asian countries and regions (Hong Kong, Macao, Taiwan, Japan, the Philippines, Thailand, Malaysia, Singapore, Indonesia, and the Republic of Korea) was US$88.179 billion.
2 McNally offers a very succinct definition of the over-accumulation crisis:

the process by which capitalist enterprises accumulate more productive capacity – factories, machines, offices, mines, shopping malls, buildings, and so on – than

Crisis of migration or struggles of labour? 111

they can profitably utilize. This is caused by intense competition to boost the productiveness of their companies by investing in new plants and technologies, which results in over-capacity.

(McNally, 2011: 196)

3 The only major labour-sending country that shows decreasing remittance was Burma, according to the World Bank data. However, it also shows the remittance total increased dramatically in 2012 to US$566 million, about five times larger than the 2005 figure. Given the high irregularity of the migration flow from Burma to Thailand, it is very likely that the remittance figure of Burma is the least reliable among the data from labour-receiving countries. For a more detailed analysis of remittance flow in East Asia, see Hugo (2012).

4 These increasing mass protests and the radicalisation of migrant workers in particular have led the party-state to address emerging discontent among the working population (Gray, 2010). Dubbed 'harmonious development', which became an official direction of Chinese development after Hu Jintao and Wen Jiabao came to power in 2003, several measures have been introduced. They include policies addressing rural-urban disparity with increasing government investment in inland areas, a more efficient system of managing minimum wages, more aggressive campaigns to establish trade unions in private enterprises, pursuit of wage negotiation through a collective contract system and finally a labour law amendment. The labour law reform has been regarded particularly pro-migrant labour by many as it was intended to improve the job security of migrant workers and provoked strong protests from business leaders.

5 Although the JCMK played a major role in supporting the migrant workers' movement, some major participants of the JCMK have also been criticised because of their view of migrant workers as passive victims to be protected by Korean citizens rather than political subjects capable of building their own movement.

6 This description of the migration process and the daily livelihoods of Burmese migrant workers in Mae Sot is based on data collected during three of the author's own field researches between 2003 and 2007.

References

Abella, M. and Ducanes, G. (2009) 'The Effect of the Global Economic Crisis on Asian Migrant Workers and Governments' Responses'. Available at: http://www.unitar.org/ny/sites/unitar.org.ny/files/Abella%20and%20Ducanes%20Economic%20Crisis%20and%20Labour%20Migration%20in%20Asia.pdf (accessed 20 May 2012).

Arnold, D. and Hewison, K. (2005) 'Exploitation in Global Supply Chains: Burmese Workers in Mae Sot', *Journal of Contemporary Asia* 35(3): 319–40.

Asian Development Bank (2007) *Asian Development Outlook 2007: Growth amid Change.* Hong Kong: ADB.

——(2010) *Asian Development Outlook 2010 Update: The Future of Growth in Asia.* Available at: http://www.adb.org/sites/default/files/pub/2010/ado2010-update.pdf (accessed 12 May 2011).

——(2012) *Key Indicators for Asia and Pacific.* Available at: http://www.adb.org/sites/default/files/ki/2012/pdf/ki2012-rt4-globalization.pdf (accessed 12 March 2013).

Breman, J. (1989) *Taming the Coolie Beast: Plantation Society and the Colonial Order in South-east Asia.* Oxford: Oxford University Press.

Castles, S. (2010) 'Understanding Global Migration: A Social Transformation Perspective', *Journal of Ethnic and Migration Studies* 36(10): 1–22.

112   Dae-oup Chang

——(2012) 'Migration, Crisis and the Global Labour Market', *Globalization* 8(3): 311–24.

Castles, S. and Vezzoli, S. (2009) 'The Global Economic Crisis and Migration: Temporary Interruption or Structural Change?', *Paradigmes* 2: 68–74.

Chalamwong, Y., Meepien, J. and Hongprayoon, K. (2012) 'Management of Cross-border Migration: Thailand as a Case of Net Immigration', *Asian Journal of Social Science* 40: 447–63.

Chan, K.W. (2010) 'The Global Financial Crisis and Migrant Workers in China: "There is No Future as a Labourer; Returning to the Village Has No Meaning"', *International Journal of Urban and Regional Research* 34(3): 659–77.

Chang, D. (2009) *Capitalist Development in Korea: Labour, Capital and the Myth of the Developmental State.* London: Routledge.

——(2012) 'The Neoliberal rise of East Asia and Social Movements of Labour: Four Moments and a Challenge', *Interface: A Journal For and About Social Movements*, 4(2): 22–51.

China Labour Bulletin (2011) 'Unity is Strength: Workers' Movement in China 2009–2011'. Available at: http://www.clb.org.hk/en/files/share/File/research_reports/unity_is_strength_web.pdf (accessed 5 January 2012).

Choi, S. (2011) 'Domestic Workers in Asia: Campaign and Organising Updates'. Available at: http://www.amrc.org.hk/system/files/Domestic%20Workers%20in%20Asia%202011.pdf (accessed 5 May 2012).

Constable, N. (2007) *Maid to Order in Hong Kong, Stories of Migrant Workers.* Ithaca, NY: Cornell University Press.

Faison, E. (2007) *Managing Women: Disciplining Labor in Modern Japan.* Berkeley, CA: University of California Press.

Gibb, H. (2009) 'Impact of the Economic Crisis: Women Migrant Workers in Asia'. Paper presented at IWG-GEM Conference 2009, July 13–14, 2009, New York. Available at: http://www.levyinstitute.org/pubs/GEMconf2009/presentations/Heather_Gibb-Panel_IV.pdf (accessed 12 December 2012).

Gills, D.S. (1999) *Rural Women and Triple Exploitation in Korean Development.* London: Palgrave Macmillan.

Globalisation Monitor (2010) 'Special Report on Honda Foshan Strike'. Available at: http://www.worldlabour.org/eng/files/u1/pecial_Report_on_Honda_Strike_gm_june 2010_1_.pdf (accessed 1 April 2012).

Gray, K. (2010) 'Labour and the State in China's Passive Revolution', *Capital and Class* 34: 449–67.

Green, T. and Winters, L.A. (2010) 'Economic Crises and Migration: Learning from the Past and the Present', Working Paper T-31, Department of International Development, University of Sussex. Available at: http://r4d.dfid.gov.uk/PDF/Outputs/MigrationGlobPov/WP-T31.pdf (accessed 5 May 2013).

Hugo, G. (2012) 'International Labour Migration and Migration Policies in Southeast Asia', *Asian Journal of Social Science* 40: 392–418.

Huguet, J.W., Chamratrithrong, A. and Richter, K. (2011) 'Thailand Migration Profile', in J.W. Huguet and A. Chamratrithrong (eds) *Thailand Migration Report 2011.* IOM Thailand.

IOM (2008) *Situation Report on International Migration in East and South-East Asia.* Available at: http://publications.iom.int/bookstore/free/Situation_Report.pdf.

Jeong, Y-C. (2009) 'Sagyegyeongjaewigiwa ijunodongja' [The Global Economic Crisis and Migrant Workers]. *Social Movement Monthly* May–June: 47–60.

Crisis of migration or struggles of labour? 113

Available at: http://www.movements.or.kr/bbs/download.php?board=journal&id=2016&idx=4.

Jung, Y-S. (2012) 'Hangukui nodongundonggwa ijunodongjaui areumdaunyeondaeneun ganeunghanga?' [Is Solidarity between the Korean Labour Movement and Migrant Workers Possible?]. e-Journal *Homo Migrans* 5(6): 65–84.

Kanapathy, V. (2010) *Impact of the Economic Crisis on International Migration in Asia a Year After: Country Report for Malaysia*. Available at: http://www.smc.org.ph/misa/uploads/country_reports/1285919888.pdf (accessed 20 April 2013).

Kang, C., Sok, S. and Liv, D. (2009) *Rapid Assessment of the Impact of Financial Crisis in Cambodia*. Available at: http://www.ilo.org/wcmsp5/groups/public/-asia/-ro-bangkok/documents/meetingdocument/wcms_101593.pdf (accessed 20 January 2013).

Kaur, A. (2004) 'Labour Dynamics in the Plantation and Mining Sector', in R. Elmhirst and R. Sapptari (eds) *Labour in Southeast Asia: Labour Processes in a Globalised World*. London: RoutledgeCurzon.

Khin, P. and Kato, R. (2010) 'The Impact of the Global Economic Crisis on Cambodia', Discussion Paper No. A-1, Centre for Risk Research, Faculty of Economics, Shiga University. Available at: http://www.econ.shiga-u.ac.jp/10/2/3/res.9/DPA1PiseyKato201008.pdf (accessed 20 January 2013).

Kim, H.M. (2001) 'Work, Nation and Hypermasculinity: The Women Question in Economic Miracle and Crisis in South Korea', *Inter-Asia Cultural Studies* 2(1): 53–68.

Kim, N. (2012) 'The Migrant Workers' Movement in the Democratic Consolidation of Korea', *Journal of Contemporary Asia* 42(4): 676–96.

Kong, D., Yoon, K. and Yu, S. (2010) 'The Social Dimension of Immigration in Korea', *Journal of Contemporary Asia* 40(2): 252–74.

Koser, K. (2009) 'The Impact of Financial Crises on International Migration: Lessons Learned', IOM Migration Research Series, Vol. 37. Available at: http://www.iom.ch/jahia/webdav/shared/shared/mainsite/published_docs/serial_publications/mrs_37_en.pdf (accessed 20 July 2013).

Kyunghyang Shinmun (2010) 2 February 2010. Available at: http://news.khan.co.kr/kh_news/khan_art_view.html?artid=201002020132275& code = 940702 (accessed 20 January 2013).

Leung, P.N. and Pun, N. (2009) 'The Radicalisation of the New Chinese Working Class: A Case Study of Collective Action in the Gemstone Industry', *Third World Quarterly* 30(3): 551–65.

Macabuag, L. (2009) *Migrants and the Global Economic Crisis*. Available at: http://www.unitar.org/ny/sites/unitar.org.ny/files/MFA%20global%20econ%20crisis%20final.pdf (accessed 20 January 2013).

Macnaughtan, H. (2005) *Women, Work and the Japanese Economic Miracle: The Case of the Cotton Textile Industry 1945–1975*. London: RoutledgeCurzon.

Manning, C. (2002) 'Structural Change, Economic Crisis and International Labour Migration in East Asia', *The World Economy* 25(3): 359–85.

McNally, D. (2011) *Global Slump: The Economics and Politics of Crisis and Resistance*. Oakland, CA: PM Press.

Pearson, R. and Kusakabe, K. (2012) *Thailand's Hidden Workforce: Burmese Migrant Women Factory Workers*. London: Zed Books.

Perrons, D. (2004) *Globalization and Social Change: People and Places in a Divided World*. London: Routledge.

Sassen, S. (2000) 'Counter-Geography of Globalization and the Feminization of Survival', *Journal of International Affairs* 53(2): 504–24.

114 Dae-oup Chang

Seol, D-H. (2012) 'The Citizenship of Foreign Workers in South Korea', *Citizenship Studies* 16(1): 119–33.

SOMO (2013) 'Outsourcing Labour: Migrant Labour Rights in Malaysia's Electronics Industry'. Available at: http://makeitfair.org/en/the-facts/news/reports/outsourcing-labour (accessed 12 May 2013).

The Economist (2009) 19 March 2009. Available at: http://www.economist.com/node/13334070/print.

Tsurumi, E.P. (1990) *Factory Girls: Women in the Thread Mills of Meiji Japan.* Princeton, NJ: Princeton University Press.

Wickramasekera, P. (2002) *Asian Labour Migration: Issues and Challenges in an Era of Globalization.* Geneva: ILO. Available at: http://www.ilo.org/wcmsp5/groups/public/–ed_protect/–protrav/–migrant/documents/publication/wcms_201784.pdf (accessed 20 March 2012).

Wong, S. (2010) *Decoding the New Generation of Chinese Migrant Workers.* Available at: http://www.eu-china.net/web/cms/upload/pdf/materialien/eu-china-hintergrundinforma tion8–10_10-09-02.pdf (accessed 3February 2012).

Yeoh, B.S.A. and Lin, W. (2012) 'Rapid Growth of Singapore's Immigrant Population Brings Policy Challenges', *Migration Information Source.* Available at: http://www.migrationinformation.org/feature/print.cfm?ID=887 (accessed 2 August 2013).

6 Crisis, enforcement and control at the EU borders

Julien Jeandesboz and Polly Pallister-Wilkins

This chapter examines the relationship between crisis and migration in the context of the border control policies of the European Union. What is a crisis? What does it look like? And what does it do? Crisis is not only an analytical category, but also a category of practice. Crisis is a powerful contemporary political symbol, and crisis labelling is a crucial modality for securing political consent (Edelman, 1977: 43–55). The practice of crisis labelling presents three claims: (1) that the particular event or sequence thus labelled 'is different from the political and social issues we routinely confront'; (2) that it 'came about for reasons outside the control of political … leaders'; and (3) that it 'requires sacrifices in order to surmount it' (ibid.: 44). Crisis labelling, however, is not only a matter of language. Examining the making of the 1973 oil crisis, Mitchell shows that shaping a 'single field of political concern and government intervention … to be known as the "energy crisis"' involves conflict and controversy among different actors (Mitchell, 2010). Crisis labelling involves contests and conflicting beliefs, 'some justifying leaders' handling of crises and others holding leaders responsible for the burdens they impose, permit[ting] both governmental regimes and the mass of citizens to live with chronic crisis and with themselves' (Edelman, 1977: 45). Considered as a category of practice, then, crisis not only involves disruption and disarray, but is also productive. Depending on the specific circumstances, it enables new patterns of action or justifies the continuation of established ones.

Our concern is the effect of crisis labelling on the handling of migration-related events at the external borders of the EU and the shaping of migration as a 'single field' of EU concern and action for bureaucrats, or professionals of politics and security professionals. We focus on the developments surrounding the so-called Arab Spring of 2011 in North Africa. The EU's dealings with what was rapidly labelled a crisis in its own terms by the European Commission (European Commission, 2011a; de Haas and Sigona, 2012) ultimately led to some soul-searching among the Union's political personnel. The EU Commissioner for Home Affairs, Cecilia Malmström, for instance, publicly commented on the fact that the Union had 'missed a historic opportunity to demonstrate its commitment to the foundations it is built on' (Malmström, 2012: 3). Such statements, however, should not be taken entirely at face value. They are,

116   *J. Jeandesboz and P. Pallister-Wilkins*

rather, indicative of how crisis labelling unfolds in the arenas where EU border control measures are shaped. Our first contention, then, is that crisis labelling has been a recurrent practice for EU policy-makers in the field of migration since the end of the Cold War.

Our second contention is that not all the actors involved in EU border control share the reasoning and framing involved in crisis labelling. Crisis labelling is conducive to the adoption of emergency or exceptional measures. Such have been, as we will show, the most visible effects following from the labelling of movements of persons across the Mediterranean during the 2011 uprisings. The pervasiveness of crisis labelling, however, should not lead to the conclusion that EU migration and border control policies operate solely through the logics of emergency and exception. This is an important finding of critical approaches to security where debates on exceptionality and security have been particularly vibrant in relation to the initial development of the securitisation framework of analysis (see e.g. Aradau, 2004; Huysmans, 2004; c.a.s.e. collective, 2006; Bigo, 2008). For securitisation analysis, the framing of an issue in security terms leads to its removal from the scope of normal politics and opens the possibility for emergency or exceptional measures (Buzan *et al.*, 1998). This conclusion has been challenged by scholarship focusing in particular on migration and security in the EU. The securitisation of migration 'comes also from a range of administrative practices such as population profiling, risk assessment, statistical calculation, proactive preparation, and what may be termed a specific *habitus* of the security professional' (Bigo, 2002: 65–6). Migration policies are formed not only through spectacular invocations of a looming crisis calling for exceptional measures, but also through discrete bureaucratic routines. These two domains coexist and are therefore in tension, between

> technocratic politics ... struggles between professionals over proper policies on the basis of the authority to produce knowledge about phenomena and their regulation, [and] the political spectacle ... a game in which the parties position themselves so as to be identifiable as having the support of the people.
>
> (Huysmans, 2006: 82)

Accounting for crisis and migration in the context of EU policies requires that we resist the appeal of the political spectacle to ask whether that which constitutes a crisis for the professionals of politics is also a crisis for the bureaucrats and security professionals.

Our third contention is that the analysis of crisis labelling and its effects cannot be limited to highlighting the disjuncture between the practical logics of professionals of politics and the bureaucrats. To do so may well contribute to the normalisation and acceptance of more banal, but no less problematic, forms of control. Encompassing migrant experiences beyond the spatio-temporal limits imposed by both crisis labelling and bureaucratic routines of control

Crisis, enforcement and control at EU borders   117

makes it possible to challenge a European approach to migration that minimises or silences such experiences elsewhere or at home.

The chapter unfolds as follows. We first examine crisis labelling in relation to the 2011 uprisings in North Africa and migration. We then discuss the relation between crisis labelling and border control activities. We finally ask whether the 2011 sequence constituted a crisis for the migrants themselves. In doing this we argue for a more nuanced understanding of the relationship between crisis and more routinised forms of control. We first critique the spectacular nature of crisis labelling that masks the everyday forms of bureaucratic forms of control that have been built up over time. Through focusing on the experiences of migrants themselves in the context of Libya and the Choucha refugee camp in Tunisia, second, we make the case for seeing European crisis labelling as being spatio-temporally limited while also challenging the normalisation and acceptance of more banal forms of control.

Throughout the chapter, we chiefly adopt an international political sociology approach, which we understand as an interpretive and relational project engaging, on the one hand, with 'the multiple processes through which political agents can encourage amnesia about the genesis of specific practices of bordering', and on the other with 'map[ping] the different fields that, like magnetic forces, attract a multiplicity of agents and polarise them around specific stakes' (Bigo and Walker, 2007: 732). We build on archival and interview materials constituted in previous research (Jeandesboz, 2008, 2011, 2013), and use compilations of migrant accounts from Tunisia's Choucha refugee camp compiled by the International Organisation for Migration (IOM) and activist group Boats4People that highlight migrants' experiences beyond the limits imposed by crisis labelling and more bureaucratic routines of control. The refugee camp here serves as a significant site of study for discussions on the spatio-temporal limits of crisis labelling and routinised forms of control.

From crisis to crisis: the 2011 uprisings and migration

The self-immolation of Mohammed Bouazizi on 17 December, 2010 was the catalyst for a series of revolutionary changes that started in Tunisia but subsequently spread to Egypt, Libya, Palestine, Yemen, Syria and Bahrain. The outbreak of political violence aimed at revolutionary change in Tunisia was to have consequences that far exceeded the demands for dignity, democracy and an end to the precarious life of the revolutionaries. The Arab revolutions focused attention on a region of critical geo-strategic importance to the European Union and many of its Member States. What they challenged, however, was the continuation of authoritarian regimes and neoliberal injustice resulting in part from policies of the EU and its Member States (Pace, 2009; Hollis, 2012; Pace and Cavatorta, 2012). This in turn led to a mixed response north of the Mediterranean. While European civil society widely expressed support for the uprisings, EU institutions and governments offered a more measured response based on their own vested interests – both political and economic – in

118   *J. Jeandesboz and P. Pallister-Wilkins*

the region (Teti, 2012). As revolution in Tunisia spread to Egypt, then, it seemed as if the people of the North African partner states were creating change for themselves. In response to increasing levels of political unrest in Tunisia, the French Foreign Affairs Minister Michèle Alliot-Marie offered the '*savoir-faire*, recognised throughout the world of [French] security forces in order to settle security situations of this type' (*Financial Times*, 2011).

The collapse of the Ben Ali regime, a crisis in Habermasian terms (Habermas, 1988) for the elites of Tunisia who saw the disintegration of the violently maintained system of rule on which they had grown fat, was also seen as a potential 'security' problem for Europe, due to Ben Ali's support for a range of European security policies built on migration and terrorism. The disintegration of Mubarak's hegemonic grip on the Egyptian security state was presented in similar terms, working to reinforce the hollow nature of previous EU attempts at democracy promotion (Hollis, 2012), and enabling the subsequent migratory flows to be constructed in similar ways. Crisis labelling about the stability of autocratic allies in the War on Terror and neoliberal expansion easily shifted into crisis labelling about migration before even the first boat landed on Lampedusa, reflecting the often loose nature of crisis labelling (Holton, 1987). In many respects the crisis of the Arab revolutions and the migration crisis that followed were the perfect storm of crisis with both working in different ways to threaten the security and territorial integrity of Europe (Boin, 2004).

The revolution in Tunisia resulted in 20,258 Tunisian migrants alone being intercepted on Europe's sea border in the first quarter of 2011 (FRONTEX, 2011a: 37). This number contrasts sharply with the last quarter of 2010, when 70 Tunisians were intercepted on Europe's sea border (ibid.: 37). David Cameron used this figure during his address in the House of Commons on 14 March 2011 to claim that doing nothing in Libya as the regime of Colonel Gaddafi lost its monopoly of violence would 'push people across the Mediterranean and create a more dangerous and uncertain world for Britain and for all our allies' (Cameron, 2011a). This figure again underpinned his speech to Parliament on the eve of the US and European enforcement of the Libyan no-fly zone on 18 March 2011 when he said: 'Libya will become ... a state from which literally hundreds of thousands of citizens could seek to escape, putting huge pressure on us in Europe' (Cameron, 2011b). It was a figure that enabled the EU Commission in May 2011 to state 'since the beginning of this year, political unrest in North Africa has brought 25,000 migrants to EU shores – mainly in Italy and Malta' (European Commission, 2011b). This framing authorised the tabling – between two communications steered by Catherine Ashton's External Action Service (EEAS) on the challenges of political upheavals in North Africa for the Union's neighbourhood and democratisation policies (EEAS and European Commission, 2011a, 2011b) – of a Commission communication on migration piloted by the Home Affairs officials headed by Commissioner Cecilia Malmström (European Commission, 2011a). Crisis labelling was also mobilised by the then Italian Minister of

Crisis, enforcement and control at EU borders 119

Foreign Affairs Franco Frattini on two accounts: to issue a request for an anticipated deployment of FRONTEX Joint-Operation Hermes Extension 2011,[1] initially scheduled in June; and to restore the agreements that had bound Italy, Tunisia and Libya in matters pertaining to migration under these countries' previous regimes (Nascimbene and Di Pascale, 2011).

The way in which the events of the spring of 2011 were dealt with in Europe highlights, on the one hand, the fluidity of crisis as a category of practice. Crisis labelling, in these circumstances, enabled the upgrading of what could have been considered a consequence of the upheavals in Tunisia and Libya as a crisis in its own right. As such, the crisis was built on a foundation of panic as can clearly be seen by the public speech acts of various European professionals of politics, claiming the 'flow' of migrants from the southern Mediterranean threatened European society and values. This panic subsequently coalesced around an apparent crisis over the EU and its Member States' capacity to enforce effective border control and led to the suspension of the Schengen Acquis governing free movement of peoples within the Schengen Area by France on 17 April 2011 and Denmark on 11 May 2011. It continued to grow in the run-up to the European Council meeting on 23–24 June in Brussels where migration was the second substantive item on the agenda after European economic policy (European Council, 2011).

If considered separately, these developments can lead to examining crisis labelling exclusively in terms of the emergency or the exceptional measures that follow it. This conclusion, however, needs to be nuanced in two ways. First, crisis labelling is not a generalised occurrence. It surfaces most strongly among professionals of politics in highly publicised and mediatised circumstances. Professionals of politics are designated here, following Max Weber's work on political vocation (Weber, 2008) and Bourdieu's analysis of the political field (Bourdieu, 2000), as those actors who 'do not live for politics but from politics' (Bigo, 2011: 246). In this regard, the notion encompasses actors who would not be considered 'politicians' in the common use of the term, such as European Commissioners such as Cecilia Malmström (on Commissioners as professionals of politics, see Joana and Smith, 2002). Crisis labelling, in other words, is a characteristic practice of professionals of politics. In this respect, crisis labelling in relation to migration has emerged over the past two decades as a routine practice in European governmental arenas. These practices have emerged in response to flows of migrants from conflicts in Yugoslavia, Somalia and Sudan among others and have elided with the inclusion of migration within an increasingly dominant security paradigm (Collyer, 2005, 2006).

A few months before the 2011 uprisings, the Greek government declared it was facing a migration-linked crisis, and called upon the EU to deploy for the first time a Rapid Border Intervention Team (RABIT) along its land border with Turkey. By the same token, the island of Lampedusa, which became the focal point for crisis labelling in 2011, has repeatedly made the headlines and been subjected to highly publicised interventions over the past decade. The visibility of the 'temporary stay and assistance centre' (CPTA) on the island

120 *J. Jeandesboz and P. Pallister-Wilkins*

led the Italian government to adopt a series of emergency measures, including the conclusion of a treaty of friendship with the Libyan government that authorised the handover of craft and passengers intercepted on the high seas by the *Guardia di Finanza* to the Libyan coastguards (Human Rights Watch, 2009; Andrijasevic, 2010). Earlier in the decade, in 2005, Ceuta and Melilla, the Spanish enclaves in northern Morocco, were sites for this routinised practice of crisis labelling during a series of migrant deaths, popularly known as *'avalanchas'*,[2] where 11 migrants lost their lives attempting to scale the fences that enclose the cities designed today to prevent migration flows. The *avalanchas* resulted in a Commission-led technical mission to Ceuta, Melilla and northern Morocco to assess the situation at the border. In its subsequent mission report, the Commission was clear to frame any changes in policy and practice due to the recent tragic events (European Commission, 2005: 3).

Introducing this perspective, second, allows us to interrogate the articulation between crisis labelling and enforcement activities associated with border control and migration policy. This involves discussing the relationship between professionals of politics, on the one hand, and security and bureaucracy professionals, on the other.

Crisis and border control

The EU's external borders agency FRONTEX notes that the increase in the number of Tunisian nationals intercepted in the first quarter of 2011

> represents one of the sharpest ever single peaks in illegal immigration pressure at the EU external border. This influx is almost exclusively due to Tunisians arriving in Lampedusa following civil unrests that spread across North Africa since the beginning of 2011.
>
> (FRONTEX, 2011a: 12)

In the narrative of the agency's officials, however, this peak is not associated with a radical disruption or a call for new measures. The view expressed in the FRONTEX 2011 general report is that the increase in arrivals in Lampedusa and Malta required 'changing the initial operational plans for the Agency' through 'fast operational decisions and contingency planning based on constant situational monitoring and developing follow-up risk assessments' (FRONTEX, 2011b: 15). The agency's analysis is framed in terms of variations (of movements of persons) and intensification (of border control activities), rather than in the dramatic terms adopted at the time by professionals of politics. The first quarter of 2011, according to the FRONTEX Risk Analysis Network (FRAN), was the year when 'for the first time since records began in early 2008 ... detections of illegal border crossings on the Central Mediterranean route exceeded those reported from both the Eastern Mediterranean and Albania to Greece routes' (FRONTEX, 2011a: 13). The agency's actions corresponded to

Crisis, enforcement and control at EU borders 121

an operational package [that] resulted in an almost 100% increase in operational days in the field of maritime joint operations compared to the Annual Programme of Work 2011, with respective implementation of additional financial resources ... based constantly on intensified monitoring and analytical work.

(FRONTEX, 2011b: 16)

This account is markedly different from the standpoints adopted by professionals of politics. Both build on the same material underpinning (the movements of persons that took place in the first quarter of 2011 between Libya, Tunisia, Italy and Malta) and communicate the same figures (proposed by FRONTEX and later used by David Cameron), but they differ in their scope and claims. The professionals of politics build on the claim that a solution to a problem, framed as a migration crisis piggybacking on a political and humanitarian crisis, is needed. The professionals of security focus on a problem that is considered unique but that should be (and has been) managed within existing frames of reference and action. In the context of the EU's migration policies, then, crisis labelling as a recurrent practice among professionals of politics co-exists with managerial concerns. While FRONTEX is often considered to be the vector of emergency and exceptional measures related to migration, this managerial logic is probably the most significant characteristic of the actions undertaken through the agency. It is, more generally, the outlook that has been sponsored by some actors in the European governmental arenas, in particular within the European Commission, since the early 2000s, and is epitomised by the term 'integrated border management'[3] that has come to encompass all EU measures in the area of border control (European Commission, 2002, 2006, 2008).

The managerial outlook of the EU border agency not only co-exists with the spectacular politics unfolding through crisis labelling; it has rather regularly been at odds with it. As Neal points out, the establishment of FRONTEX in 2004 may well have initially been sustained in the name of the proclaimed crisis instigated by the attacks of 11 September 2001 in the United States, but this notion of urgency soon gave way to the 'regular dynamics of EU politics' (Neal, 2009: 340). By the same token, the management model advocated by the agency in relation to border control, grounded in the conduct of risk analysis, is the opposite of the spectacular logic of crisis labelling and securitisation 'in that it aims to regulate and harmonize the border practices of individual states' rather than enforce emergency and exceptional measures (ibid.: 347). The contrast surfaced very strongly during the agency's first years of operation. It comes out quite explicitly in the diverging evidence provided by witnesses in the investigation on FRONTEX in 2007–2008 undertaken by the UK House of Lords' Committee on European Union. Asked about his evaluation of the agency's work so far, conservative Maltese MEP Simon Busuttil, at the time rapporteur for the European Parliament's LIBE Committee[4] on the European Commission's 'border package' (European Commission, 2008), commented that his assessment was 'negative to the extent that I do not think

122   *J. Jeandesboz and P. Pallister-Wilkins*

that Frontex is doing enough, in particular to stem the immense wave of migration that is coming northwards from Africa at the moment' (House of Lords, 2008: 21). Questioned on the European Parliament's decision to increase the agency's budget beyond what the European Commission and FRONTEX had actually requested over several years, Busuttil added that 'we [the European Parliament] have no interest in seeing Frontex walk. We want it to run at great speed and this explains why we have done this' (ibid.: 24). In the same hearing, the agency's Executive Director Ilkka Laitinen claimed in the hearing by the Lords that:

> [FRONTEX had] been struggling with the more or less realistic or unrealistic expectations from different sectors towards Frontex. The common denominator in this case is that the role and the remit of Frontex have not been entirely understood, either by accident or deliberately. Very often we have felt that Frontex is considered to be a European panacea for all border-related issues and if there are some problems at the external borders, it is Frontex who is in charge of that instead of considering Frontex to be a co-ordinator to co-ordinate such co-operation where the Member States participate of their own volition.
>
> (ibid.: 54)

The tension between the spectacular politics of crisis labelling in relation to migration and the managerial outlook of border control is important to address when discussing the effects of the former. It suggests, as Neal argues, that:

> [the] complexity [of EU border control policies] far exceeds that of the political theatre of securitization ... We should be less concerned with a spectacular dialectic of norm/exception and more concerned with an ongoing process of incremental normalization that is not quite spectacular or controversial enough to draw attention to itself.
>
> (Neal, 2009: 353)

Crisis labelling is overbearing, and as such can be misleading for analysis. It can lead in particular to overstating the centrality of emergency and exceptional measures in the handling of migration events. What needs to be stressed, in this regard, is that the events of 2011 did not fundamentally change the overall rationale of EU external border control.

Most of the measures proposed and adopted in relation to EU border control after the 2011 events indeed followed from earlier discussions and pertained to the normal EU policy-making process. These include the proposal for a revision of the FRONTEX regulation (European Commission, 2010), which had been tabled by the European Commission in February 2010 and was adopted in October 2011 without any significant modification. The only addition alluding to the 2011 developments in the Mediterranean is found in

Crisis, enforcement and control at EU borders 123

the regulation's first recital that makes reference to '[t]he development of a forward-looking and comprehensive European migration policy based on human rights, solidarity and responsibility, especially for those Member States facing specific and disproportionate pressures' (OJEU, 2011: 1). The insert was introduced by the European Parliament at the behest of MEP Simon Busuttil, rapporteur for the proposal, who recalls in his report the situation of 'frontier Member States that, owing to their geographic or demographic situation, face severe migratory pressures at their borders' (European Parliament, 2011: 36). The other major policy development in the field of border control, the deployment of the European Border Surveillance system (EUROSUR, see Jeandesboz, 2011) has so far unfolded without any significant change due to the 2011 events. The European Commission's Directorate General for Home Affairs (DG Home, also responsible for the aforementioned May 2011 Communication on Migration) tabled a legislative proposal in December 2011 (European Commission, 2011b). The impact assessment document transmitted alongside the proposal uses the figures published by FRONTEX to make the case for the necessity of setting up EUROSUR, but without invoking notions of exceptionality or crisis:

The EU faces pressure from irregular migration at its external borders. Over 100,000 unauthorised border crossings were detected … in 2009 and 2010. During the first six months of 2011, 74,300 unauthorised border crossings were detected, of which over 96% took place at the external borders of Spain, Greece, Italy and Malta.

(European Commission, 2011c: 8)

This point can be discussed further. What crisis labelling brings to the fore, beyond the specific tension between the 'practical reason' (Bigo, 2011) of professionals of politics and security professionals, is the broader tension between the former and the professionals of bureaucracy. That politics and bureaucracy are separate and autonomous social realms has been a familiar notion to sociologists and political scientists since Weber. In the circumstances discussed here, this separation and autonomy are also observable through the measures advocated in the communications hastily tabled by the European Commission amidst the unfolding events of the Spring of 2011. The measures envisaged in the May 2011 communication on migration, for one, overwhelmingly relate to initiatives already put in place or that were being discussed before the 'Arab Spring'. For instance, the establishment of an Entry/Exit system (EES) and Registered Traveller Programme (RTP), the extension of visa facilitation agreements, or the development of labour migration schemes, which were all proposed under the third heading of the communication (European Commission, 2011a: 10–14), are initiatives that had been considered for some time already. The EES and RTP had been officially presented as policy options in the Commission's 'border package' three years previously (European Commission, 2008). Visa facilitation

124 *J. Jeandesboz and P. Pallister-Wilkins*

agreements had been discussed with third countries since 2002. As for labour migration schemes, the communication stresses that 'the time has come to find an agreement on the 2007 proposal on the "Single permit" which will simplify administrative procedures for migrants and give a clear and common set of rights' (European Commission, 2011a: 12–13). With the explicit aim of moving 'beyond the crisis' (ibid.: 16), the communication reflects an attempt by bureaucratic actors within the European arenas to normalise the emergency, and to use the sense of urgency built up by the professionals of politics to make a concrete case for the normalisation of EU migration policy.

The relative banality and routine-like characteristic of European migration and border policies imply that the crisis loses credibility as an explanatory factor. Crisis labelling does affect, or inflect, policy, but is only one factor among others in this regard. In the meantime, placing emphasis on management and normalisation does not render European border control practices less problematic. As the next section argues, both crisis labelling and management decrease when we look at the subjects of the policies and practices and their experiences of 'crisis'.

Migration crisis, categorisation and migrant experiences

Thus far, we have focused on the construction of crisis labelling by professionals of politics and the fact that it overshadows more everyday routines of control. Further, we have shown how these routines of control have served to consolidate the European border over time. It would be easy to inadvertently reinforce and endorse the bureaucratic and routine forms of control that migrants face on a daily basis though critiquing the spectacular politics behind crisis labelling. But both crisis labelling and routines of control are co-constitutive of a wider European migration order built on policies and practices of exclusion. By widening the spatio-temporal lens to encompass migrant experiences beyond the limits imposed by both crisis labelling and bureaucratic routines of control, we are able to challenge a European approach to migration that minimises or silences migrant experiences elsewhere or 'at home'. Challenging the spatio-temporal limits of crisis labelling attempts to re-politicise the migrant experience, drawing attention to the systemic forms of violence, that structural migrants, through exercising their agency, are attempting to overcome.

Migration is both a spatial and a temporal phenomenon. It involves movement between distinct places – the spatial element – and this movement is understood to occur in and over specific periods of time – the temporal element. However, these spatial and temporal boundaries are fluid while crisis labelling attempts to fix them in particular places at particular times. So the migration crisis following the Arab revolutions attempted to fix the experience of those migrants involved to the European Mediterranean in the year of 2011 (Marfleet and Hanieh, Chapter 2 in this volume). The dominant European narrative paid little attention to the 644,000 people who crossed Libya's land

Crisis, enforcement and control at EU borders 125

borders between February and October 2011. The crisis created in Tunisia when, after the downfall of Ben Ali, it became itself a destination for migrants leaving neighbouring Libya, with tens of thousands of migrants gathering in the Choucha refugee camp, many of whom remained there until 2013, received scant media coverage. Nor was much attention paid to those refugees who left Libya for Egypt, another destination country that had recently staged its own revolution.

Furthermore, as explored by Philip Marfleet and Adam Hanieh in Chapter 2 in this volume, structural inequalities wrought by neoliberal policies have had and continue to have large-scale repercussions for migration outside of the crisis wrought by the Arab revolutions. Thus, there is a 'crisis-multiplier' where events in the past in 'far-away' places constituted the primary crisis for migrants in the here-and-now. In this sense, the crisis is not the political violence of the Arab revolutions or the 'flows' of people taking to the Mediterranean, but the systemic, transnational structures that render life in certain places untenable, making mobility and migration a tactic in the struggle for survival in the face of economic violence (Duffield, 2007). These systemic structures are quietly written into the categories used by bureaucratic routines to determine who is allowed to enter and who is not (De Genova, 2002; van Houtum, 2010).

Both crisis labelling and bureaucratic routines of control assign different values to voluntary and involuntary migration. Voluntary migration is generally considered to be apolitical and the result of an individualised pursuit of increased opportunity in the economic sphere. This places voluntary migration within a liberal paradigm that understands the migrant and their motivations through individualistic and economic forms of rationality. Meanwhile involuntary migration and its assumed attachment to political violence create a false dichotomy between political and structural violence and therefore opens a dichotomy between migrants. Additionally, as emphasised in Chapter 1 of this book, this dichotomy assumes that the migrant falls neatly into one of these two categories, when in fact migrants can be both simultaneously or at different times throughout their life. In the case of the 2011 Mediterranean migration crisis, the revolutions caused a mixture of forced involuntary migration from political violence and economic migration by those taking advantage of the temporary collapse of certain externalised and routinised European migration controls carried out by North African partner states. Seeing these migrants' experiences exclusively through crisis labelling practices placed clear spatio-temporal limits and a clear line of causation on the flows of people crossing the Mediterranean.

One can begin to grasp the limits imposed by crisis labelling from an analysis of the language used by the migration control professionals tasked with handling the crisis under, as we have seen, pre-existing control mechanisms. A key piece of policy terminology that is suggestive of the underlying complexity is the term 'mixed flow'. 'Mixed' here refers to both the nationalities and the reasons behind the migrants undertaking the journey. Further investigation

126 *J. Jeandesboz and P. Pallister-Wilkins*

reveals that the majority of the persons forming the 'flows' recorded by the EU authorities in 2011 did not originate from North Africa, but may well have left their countries of origin in an earlier attempt to escape political violence and/or economic inequalities. As Figure 6.1 suggests, the very figures provided to EU policy-makers and the interested public by FRONTEX remain inconclusive. While, in 2011, Tunisian nationals constituted a significant proportion of detected unauthorised entries at all EU borders and at sea borders in particular, they and nationals from other North African countries did not represent the majority of people crossing EU external borders through unauthorised channels.

What these 'mixed flows' and the complex migrant experiences hidden within them effectively convey is the spatio-temporal limits of both crisis labelling, that restricted the 'crisis' to one concerning migration in response to the Arab revolutions in 2011, and a bureaucratic logic that attempts to categorise migrants into easily processable parts that results in the term 'mixed flow'. Yet such categories veil the specificities, motivations, experiences, wants and desires of migrants or the larger structural system in which they find themselves when they are reduced to quantifiable pieces of data.

Analysis of migration as it relates to the Libyan case before the outbreak of political violence, during the revolution and up to the present day, demonstrates very convincingly the need for a widening of the spatio-temporal lens and a consideration of migrant experiences beyond the categories created for them by bureaucratic routines of control. Particular emphasis will be placed on Libya's role as a migrant-receiving and migrant-transit country, its role in

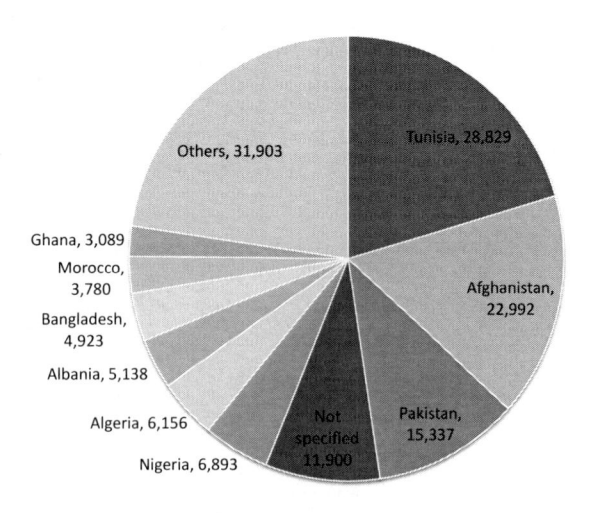

Figure 6.1 Unauthorised entries in 2011: detections by nationality, all EU borders
Source: Compiled from FRONTEX (2011b: 47).

Crisis, enforcement and control at EU borders   127

the consolidation of routinised forms of control and the experiences of migrants in Libya and some of the hundreds of thousands who left to go to neighbouring countries during the violence. Here the testimonies of migrants in the Choucha refugee camp in Tunisia will be used to show the multi-layered nature of crisis both spatially and temporally, and the ongoing struggles they are experiencing in relation to their categorisation as migrants, asylum seekers and refugees.

Prior to the outbreak of political violence against the dictatorship of Muammar Gaddafi, Libya was 'home' to between 1.5 million and 2 million foreign nationals, while the Libyan government put the number closer to 3 million, roughly 10 per cent of the population (Fargues, 2009: 3; Amnesty International, 2011: 79). Libya's migration history is closely tied to changes in its political economy over time and can be broken down into what we can term the Pan-Arab period from the 1960s to the 1980s, the Pan-African period of the 1990s, and the Pan-European period following 2004's rapprochement. It was during the Pan-Arab period that Libya became a migrant-receiving country as its political economy was built on a model of state-led capitalist growth and the number of migrants in Libya steadily grew, with almost half coming from Egypt and the rest from Tunisia, other Arab states and Asia. These policies enabled Libya to fill gaps in its agricultural, education and wider welfare sectors from the surplus labour populations in other Arab states.

This changed during the Pan-African period of the 1990s as a result of the UN embargo and a perceived lack of Arab solidarity that saw Gaddafi recast himself as an African leader and the rise of neoliberalism that saw the creation of an open-door policy and migration agreements between Libya and various other African countries to provide a newly neoliberalising economy with the necessary cheap, unskilled labour. Skilled migrants from other Arab states were no longer in as much demand as cheap unskilled African workers, many of whom were driven by structural inequalities elsewhere to seek employment in Libya. Libya, while it may have offered economic opportunities not available in Sub-Saharan Africa, was not a space free from violence of various kinds. The open-door policy of a neoliberalising Libya might have offered migrants an opportunity to escape the ravages of economic violence during the Pan-African period; however, they were not always safe in their new home. The increasing numbers of Sub-Saharan migrant workers in Libya, coupled with Libya's growing role as a transit country, led to the outbreak of racist violence against Sub-Saharans in the 2000s in which 130 migrants were killed (Abdelfattah, 2011: 3).

In fact, during the 2000s, as Libya entered its Pan-European period, it became an increasingly precarious place for both the regular and irregular migrants, who had helped build a neoliberal Libyan economy. Having scaled back the Pan-African open-door policies, following Libya's reconciliation with the West in 2004, Libya began to actively and violently prevent irregular migration. This led to the return of hundreds of thousands of Sub-Saharan migrants, with 64,000 being returned in 2006 alone (Abdelfattah, 2011: 3).

128   *J. Jeandesboz and P. Pallister-Wilkins*

This change in migration policy served two main purposes. The first relates to changing Libyan economic needs, whereby the Libyan economy no longer needed such high levels of migrant labour and the Libyan state did not want responsibility for the welfare of such large numbers of migrant workers. The second relates to Libya's improving political and economic relations with Europe, its increasing role as a transit country and its steadily increasing co-operation with the European migration control nexus (Bialasiewicz, 2012).

During this push to facilitate stronger relations with Europe, Libya's migration policies gradually changed and came to be more firmly in line with those of Europe. Meanwhile Libya's role as a transit country for those attempting the journey to Europe from Sub-Saharan Africa, the Middle East and Asia steadily grew. Throughout this period Libya remained outside of the multilateral, bilateral and intergovernmental frameworks governing Euro-Mediterranean relations, yet it was considered a working partner on a wide range of issues relating to European security, broadly defined (see Paoletti, 2010; Bialasiewicz, 2012). On issues of migration control, the EU provided training and technology for maritime monitoring, as well as encouraging joint sea-patrol operations (Human Rights Watch, 2009: 31). From 2004 onwards, the EU repeatedly attempted to negotiate a specific package of funding worth upwards of €80 million with Libya (EU Business, 2009) that was designed to fund the construction of detention centres and maritime patrols along Libya's coastline and to tie Libya into more routinised forms of control. This was evidenced in the 'business as usual' discourse of the now disbanded Libyan National Transitional Council when signing a migration control agreement with Italy, following the overthrow of Gaddafi during the Arab revolutions (ANSAmed, 2011).

It was 'business as usual' as well for migrants where danger and violence continued to be ever present. Danger was found not only on the boats heading across the Mediterranean, and large flows of people were arriving not only in Europe. The migration 'crisis' was much larger in scale with far greater spatio-temporal reach than that constructed by European labelling. In Libya itself, there were reports of violence against Sub-Saharan migrants (Amnesty International, 2011: 79–82) – some of whom had come to Libya years before through the open-door policies, others who had considered Libya a space of transit, just one more country on their journey to Europe. For example, Faraj Mohammed Omar from Eritrea told Amnesty International that he had been in Libya since 2007 and that he had decided to leave Tripoli after 'eight men in plain clothes, two of them armed with Kalashnikovs, broke down his door in the middle of the night on 26 February' (ibid.: 80). Migrants found themselves in increasingly precarious positions in the fighting between pro- and anti-Gaddafi factions where their loyalties were questioned and many Sub-Saharans were labelled mercenaries. Later in March, Ali Youssef from Niger, along with his cousin Nasser Ider were trying to leave their home in Misratah to a place of safety during fighting, when they were captured by forces loyal to Gaddafi, tied up and shot at. Nasser Ider was killed by a shot in the back of

Crisis, enforcement and control at EU borders 129

the head, while Ali Youssef was shot in the side of the head but survived. He lay in the street for 11 days until he was finally rescued by an Egyptian migrant worker who took him to the safety of a building used by other migrant workers (ibid.: 81–2).

The revolution in Libya was to create multiple migrant realties. It created migrants in the form of Libyans fleeing violence; it forced migrants in Libya, such as Faraj Mohammed Omar, to become migrants once more; it turned economic migrants into political refugees; and many more combinations in between. As already mentioned, it is estimated that between February and October 2011, 644,000 people crossed one of Libya's land borders, compared with 112,726 intercepted crossing into Europe from January to October 2011 (FRONTEX, 2012). Thus regional migration dwarfed migration from Libya into the European space. A major destination was Tunisia (a country itself in upheaval and whose 20,000 migrants had precipitated the crisis labelling in Europe in early 2011). It is estimated by the UNHCR that up to 1 million people crossed into southern Tunisia in 2011, 200,000 of whom were non-Libyan, secondary migrants (UNHCR, 2013). One of the key destinations was Choucha refugee camp, where migrants' accounts capture the multi-layered and intersectional nature of migrant experiences across time and space.

As a tool for controlling and governing the displaced in times of crisis (see Agier, 2011), the refugee camp often ends up challenging the spatio-temporal logic created by crisis labelling. As camps become semi-permanent and permanent settlements over time – as is the case with many Palestinian UNRWA-run camps – and as they simultaneously remove migrant subjects from the perceived site of crisis, they become sites of crisis themselves. Camps, like borders, are sites of enactment for many of these routine forms of control such as identity checks (name, age, nationality) and the categorisation of migrants according to where they fit on a pre-determined set of criteria relating to their migrant status (economic migrant, asylum seeker, refugee, stateless person, unaccompanied minor, at general risk).[5]

Choucha during the immediate 'crisis' was a major destination for people fleeing Libya, holding at its peak between February and May 2011 approximately 135,000 people. The camp was established on 24 February 2011, and situated in the remote desert 6 km from the Libyan border between the border towns of Ras Ajdir and Ben Gardane. Choucha was run by the UNHCR, which provided food and medical care in line with international humanitarian obligations. The camp soon also became a holding site for people intercepted in the Mediterranean by Tunisian authorities, and for asylum applicants as their futures were negotiated between states and international organisations attempting to determine nationality and/or the validity of asylum claims within the liberal dichotomy of political and economic/involuntary and voluntary migrants. Technically free to leave the camp at any time, the remoteness of the location, combined with many residents' lack of documentation or anywhere else to go, meant that Choucha was effectively a

130   *J. Jeandesboz and P. Pallister-Wilkins*

prison (see Agier, 2011, for more on the camps as places of inadvertent control).

For all non-Libyan residents, however, Choucha was only one staging post within lives spent navigating moments and extended periods of crisis. The largest communities in Choucha hailed from Somalia, Darfur, Eritrea, Nigeria, Ghana, Chad and Bangladesh. In the compilation of migrant stories collected and published by IOM, the case of Osman, a Somali who had spent ten years previously in Libya, is indicative of the experiences of many. Osman had first left Somalia in the 1980s for Kenya where he had been granted refugee status by the UNHCR in the Dadaab refugee camp in north eastern Kenya, from where he worked his way to Libya through a series of odd-jobs and camp-trading. Osman told IOM that:

> Going back to Somalia is a non-starter. None of us would even entertain the thought. When the violence [in Libya] started, soldiers came into our house at midnight and took me and others to a detention centre. We were not told of our crime. They only repeated the word Somali ... Libyans don't like blacks like me. They treat us with contempt and often with hostility ... One night they threw four bodies of Nigerians into our cell ... We stayed with them for the whole night until when they came to remove them in the morning ... Just as they detained us with no explanation, they released us without one.
>
> (IOM, 2011)

Alongside the IOM's collection of migrant stories, narrative interviews with separate national and sub-national groups collected by activist project Boats4People in May 2011 clearly challenge the spatio-temporal limits generated by European crisis labelling and the frustrations that arise from more bureaucratic forms of control unable to deal with the specificities of migrant experiences. For example, Somalis in Choucha stressed that they 'have been experiencing civil war in their country for more than 23 years' and 'that most of them have lost their families and loved ones' in what they term the 'Somali crisis' (see also Lindley and Hammond, Chapter 3 in this volume). They did not see returning to Somalia as an option because of the war, and emphasised their precarious situation in Libya, and now in Tunisia, with even those like Osman who are recognised as refugees by UNHCR unable to access resettlement opportunities (Boats4People, 2011). As the IOM suggests, 'unlike migrant workers from Asia or sub-Saharan Africa who can return home safely, the Somalis and other vulnerable groups will continue to need special protection and a new home' (IOM, 2011). With the closure of the camp by the UNHCR in July 2013, those who could not be resettled in their home countries, some 250 remaining residents, were offered temporary residence by the new Tunisian government. In the two years since 2011, more than 3,170 were resettled in third countries, such as the United States, Norway, Germany, Canada and Australia (UNHCR, 2013).

The testimonies of migrants in Choucha also demonstrate loss of agency and their struggle with bureaucratic forms of control in the camp:

> The situation is [one] of turmoil and horrible, hence we cannot return back to Libya due to the political instability, neither back to our country, nor remain here. Our fate we cannot determine. We are making a general appeal for legal solicitors to advocate our cases and for the attention of the civil society ...
>
> (Boats4People, 2011)

The routines of control designed to determine the status of the residents of Choucha in relation to nationality, immigration and refugee frameworks, and thus their futures, rely on accurate information in order to categorise people precisely and determine people's 'correct' status. Typically, this relies on documentation such as a passport or national population records that can be cross-checked to determine identity (see Torpey, 2000) along with information on past events that can be 'verified' if the migrant is applying for asylum. Such a system was extremely difficult to comply with for many of the residents of Choucha, who were secondary migrants from Libya, lacked documentation, had initially been voluntary migrants or had left violent conflicts many years before. Furthermore, residents complained about the ways in which their personal data and testimonies were collected, citing errors in translation and poor interview conditions, where the interviewees did not feel safe and were often reliant on an interpreter involved somehow in the conflict situations that they had left behind. In addition, many of the migrants felt that the complexity of the system they were exposed to and categorised by was not adequately explained. Categorisation based on dichotomies between political/economic violence or based on nationalities pre-determined to be at risk worked here to obscure the multiple forms of 'crisis' experienced by migrants across various spatio-temporal zones. In sum, the experiences of the migrants from Libya to Choucha articulate very different crisis narratives to the one constructed by European professionals of politics around the Arab revolutions and migration in 2011 and are suggestive of complex identities that cannot be fully grasped by the categories designed to determine status and/or entry that currently exist to govern migration.

Conclusion

What is a crisis? What does it look like? And what does it do? Examining these questions in relation to migration and border control in the EU allows us to propose three conclusions. First, asking what a crisis is and looks like directs our attention towards the practice of crisis labelling. Although crisis labelling can involve multiple actors, it is first and foremost the precinct of the professionals of politics. Crisis is a powerful political symbol in contemporary European societies. In the context of the 2011 uprisings, second, crisis

132   J. Jeandesboz and P. Pallister-Wilkins

labelling has enabled the translation of the political crisis in North Africa into a migration crisis on the southern shores of the European Union. It has authorised the adoption of emergency and exceptional measures. While such initiatives are highly visible, however, they do not reflect the full scope of EU policies and practices related to migration and border control. Routine and banal activities associated with a managerial logic of enforcement continued to unfold alongside crisis labelling and emergency measures, and were not affected significantly. This suggests that crisis does not offer sufficient analytical leverage to account fully for the way in which migration control is carried out in the EU today. Highlighting the managerial outlook of border control and the normalising effects stemming from EU activities, however, does not imply that such practices are harmless. The third conclusion of the chapter, in this regard, is that both crisis labelling and bureaucratic/managerial everyday border control practices fail to take account of the diversity of migrant experiences. Crisis labelling works to spatio-temporally fix migrant experiences in particular moments understood by professionals of politics as 'crisis', while more banal managerial border control practices work to manage migrants according to pre-determined identity categories that additionally fail to take account of the diversity of their experiences.

Notes

1 Established in 2004, FRONTEX is the EU's agency responsible for coordinating operational cooperation (so-called joint operations) between the national border control services of EU Member States and Schengen Area countries. FRONTEX is often mistakenly presented as a European corps of border guards. The agency's staff, however, do not currently hold any enforcement competence. The two main tasks of FRONTEX are the planning and co-ordination of joint operations (on the ground and from the agency's headquarters in Warsaw), as well as the collection and analysis of information on persons, goods and vehicles crossing the EU's external borders via its own risk analysis unit and the risk analysis network of the national units it coordinates (FRAN). For further details, see Jeandesboz (2008) and Neal (2009).
2 The use of metaphors drawn from natural catastrophes may well be another recurrent pattern within crisis labelling (see Lindley, Chapter 1 in this volume).
3 A notion contiguous to that of 'migration management' (see Geiger and Pécoud, 2010).
4 Committee on Civil Liberties, Justice and Home Affairs.
5 Migrants may find themselves in more than one of these categories at a time or may move between categories.

References

Abdelfattah, D. (2011) 'Impact of Arab Revolts on Migration', *CARIM AS*, 68.
Agier, M. (2011) *Managing Undesirables: Refugee Camps and Humanitarian Government.* Cambridge: Polity Press.
Amnesty International (2011) *The Battle For Libya: Killings, Disappearances and Torture.* London: Amnesty International.

Crisis, enforcement and control at EU borders 133

Amoore, L. (2011) 'Data Derivatives: On the Emergence of a Security Risk Calculus for Our Times', *Theory, Culture & Society* 28(6): 24–43.

Andrijasevic, R. (2010) 'Deported: The Right to Asylum at EU's External Border of Italy and Libya', *International Migration* 48(1): 148–74.

ANSAmed (2011) 'Frattini Signs Agreement with New Libya', 17 June.

Aradau, C. (2004) 'Security and the Democratic Scene: Desecuritization and Emancipation', *Journal of International Relations and Development* 7(4): 388–413.

Bialasiewicz, L. (2012) 'Off-shoring and Out-sourcing the Borders of Europe: Libya and EU Border Work in the Mediterranean', *Geopolitics* 17(4): 843–66.

Bigo, D. (2002) 'Security and Immigration: Toward a Critique of the Governmentality of Unease', *Alternatives* 27: 63–92.

——(2008) 'Security: A Field Left Fallow', in M. Dillon and A. Neal (eds) *Foucault on Politics, Security and War*. Basingstoke: Palgrave Macmillan, pp. 93–114.

——(2011) 'Pierre Bourdieu and International Relations: Power of Practices, Practices of Power', *International Political Sociology* 5: 225–58.

Bigo, D. and Walker, R.B.J. (2007) 'Political Sociology and the Problem of the International', *Millennium: Journal of International Studies* 35(3): 725–39.

Boats4People (2011) *A Report from the Choucha Refugee Camp – Tunisia*, 11 May.

Boin, A. (2004) 'Lessons from Crisis Research', *International Studies Review* 6: 165–94.

Bourdieu, P. (2000) *Propos sur le champ politique*. Lyon: Presses universitaires de Lyon.

Buzan, B., Waever, O. and de Wilde, J. (1998) *Security: A New Framework for Analysis*. Boulder, CO: Lynne Rienner.

Cameron, D. (2011a) Speech, available at: http://news.bbc.co.uk/democracylive/hi/house_of_commons/newsid_9424000/9424225.stm.

——(2011b) Speech, available at: http://news.bbc.co.uk/democracylive/hi/house_of_commons/newsid_9428000/9428723.stm.

c.a.s.e. collective (2006) 'Critical Approaches to Security in Europe: A Networked Manifesto', *Security Dialogue* 37(4): 443–87.

Collyer, M. (2005) 'Secret Agents: Anarchists, Islamists and Responses to Politically Active Refugees in London', *Ethnic and Racial Studies* 28(2): 278–303.

——(2006) 'Migrants, Migration and the Security Paradigm: Constraints and Opportunities', *Mediterranean Politics* 11(2): 255–70.

De Genova, N. (2002) 'Migrant "Illegality" and Deportability in Everyday Life', *Annual Review of Anthropology* 31: 419–47.

de Haas, H. and Sigona, N. (2012) 'Migration and Revolution', *Forced Migration Review* 39. Available at: http://fmreview.nonuniv.ox.ac.uk/north-africa/dehaas-sigona.html.

Duffield, M. (2007) *Development Security and Unending War: Governing the World of Peoples*. Cambridge: Polity Press.

Edelman, M. (1977) *Political Language: Words That Succeed and Policies That Fail*. Chicago: University of Chicago Press.

——(1988) *Constructing the Political Spectacle*. Chicago: University of Chicago Press.

EEAS and European Commission (2011a) *A Partnership for Democracy and Shared Prosperity with the Southern Mediterranean*. COM(2011) 200, Brussels: EU.

——(2011b) *A New Response to a Changing Neighbourhood: A Review of the European Neighbourhood Policy*. COM(2011) 303, Brussels: EU.

EU Business (2009) 'EU Wants Turkey, Libya to Help Fight Illegal Immigration', *EU Business News*, 17 July.

134   J. Jeandesboz and P. Pallister-Wilkins

European Commission (2002) 'Towards Integrated Management of the External Borders of the Member States of the European Union', COM(2002) 233, Brussels.
——(2005) 'Visit to Ceuta and Melilla – Mission Report Technical Mission to Morocco on Illegal Immigration', MEMO/05/380, Brussels.
——(2006) 'Reinforcing the Management of the European Union's Southern Maritime Borders', COM(2006) 733, Brussels.
——(2008) 'Preparing the Next Steps in Border Management in the European Union', COM(2008) 69, Brussels.
——(2010) 'Proposal for a Regulation of the European Parliament and of the Council Amending Council Regulation (EC) No 2007/2004 Establishing a European Agency for the Management of Operational Cooperation at the External Borders of the Member States of the European Union (FRONTEX)', COM(2010) 61, Brussels.
——(2011a) 'Communication on Migration', COM(2011) 248, Brussels.
——(2011b) 'Proposal for a Regulation of the European Parliament and of the Council Establishing the European Border Surveillance System', COM(2011) 873, Brussels.
——(2011c) 'Impact Assessment Accompanying the Proposal for a Regulation of the European Parliament and of the Council Establishing the European Border Surveillance System (EUROSUR)', SEC(2011) 1536, Brussels.
European Council (2011) 'Provisional Agenda European Council Meeting 23–24 June', EUCO 17/11, Brussels.
European Parliament (2011) *Report on the Proposal for a Regulation of the European Parliament and of the Council Amending Council Regulation (EC) No 2007/2004 Establishing a European Agency for the Management of Operational Cooperation at the External Borders of the Member States of the European Union (FRONTEX)*. A7–0278/2011, Brussels.
Fargues, P. (2009) 'Irregularity as Normality among Immigrants South and East of the Mediterranean', *CARIM AS*, 2.
Financial Times (2011) 'France Regrets Misjudgment over Ben Ali', 18 January.
FRONTEX (2011a) *FRAN Quarterly Issue 1, January–March 2011*. Warsaw: FRONTEX.
——(2011b) *General Report 2011*. Warsaw: FRONTEX.
——(2012) *Annual Risk Analysis 2012*. Warsaw: FRONTEX.
Geiger, M. and Pécoud, A. (eds) (2010) *The Politics of International Migration Management*. Basingstoke: Palgrave Macmillan.
Habermas, J. (1988) *Legitimation Crisis*. Cambridge: Polity.
Hollis, R. (2012) 'No Friend of Democratization: Europe's Role in the Genesis of the "Arab Spring"', *International Affairs* 88(1): 81–94.
Holton, R.J. (1987) 'The Idea of Crisis in Modern Society', *The British Journal of Sociology* 38: 502–20.
House of Lords (2008) *FRONTEX: The EU External Borders Agency, Report with Evidence*. London: The Stationery Office.
Human Rights Watch (2009) *Pushed Back, Pushed Around: Italy's Forced Return of Boat Migrants and Asylum Seekers, Libya's Mistreatment of Migrants and Asylum Seekers*. Washington, DC: Human Rights Watch.
Huysmans, J. (2004) 'Minding Exceptions: Politics of Insecurity and Liberal Democracy', *Contemporary Political Theory* 3(3): 321–41.
——(2006) *The Politics of Insecurity: Fear, Migration and Asylum in the EU*. London: Routledge.

IOM (2011) *Enter the Somalis*, 9 March. Available at: http://www.iom.int/cms/en/sites/
iom/home/news-and-views/feature-stories/feature-story-listing/enter-the-somalis.html.

Jeandesboz, J. (2008) *Reinforcing the Surveillance of EU Borders: The Future Development
of FRONTEX and EUROSUR*. Brussels: CEPS.

——(2011) 'Beyond the Tartar Steppe: EUROSUR and the Ethics of European Border
Control Practices', in J. P. Burgess and S. Gutwirth (eds) *A Threat Against Europe?
Security, Migration and Integration*. Brussels: Brussels University Press, pp. 77–89.

——(2013) 'Sécurité, technologie et contrôle des frontières européennes: éléments pour
un regard sociologique', in D. Duez, O. Paye and C. Verdure (eds) *L'européanisation,
à la croisée des sciences et de nouveaux enjeux*. Brussels: Bruylant.

Joana, J. and Smith, A. (2002) *Les commissaires européens: technocrates, diplômats ou
politiques?* Paris: Presses de Sciences Po.

Malmström, C. (2012) 'Responding to the Arab Spring and Rising Populism: The
Challenges of Building a European Migration and Asylum Policy', SPEECH/12/
312, Brussels.

Mitchell, T. (2010) 'The Resources of Economics: Making the 1973 Oil Crisis', *Journal
of Cultural Economy* 3(2): 189–204.

Nascimbene, B. and Di Pascale, A. (2011) 'The "Arab Spring" and the Extraordinary
Influx of People Who Arrived in Italy from North Africa', *European Journal of
Migration and Law* 13(4): 341–60.

Neal, A. (2009) 'Securitization and Risk at the EU Border: The Origins of FRONTEX',
Journal of Common Market Studies 47(2): 333–56.

OJEU (2011) *Regulation (EU) No 1168/2011 of the European Parliament and of the
Council Amending Council Regulation (EC) No 2007/2004 Establishing a European
Agency for the Management of Operational Cooperation at the External Borders of
the Member States of the European Union (FRONTEX)*. L 304/1, Brussels.

Pace, M. (2009) 'Paradoxes and Contradictions in EU Democracy Promotion in the
Mediterranean: The Limits of EU Normative Power', *Democratization* 16(1): 39–58.

Pace, M. and Cavatorta, F. (2012) 'The Arab Uprisings in Theoretical Perspective: An
Introduction', *Mediterranean Politics* 17(2): 125–38.

Paoletti, E. (2010) *The Migration of Power and North–South Inequalities: The Case of
Libya and Italy*. Basingstoke: Palgrave Macmillan.

Teti, A. (2012) 'The EU's First Response to the "Arab Spring": A Critical Discourse
Analysis of the Partnership for Democracy and Shared Prosperity', *Mediterranean
Politics* 17(3): 266–84.

Torpey, J. (2000) *The Invention of the Passport: Surveillance, Citizenship and the State*.
Cambridge: Cambridge University Press.

UNHCR (2013) 'UNHCR Closes Camp in South Tunisia, Moves Services to Urban
Areas', 2 July. Available at: http://www.unhcr.org/51d2a40e9.html.

van Houtum, H. (2010) 'Human Blacklisting: The Global Apartheid of the EU's
External Border Regime', *Environment and Planning D: Society and Space* 28(6):
957–76.

Weber, M. (2008) *Complete Writings on Academic and Political Vocations*.
New York: Algora.

7 The social construction of (non-)crises and its effects

Government discourse on xenophobia, immigration and social cohesion in South Africa

Iriann Freemantle with Jean Pierre Misago

In May 2008, South Africa made global headlines with images reminiscent of the country's intense civil unrest of the 1980s and early 1990s: of townships in flames and youngsters swinging knobkerries and pangas;[1] of people being burnt alive; and of soldiers patrolling informal settlements in heavily armoured vehicles. These images were gory snapshots of a wave of large-scale violence against foreigners and other 'outsiders' that had erupted in the Johannesburg township of Alexandra, and from there rapidly spread across the country. In the eyes of many academic and civil society observers, the situation constituted an acute crisis in need of decisive immediate action as well as more sustainable policy change for the future: South Africa's rampant and long-standing xenophobia had apparently passed a critical threshold that now made it dangerous on a hitherto unprecedented scale, threatened thousands of lives and livelihoods, revealed the cracks in the legitimacy and sovereignty of the South African state, and tainted the country's international reputation (Hassim *et al.*, 2008; Hawabibi, 2009; Nyar, 2010; Landau, 2010). However, the South African government was not only remarkably slow in acknowledging the severity of the situation and taking action to stop the violence, but also went to great lengths in emphasising that these attacks were *not* xenophobic or political, but simply 'criminal' in nature. The vast majority of government officials also characterised the events as 'one-off' and unexpected: an unfortunate fluke that was unlikely to recur, and, rebutting the voices of civil society and human rights organisations, explicitly downplayed what had happened as being a 'non-crisis'.

With well-documented, high levels of xenophobia across all levels of South African society and over 60 dead, hundreds injured and up to 200,000 displaced by the May 2008 attacks, the government's somewhat puzzling denial and inaction warrant some unravelling, and this is what this chapter attempts to do. We suggest that just as crises need contextualisation in order to make sense of them (Roux-Dufort, 2007), so do situations in which political actors counter-construct apparently 'unambiguous' empirical facts of disaster or emergency as 'non-crises' (see also Rubio Díaz-Leal and Albuja, Chapter 4 in

Xenophobia, immigration, social cohesion 137

this volume). More specifically, we adopt a social constructionist perspective and argue that what is *not* considered a crisis can only really be understood in the context of what *is* constructed as a crisis in any given context, and that these constructions collectively produce particular 'versions' of truth which in turn enable and legitimise certain practices while inhibiting or pathologising others (see Wooffitt, 1993; Potter and Wetherell, 1987; Harris, 2008). Applied to our South African example, we thus suggest that the narrative of the 'non-crisis' of xenophobia and the 2008 events is intimately related to two other constructions of 'threatening crises' forcefully prevailing in contemporary South Africa: the *immigration crisis*, on the one hand, and the *social cohesion crisis*, on the other. Collectively, these constructions 'work' to gloss over rifts within the South African population that are unrelated to inherited racial inequalities as well position foreign nationals as outside of, and even menacing to, the well-being and stability of the South African nation. While likely intended to maintain an image of the South African state as capable, sovereign and successful, the government's constructions of these (non-)crises of xenophobia, social cohesion and immigration thus simultaneously enable – and in the case of unofficially 'state-sanctioned' xenophobia even help create – a climate conducive to ongoing violence.

After a brief methodological note, this chapter proceeds to document and support this line of argumentation in four parts. Drawing on past and ongoing research conducted by the African Centre for Migration & Society, the substantial literature on xenophobia and immigration in South Africa, as well as analyses of newspaper articles, policy documents and official governmental press statements between 2008 and 2013, we begin with a description of the 2008 events, the generalised xenophobia in South Africa as well as an analysis of the effects resulting from (the lack of) governmental response to it. The second section discusses the official construction of the 'immigration crisis'. This 'crisis' is constructed through a discourse of the migrant as a threat, accompanied by a range of exclusionary practices (restrictive immigration legislation, the targeting of foreigners by the police, an impressive deportation record and poor implementation of the rights of non-citizens in the country). Both discourse and practices work to retain the figure of the foreigner as a major or even principal threat to South African jobs, public health, prosperity and security. The third part of the chapter focuses on narratives of the 'cohesion crisis', a recently reinvigorated debate focused primarily on the need to 'unite' a country riddled by inherited racial inequality and division while obscuring the fluid and multi-faceted nature and causes of inter-group (including xenophobic) tensions across the country. In the concluding section, this chapter looks at the effects of these various (non-)crises, and suggests that in their efforts to promote and uphold the legitimacy, sovereignty and relative success of the South African post-Apartheid project, they simultaneously sustain – and in the case of xenophobia to a certain degree even necessitate – a climate of perpetual anti-outsider violence in the country.

138   *Iriann Freemantle with Jean Pierre Misago*

Methodological note

When it comes to the recognition of a situation as a crisis, 'brute facts matter ... but require an interpretive framework for actors to make sense of them' (Broome *et al.*, 2012: 11; see also Boin, 2004). Informed by the ontological principles of social constructionism and loosely building on Roux-Dufort's notion of crisis as *process*, this chapter considers crisis as a contextually embedded, contested, politicised and 'produced' narrative rather than an event with a fixed, singular meaning (Rosenthal, 2003; Roux-Dufort, 2007; Fierke, 2007; Broome *et al.*, 2012). The way crisis is 'talked about' and discursively constructed is central to our analysis, since social constructionists consider language to be productive of social reality rather than as a separate, objective tool to describe it: we take as our point of departure that whatever people talk about, they selectively choose one 'version' of representing reality over a number of alternatives, and through this enable and legitimise certain practices while inhibiting or even pathologising others (Berger and Luckmann, 1967; Potter and Wetherell, 1987; Wooffitt, 1993; Harris, 2008). As outlined in the introductory chapter of this book, conceptualising crisis in this way challenges many of our common assumptions about their nature as inevitable turning points or ruptures from normality, or as exceptional events (see also Rosenthal *et al.*, 1989; Roux-Dufort, 2007). Instead, we suggest that emergence of particular situations as 'social problems' or crises as well as the promotion of certain causes, solutions and interventions is constructed by dominant actors to serve certain goals rather than as objectively 'given' (Stone, 1989; Bacchi, 1999; Broome *et al.*, 2012).

The 2008 events, xenophobia and the government response

From the Johannesburg township of Alexandra, violent attacks against foreign nationals and South Africans considered 'outsiders' spread rapidly to other locations around the country in the beginning of May 2008 (Hadland, 2008). In less than a month, 135 separate incidents had been reported (Bekker *et al.*, 2008); 62 people died; at least 670 were wounded; dozens were raped; more than 100,000 became displaced; and millions of Rand worth of property was looted, destroyed or appropriated by local residents (CoRMSA, 2008a). Graphic images of knife- and stick-wielding aggressors, wounded victims, destroyed dwellings and even of a Mozambican man burnt alive made headlines around the world (*New York Times*, 2008; *Die Welt*, 2008; *Le Figaro*, 2008). Although the majority of those attacked were foreign migrants, a third of those killed were South African citizens 'who had married foreigners, refused to participate in the violent orgy, or had the misfortune of belonging to groups that were evidently *not South African enough* to claim their patch of urban space' (Landau, 2011: 1, emphasis added), a fact indicative of the volatile and varied configurations of exclusion typical of anti-outsider violence in the country.

Xenophobia, immigration, social cohesion 139

Although explanations for the violence differed, academic and civil society observers alike considered these events an acute, serious crisis that brutally exposed the failures of South Africa's approach to nation-building, social cohesion and immigration. They also argued that this crisis required not only immediate and decisive action to stop ongoing attacks but long-term strategies to prevent future recurrences (see, for example, CPS, 2009). Reflecting the sentiments shared by many non-governmental observers at the time, a prominent South African migrant rights organisation declared that there was 'little doubt that this is in fact a national crisis requiring urgent attention at the most senior level of government' (CoRMSA, 2008b: 1).

Yet the South African government was slow in its acknowledgement of the problem and the necessity for it to act. On 14 May 2008, amidst a noticeable increase in the frequency of attacks on foreigners, the country's Minister of Safety and Security dismissed what was going on as 'only a problem', and declared that 'if it were a crisis, it would be happening right across the country' (Nqakula, cited in CoRMSA, 2008b). Warnings about the severity and indeed critical nature of the situation went unheeded. Within days of the Minister's statement, attacks and violence, however, did spread to the rest of the country. Once the attacks were underway, civil society organisations and opposition parties repeatedly called on the government to declare a state of emergency (*Mail and Guardian*, 2008a) but were continuously rebutted. The Premier of Gauteng, the country's most densely populated and richest province and home to Alexandra township where the violence had first erupted, declared that a 'state of emergency implies ... that the life of the nation is threatened by war, invasion or general insurrection, disorder, natural disorder or other public emergency' and that he did not consider ongoing events to fulfil this definition. He added that 'the decision to deploy the army should not be a political one' and that 'it is important that such a declaration not be made lightly and in haste' (Shilowa, quoted in Sowetan, 2008a). When the police force eventually signalled its inability to cope with the violence and several appeals to restore public peace went unheeded, the South African President finally approved the deployment of the National Defence Force on 21 May, after nearly two weeks of murder and looting (The Presidency of the Republic of South Africa, 2008a; *Mail and Guardian*, 2008b). However, when the army arrived, most of the damage to lives and livelihoods had been done, and perpetrators had 'silently slipped back into the townships' embrace' (Landau, 2011: 1). Displaced migrants remained in temporary camps for several months until all but one were dismantled at the end of 2008 (*Mail and Guardian*, 2008c). Soon after violence subsided, the government started encouraging (and, by closing down shelters, to a certain extent coercing) displaced migrants to 'reintegrate' into the communities they had originally fled from (IOL, 2008), despite evidence that conditions were not conducive to do so. Actual reintegration activities were far and few and largely ad hoc measures, limited in number and carried out almost exclusively by civil society organisations, not the government (see, for example, UNICEF, 2008).

140   *Iriann Freemantle with Jean Pierre Misago*

Although some government officials publicly condemned the attacks as they were ongoing (Monson *et al.*, 2009), President Thabo Mbeki waited to deliver an official national address until 25 May (somewhat ironically, national 'Africa Day'). A national day of mourning was planned for 24 June but then postponed and eventually replaced by a 'national tribute' held by the President and various church organisations 'in remembrance of the victims of attacks on foreign nationals' on 3 July (Mbeki, 2008; Monson *et al.*, 2009). The president's speech to commemorate the victims is emblematic of the government's discourse surrounding the 2008 attacks, in particular in the emerging construction of the violence as criminal in nature, and *not* xenophobic. He referred to the events as 'criminal onslaught', 'murderous criminal activities' and 'violent attacks for criminal purposes and personal gain' and emphasised repeatedly that the violence was not motivated by prejudice. According to Mbeki, South Africans and foreign nationals had 'lived peacefully as fellow-Africans, until the dark days of May that descended upon them without warning'. He asserted that 'the masses who have consistently responded positively to the Pan-African messages of the oldest liberation movement on our continent, the African National Congress, are not xenophobic' (Mbeki, 2008). Mbeki further promised to 'isolate and defeat the evil elements in our midst who target vulnerable African migrants'.

Following Mbeki's example, construing the 2008 attacks as the work of a small group of criminals, rather than as committed or at least condoned by a significant part of the South African population, has by now become the singular and dominant official narrative of past and ongoing violence (for a detailed account of the 'just crime' discourse, see Polzer and Takabvirwa, 2010). A South African Communist Party[2] statement on a series of attacks on foreigners in the Western Cape in 2010, for example, reads that 'these are no xenophobic attack … but acts of criminality to loot and destabilise our communities to provide cover for these criminals' (*Mail and Guardian*, 2010). Also in 2010, the Minister of the Police warned against xenophobia 'hysteria' and urged 'the people and the media not to be part of peddling this hysteria of a possible outbreak', emphasising that 'there is no such systematic thing as xenophobia in the country' (*News 24*, 2010). After new attacks on foreigners in several informal settlements around Johannesburg in mid-2013, a police spokesperson declared that 'when we see children looting shops and people robbing people of their goods it is to us a blatant sign of crime that is being *excused* as xenophobia' (Mnisi, quoted in *Mail and Guardian*, 2013, emphasis added).

At all levels, the government also ignored the fact that violence against foreign nationals and other outsiders has been documented since and even before South Africa's transition to democracy (Crush, 2000; Nyar, 2010; Nieftagodien, 2011) and treated the attacks as one-off incidents that were adequately dealt with then and there, and would never occur again. The government did not institute an official enquiry into the events to establish the nature and root causes of the violence or addressed the responsibilities and accountability of perpetrators, instigators and mandated institutions that failed to prevent or stop the attacks. Instead, it supported the findings of a parliamentary 'Rapid Task Team',

Xenophobia, immigration, social cohesion 141

which, in line with existing dominant constructions, emphasised criminal opportunism and socio-economic inequality as the causes of the violence (Monson *et al.*, 2009). Combined with the government's slow response and lack of political will to protect foreign nationals in the country, the emphasis on poverty as an explanation for attacks on foreigners effectively legitimised the violence as a justifiable, understandable reaction of those whose livelihoods are threatened. As such, the 2008 violence became amalgamated into the overall high levels of impoverishment, criminality and violence in South Africa, a small part of a larger structural problem and as such not warranting a specific response beyond already existing, more general government policies (Polzer and Takabvirwa, 2010). It was only in November 2009, upon insistent request from the country's leading migrant rights consortium that the South African Human Rights Commission initiated an investigation specifically into the events (CoRMSA, 2010b). The final report of the investigation was published over two years after the violence had taken place, but its findings and recommendations were not taken up by the government. Even after 2008, governmental xenophobia task teams and committees continue to operate largely on an ad-hoc basis or even exist merely on paper. There also remains a near complete lack of interdepartmental coordination and as well as little cooperation with civil society and research organisations on the issue of xenophobia. Despite on-going anti-outsider sentiments and repeated occurrences of attacks on foreign nationals, research conducted on municipal government shows that even at the local level there are no long-term, sustained initiatives to work towards social cohesion or to respond to and/or prevent future outbreaks (Landau *et al.*, 2011). However, it is not only hostility towards foreigners that remains unaddressed, but there is also a near complete official silence about 'anti-outsider violence' directed against South African citizens who, after all, constituted a third of those killed in 2008. In line with the treatment of the events as a one-off occurrence, there have been no official days of remembrance for the 2008 attacks, since, as Presidential spokesperson Masebe explained in 2009, the government's opinion is that 'there is no such anniversary – we have moved forward' (Black Sash, 2009).

Most independent analysts and observers have described the government's official response to the May 2008 violence as severely wanting, characterised by a number of failures: the failure to prevent violence, the failure to protect victims during the attacks both from victimisation and from deportation, the failure to prioritise prosecution of the offenders throughout the judicial process, and a reluctant approach to humanitarian assistance and lack of assistance with reintegration. A 2011 report by the African Peer Review Mechanism Monitoring Project thus gave South Africa a 'red rating'[3] for its failure to address, and indeed denial of, xenophobia (SAIIA (South African Institute of International Affairs), CPS (Centre for Policy Studies) and AGMAP (Africa Governance Monitoring and Advocacy Project), 2011; see also Nyar, 2010). The shortcomings of the government in 2008 have, many argue, deliberately or otherwise supported the intentions of perpetrators, further criminalised the victims,[4] and promoted future security risks for non-nationals, other outsiders

142 *Iriann Freemantle with Jean Pierre Misago*

and by extension the South African communities in which they live (Monson and Misago, 2009). A newspaper editorial in August 2008 provocatively asked: 'We might well ask how the government's haughty attitude differs from the actions of the communities that forced these refugees out' (Sowetan, 2008b).

In summary, the South African government has consistently downplayed the severity of the acute displacement and violence, 'normalised' or even to a certain extent justified the attacks by characterising them as either purely criminal and/or caused by poverty, and has denied the structural existence of xenophobia in South African society. Through this, the 2008 events were officially rendered a 'one off event' that erupted without warning, a 'non-crisis' with no need for further attention or intervention in the future. Although not officially condoning it, state institutions have thus 'provided an environment wherein such xenophobic violence has effectively been legitimised by the state' (Neocosmos, 2008). Without overstating the power of the state in the lives of ordinary South African citizens – who are, after all, 'the *real* agents that promote or restrict access to the cities' (Landau, quoted in Hadland, 2008: 33, emphasis added) – this does mean that there is considerable mutuality between official discourses on immigration with those of the general public, providing an ideal climate for future violence and impunity for perpetrators. Such a reading enabled the continued lack of policies and interventions aimed at integrating foreign (and other) migrants in the aftermath of May 2008. Since the government does not acknowledge any particular vulnerability of foreign migrants and other outsiders, the denialist approach has also prevented migrant rights organisations from carving out a legitimate political space and opportunity for a sustained mobilisation for the rights of non-citizens in the country (Polzer and Segatti, 2011). As such, the 2008 events, while empirically rather unambiguously a crisis, did not constitute a 'turning point' for the vulnerable groups affected. If anything, official practices and policies of exclusion (including increasingly restrictive legislative frameworks) have intensified in the years following 2008. Meanwhile, xenophobia and violence against foreign nationals and other outsiders continue (HSRC, 2008, 2011; Misago *et al.*, 2009; BBC, 2010; CoRMSA, 2010a; Nieftagodien, 2011; SABC, 2011; Segatti, 2011a, 2011b; Sowetan, 2012; *Mail and Guardian*, 2012; *The Star*, 2012).

Having described the events of 2008 and official responses to it, the chapter now turns to an analysis of two crises central to official discussions of the well-being and 'condition' of the South African social fabric: the immigration crisis and the social cohesion crisis. Both of these narratives of crises, we suggest, help explain South Africa's unwillingness to intervene in xenophobic violence and protect foreign nationals and other outsiders from discrimination and attacks.

The immigration crisis

Although South Africa has always been a major hub within a historically entrenched system of regional labour mobility, migration has diversified and increased since the country's transition to democracy and reintegration into

Xenophobia, immigration, social cohesion 143

the global economy in 1994. While domestic mobility remains numerically much more significant (Polzer, 2010), South Africa has become a magnet for (predominantly African) migrants seeking a better socio-economic future but also protection from civil wars and/or political persecution. However, while there is no doubt that the scale of both documented and undocumented migration in South Africa has increased since 1994, particularly following the political and economic crisis in neighbouring Zimbabwe, there is no evidence to support popular perceptions of an 'invasion' (Crush, 2008a: 8). Yet inflated estimates abound and concepts of migration as an overwhelming burden dominate both public opinion and the views of government officials and policy-makers (ibid.), despite the fact that realistic estimates for 2012, for example, state that less than 4 per cent of the population was foreign (UNDESA, 2010). Metaphors of a human 'tsunami', or the 'flooding' of the country by millions of undocumented migrants or 'illegal aliens' (as they are still commonly referred to in the country), are central to the discourse of the 'immigration crisis'. There is a general popular impression that South Africa is allowing too many immigrants into the country – either through a lack of border control, or through policies that are too generous. De Freitas, currently Shadow Minister of Home Affairs in the Democratic Alliance (one of the opposition parties in South Africa), for example, stated:

> You've got to be a sieve. You can't accept every Tom, Dick and Harry – which frankly, is what South Africa has been doing. You need to put in certain measures to say, we need to sift you out. South Africa has been accepting everybody and that's part of the problem.
>
> (*The South African*, 2012)

Apart from opposition to immigration, a more generalised xenophobia is also pervasive in South Africa. A 2006 survey found that 'South Africa exhibits levels of intolerance and hostility to outsiders unlike virtually anything seen in other parts of the world', with 76 per cent in favour of electrified border fences and almost 50 per cent in support of deporting *all* foreign nationals (Crush, 2008a: 1–2). Migrants are assumed to 'steal' jobs, opportunities and resources, pose a threat to the country's security, are generally prone to criminality and constitute a major obstacle to social and economic transformation.

Accordingly, and with striking continuity with previous (colonial and Apartheid) regimes, the government treats human mobility with great suspicion and largely considers it a threat to the citizenry's economic and physical well-being (Misago *et al.*, 2009) despite the occasional nod to the migration-development nexus. Former Director-General of Home Affairs, Billy Masetlha (2002), for example, commented on migrants' (alleged) involvement in criminal activities in the following way:

> Approximately 90 per cent of foreign persons who are in RSA with fraudulent documents, i.e., either citizenship or migration documents, are involved in

144 *Iriann Freemantle with Jean Pierre Misago*

other crimes as well ... it is quicker to charge these criminals for their false documentation and then to deport them than to pursue the long route in respect of the other crimes that are committed.

The premise that 'free movement of people spells disaster for our country', made by former Home Affairs Minister Mangosuthu Buthelezi in 1997 (Buthelezi, 1997) remains to inform all policy and legislation related to asylum and immigration. In fact, for over a decade into the 'new South Africa', the government retained what has become known as 'Apartheid's last Act', the 'Alien Controls Act' of 1991. But even when the new immigration law finally came into power in 2002 which brought some (if poorly implemented) changes with regards to avenues for highly skilled foreign labour and foreign investment, the new government essentially maintained the previous 'policing vision' of Apartheid migration policies (Black *et al.*, 2006; Wa Kabwe Segatti, 2008). It also sanctioned measures and practices, such as arrest, detention and deportation, which were a direct continuation of those deployed by the apartheid regime to control and exclude 'illegal aliens' (Crush, 2008b).[5] As Hammerstad (2012: 2) notes, the belief that blames (African) migrants for most of South Africa's ills is widespread and

[is] often affirmed by the actions of the police, treating immigrants as criminals by swooping on their settlements in paramilitary style raids, using crude versions of racial profiling (determining who 'looks like a migrant') for stop and search on the streets, arresting those not carrying papers.

Influenced by its own discourse of the 'immigration crisis' and responding to growing public concerns over the government's alleged failure to protect the country's borders, in 2010, the South African government amended the Act of 2002 to an even more narrowly protectionist and restrictive approach in terms of labour market access and asylum. According to the former Minister of Home Affairs Dlamini-Zuma, these most recent legislative changes were designed to 'stop the spread of organised crime, trafficking in persons and corruption' as well as to accelerate employment creation for South Africans (Dlamini-Zuma, 2011), creating the impression that migration is a major source of both crime and unemployment and perpetuating stereotypes of migrants as a threat to South African jobs, prosperity, and security. In 2011, the government began to shut down refugee reception offices – situated in the country's major urban centres – with plans to move all of them to the borders, presumably in a bid to stem the 'flood' of asylum seekers right at the point of entry rather than allowing people already 'into' the country before assessing their claims (Amit, 2012; CoRMSA, 2012).[6] In a further attempt to control and contain asylum seekers and refugees, there is also an on-going discussion about discontinuing the country's long standing 'non-encampment' policy for

Xenophobia, immigration, social cohesion   145

recognised refugees which allowed refugees to settle wherever they liked in the country (LHR, 2012).

The ruling party's policy discussion documents, published in 2012, discuss further restrictions not only on immigration itself but on what foreigners are allowed to do once they are already in the country. For example, the 2012 ANC discussion document on 'Peace and Stability' characterises migration as a burden and threat and alleges the illegality of foreign-run businesses in many townships. While at the moment asylum seekers and refugees have the right to work in South Africa, the document also suggests restrictions on the ability of foreigners to run shops and other businesses. The document also questions the legitimacy of the asylum claims the country receives, suggests the 'monitoring' of asylum seekers once they are in the country, and generally advocates for more restrictive immigration management to 'minimize the risk to national security and stability' (ANC, 2012a). The ANC's official report on its 2012 policy conference in Mangaung echoes these fears, raising as cause for 'concern' 'the relatively high number of cases of crime involving foreign nationals', 'the number of undocumented foreign nationals who have jobs in certain sectors in the face of high unemployment' and 'the negative impact on small businesses by competition from nationals from Asian countries in the main'. The unemployment rate among South Africans is once again juxtaposed with the influx of foreigners and demands that 'the ANC must boldly deal with questions of competition for limited resources and opportunities in a country where the main challenges are high unemployment, poverty and growing inequality' (ANC, 2012b: 30). Beyond its own national domestic realm, South Africa has also consistently stalled the development of a regional policy framework of free movement of people, an initiative of the Southern African Development Community (SADC) to promote regional stability and economic growth (Crush and Oucho, 2001).

In summary, official discourses on the immigration crisis construct foreigners as a threat and burden, whose presence in South Africa is undesirable, illegitimate and needs to be curbed. Given their considerable overlap with popular discourses, this feeds into, strengthens and legitimises popular practices of xenophobic violence and exclusion and helps explain the government's lack of action to address anti-foreign sentiment. The next section of this chapter will detail the social cohesion crisis, which we will argue further positions foreign nationals as 'outside' of the state's responsibility and concern for the South African national community.

The social cohesion crisis[7]

According to many key national strategic documents published during the late 2000s and early 2010s, the South African 'social fabric' is in a state of fundamental crisis because it remains deeply 'divided'. The country's major social pathologies – exorbitant crime, poverty, domestic violence, inequality, unemployment, the presence of a disempowered and often violently protesting

146　*Iriann Freemantle with Jean Pierre Misago*

citizenry – are all linked directly to a lack of national unity, a set of national values all citizens abide by and social cohesion among them. South Africa's recently established National Planning Commission, responsible for the broader strategic vision of the country, strongly emphasises the importance of social cohesion: 'Without a high degree of social cohesion, without unity of purpose, it is difficult to envisage South Africa overcoming the significant obstacles that stand in the way of prosperity and equity' (NPC, 2011b: 1). With national unity viewed as a pre-condition for social transformation and economic progress, the South African government has recently reinvigorated the discussion on the issue. In 2011 and 2012, it launched two nation-wide campaigns (*South African@Heart* and *Formula SA*), published a new draft social cohesion strategy, and hosted the first national 'social cohesion summit'.

Notably, the national debate on the topic focuses almost singularly on the fault lines of race and class as the impediments to social cohesion in South Africa: building social cohesion first and foremost means bridging economic inequalities and instilling a shared sense of belonging and national identity among black and white South Africans (The Presidency of the Republic of South Africa, 2009; NPC, 2011a: 1, 26; 2011b: 4, 22; 2011c: 412). The concept of unity, for the most part used synonymously with 'social cohesion', is central to these discussions (The Presidency of the Republic of South Africa 2008b: 40; NPC, 2011a, 2011b: 16). To achieve it, the government promotes the notions of an empowered citizenship, patriotism, and 'South Africanness' as the common denominators able to bond all citizens, black and white (The Presidency of the Republic of South Africa, 2008b: 15, 2010, 2011; DAC, 2011a: 8–9, 12; DAC, paraphrased in PMG 2010). Congruent with the more long-standing objectives of nation building, South Africans are encouraged to consider themselves members of a national community of mutual sacrifice, trust, recognition, and collaboration for the greater good and long-term goals of the country. South Africans are thus to enter into, and honour, a symbolic social contract with one another, with a concern for the South African 'downtrodden' and poor in particular at its heart (NPC, 2011b: 4, 14, 15, 27, 28; Nchoba, 2011; DAC, 2011b, see also NPC, 2011a: 13, 27).

In this official vision of social cohesion, society is seen as legitimately and exclusively composed of all South African citizens: social cohesion is envisaged as something *for* South Africans which needs to be built *by* all of them. Citizenship is defined as the central relationship enabling cohesion. Notions of participation, responsibilities, rights, legitimacy, and accountability are exclusively associated with citizens in their relationships with government and with one another (The Presidency of the Republic of South Africa 2008b: 40; DAC and DPAS, 2010: 85–9). In addition to citizenship, social cohesion is associated with the absolute primacy of national identity. While the country's cultural and linguistic diversity is to be respected (DAC, 2011a), the general premise is that citizens are 'South Africans first, before race, language or

Xenophobia, immigration, social cohesion 147

ethnicity' (NPC, 2011a: 14). While respect for 'diversity' and 'non-racialism' occupy a prominent position within the overall set of values that are to inform nation-building, these values are – either explicitly or subtly – typically presented within a national, domestic frame of reference: diversity is understood as the cultural differences between South African citizens, and non-racialism as the refusal to discriminate between South Africans of different skin colours (DAC, 2010: 8, 14,17,19; DAC, 2011a: 12; DAC and DPAS 2010: 82, 84; Nchoba, 2011; NPC, 2011b: 14; 2011c: 428). Diversity within the country's population groups is almost exclusively considered non-conflictual (discussed only in terms of different cultural traditions, customs, and languages) without mention of the ways in which cultural, ethnic, political, or other forms of difference can be/are mobilised to create division and foster prejudice in the country.

Foreign migrants are not considered part of the social cohesion project, and regardless of the pervasiveness of xenophobia in South Africa, hostilty towards foreigners is rarely mentioned in official social cohesion strategies. This manifests in two different ways. The first is very direct: most South African social cohesion strategies do not discuss migration, integration, xenophobia, and xenophobic violence as relevant to social cohesion. The second is more indirect: social cohesion discussions draw the boundaries of societies around a domestic South African citizenry, which excludes foreign nationals from the social cohesion project. While the dominant national social cohesion strategy is about getting all South Africans to form and feel part of a 'united whole', foreign nationals/non-citizens are symbolically and materially positioned 'outside' of the South African (comm)unity of citizens. Making membership in South African society dependent on patriotic attachment, South African identity, nationality, and citizenship, the national strategy directly excludes foreign migrants who, for a variety of practical, social, and legal reasons, rarely hold citizenship or consider themselves to be South Africans. Positioning patriotism and identification with the nation and its symbols (such as proudly singing the anthem or displaying the flag) as central to social cohesion directly excludes all those residents of the country who are not South African. While promoting the notion of a shared 'new' history of the liberation struggle as a powerful source of solidarity among South Africans, the national strategy rarely mentions the support given by other African countries in the fight against apartheid. Foreign nationals are thus not considered to be part of this shared history and are excluded from the solidarity and sense of belonging that is to arise from it. While South Africans are encouraged to collaborate with one another across the various divides to accelerate development in the country, foreign migrants are neither considered part of, nor beneficiaries of, this 'social contract'. Although respect for diversity is considered to be a key feature of what it means to be South African, diversity is only to refer to the cultural and linguistic differences of South Africa's various ethnic groups. The diversity added by migrants is not mentioned anywhere, and respect for the cultural differences between South

148   *Iriann Freemantle with Jean Pierre Misago*

Africans and non-citizens is not discussed. While the national strategy frequently refers to the constitution to highlight the importance of the norms, values, rights, and responsibilities of South African citizens, it is overwhelmingly silent about the rights of non-citizens (irrespective of the fact that the South African Constitution grants basic socio-economic rights to everyone and enshrines the right to dignity irrespective of nationality or legal status). While the norms and values of citizenship are meant to provide South Africans with a moral compass on how to relate to fellow citizens, the national strategy does not speak about the responsibilities South Africans have towards non-citizens.

The social cohesion strategy is similarly silent about rifts *within* South African population groups – zooming in on racial divides, the discourse effectively prevents and shuts down even just the possibility of the existence of other salient sources of conflict that might hinder social cohesion. However, South Africa's fault lines are complex, multiple and centred around often vague notions of autochthony and territorial entitlement, and the criteria of who becomes subject to (violent) exclusion, intolerance, and discrimination are flexible within and across locations and over time. In fact, with anxieties about protecting access to resources against 'undeserving' outsiders high (Monson *et al.*, 2012: 5–6), South Africa's poor urban settlements are regularly the sites of territorial exclusion and tensions between groups that consider themselves established locals and those new arrivals or different 'Others', be they from within or beyond South Africa's borders. In some places, Somali shopkeepers or Zimbabwean farmworkers are excluded; elsewhere, Zimbabweans are left alone but Bangladeshis are attacked; in other places, Mozambicans are singled out or South Africans of the 'wrong' ethnicity, community of origin, domestic migrant status or political affiliation (Valji, 2003; Akileswaran, 2005; IRIN, 2008; Sharp, 2008; HSRC, 2008: 23–4; Misago, 2009: 7; Misago with Landau and Monson, 2009; Nieftagodien, 2011). Constructions of 'outsiders' and 'insiders' are thus fluid and complex, and do not overlap with homogeneously conceptualised groups of 'foreigners' versus 'citizens' (Monson and Arian, 2011: 53). Much of this autochthonous dynamic is rooted in the spatial practices of Apartheid policies, which enforced the idea that the rights of groups were linked to a certain territory only, with strict controls and limitations on movement between these territories. This legacy is clearly linked to contemporary hostilities towards those 'invading' from other places in the country or beyond South Africa's borders under conditions of widespread unemployment and poverty. Exploiting popular anxieties towards outsiders, both formal and informal local political entrepreneurs in these contexts often further promote prejudice between different groups, sow suspicion, or even trigger violence directly to consolidate their own power and support base (Monson *et al.*, 2012).

As Jackson eloquently describes, autochthonous discourses are characterised by 'a slipperiness between different scales of meaning [that] permits the speaker to leave open multiple interpretations. This indefiniteness is a paradoxical source of the discourse's strength and weakness, suppleness and nervousness, its declarative mood and attendant paranoia' (Jackson, 2006: 95). Similarly, Ceuppens and Geschiere (2005: 385) write that 'autochthony is subject to constant redefinition against new "others" and at ever-closer range'. However, this nervous uncertainty does not feature in dominant official narratives of what social cohesion means in the South African context. While of course the legacies of colonialism and Apartheid continue to unequally define and limit life chances, opportunities, and interactions for black and white South Africans, and racial inequality is important to tackle, the country's current exclusive focus on race and class means that a host of other divisions that manifest particularly in the country's many poor informal settlements remain unaddressed. As such, the construction of the cohesion crisis around the notion of racial division is not empirically unfounded, but highly selective nonetheless.

Conclusion

Mutually reinforcing one another, the various constructions of (non-)crises – of xenophobia, immigration and social cohesion – define the condition, state and boundaries of the South African nation in a way that positions foreign nationals as outside of and threatening to the South African community. This renders xenophobic violence not only 'invisible' and unworthy of the government's intervention but at the same time justified since it is taking place beyond the boundaries of the national community for whom the South African state is responsible. However, official discourses of these three (non-)crises not only legitimise xenophobic violence, but also deny the existence of antagonism *among* black South Africans, rather than just between an impoverished black and a privileged white citizenry. In combination, this renders the vulnerability of foreign nationals and other outsiders invisible, pathologises those 'without' and projects an (albeit unrealistic) image of consolidation and sameness 'within'.

Taken together, these constructions have a variety of effects. On the one hand, they work for the government to legitimise the post-Apartheid project by glossing over rifts within the South African population and de-politicise the claims inherent to this type of violence that target the legitimacy, representativeness, territorial control and sovereignty of the South African state. On the other hand, these official constructions also work to maintain the figure of the foreigner as a convenient scapegoat for the state's inability to deliver employment and welfare to all. As an effect on the country's population, these constructions, however, come at the cost of on-going instability, since anti-outsider violence in its nervous, autochthonous volatility puts virtually everyone at risk (Crush and Ramachandran, 2010). While likely intended to maintain an image of the South African state as capable, sovereign and successful, the government's constructions of the (non-)crises of xenophobia, social cohesion

150 *Iriann Freemantle with Jean Pierre Misago*

and immigration thus simultaneously enable – and, in the case of unofficially 'state-sanctioned' xenophobia, even help create – a climate so conducive to violence that the idea of a diverse yet reasonably inclusive and peaceful South Africa remains a distant aspiration.

Notes

1 A knobkerrie is short club with one knobbed end, a panga is a broad-bladed knife.
2 The SACP is part of the tripartite alliance with the ANC.
3 Red rating = 'no progress has been achieved on addressing the issue; or very little progress has been achieved and the government does not seem to be on track to complete it in the near future' (SAIIA, (South African Institute of International Affairs), CPS (Centre for Policy Studies) and AGMAP (Africa Governance Monitoring and Advocacy Project), 2011: 13).
4 On at least two occasions during the violence, immigration officials (sent by the Department of Home Affairs) raided shelters to arrest and deport undocumented victims including those who had just lost papers during the flight. These unlawful arrests and deportations criminalised 'undocumented' victims rather than their assailants (see details in Monson and Misago, 2009).
5 From 1994 to 2008, South Africa deported 1.7 million undocumented migrants to neighbouring states like Mozambique, Zimbabwe, and Lesotho. In 2006 alone, 260,000 migrants were arrested and deported (Crush, 2008b).
6 The government has, however, successfully been taken to court in some cases and was forced to re-open some offices (*Western Cape News*, 2012).
7 This section draws heavily on Freemantle (2012).

References

Akileswaran, C. (2005) 'Bridging Migration, HIV/AIDS, and Violence Among Women in Rustenburg, South Africa'. Available at: http://www.bafokeng.com/sites/default/files/reports/akileswaran.pdf (accessed May 2012).

Amit, R. (2012) *No Way in. Barriers to Access, Service and Administrative Justice at South Africa's Refugee Reception Offices.* ACMS Research Report, African Centre for Migration and Society. Johannesburg: University of the Witwatersrand.

ANC (2012a) 'Policy Discussion Document on Peace and Stability', March 2012. Available at: http://www.anc.org.za/docs/discus/2012/peacev.pdf (accessed December 2012).

——(2012b) 'Unity in Action. Towards Socio-Economic Freedom', Organisational Report by General Secretary Gwede Mantashe. Available at: www.anc.org.za/docs/reps/2012/organisational_reportk.pdf (accessed 4 January 2013).

Bacchi, C.L. (1999) *The Construction of Policy Problems.* London: Sage.

BBC (2010) 'South Africa: Foreigners Injured in Xenophobia Clashes'. Available at: www.bbc.co.uk/news/world-africa-10696292 (accessed 28 July 2010).

Bekker, S., Eigelaar-Meets, I., Gary, E. and Poole, C. (2008) 'Xenophobia and Violence in South Africa: A Desktop Study of the Trends and a Scan of Explanations Offered', unpublished report, University of Stellenbosch.

Berger, P.L. and Luckmann, T. (1967) *The Social Construction of Reality: A Treatise in the Sociology of Knowledge.* New York: Anchor Press.

Xenophobia, immigration, social cohesion 151

Black, R., Crush, J., Peberdy, S. with Ammassari, S., McLean Hilker, L., Mouillesseaux, S., Pooley, C. and Rajkotia, R. (2006) *Migration and Development in Africa: An Overview.* Queens University, Ontario: Southern African Migration Project.

Black Sash (2009) 'Khumbula Ekhaya' [Remember Your Home], 11 May 2009. Available at: www.blacksash.org.za/index.php?option=com_content&view=article&id=582 (accessed 13 January 2013).

Boin, A. (2004) 'Lessons from Crisis Research', *International Studies Review* 6, 165–94.

Broome, A., Clegg, L. and Rethal, L. (2012) 'Global Governance and the Politics of Crisis', *Global Society* 26: 3–17.

Buthelezi, M.G. (1997) 'Keynote Address at the Southern African Migration Project's Conference: After Amnesty, The Future of Foreign Migrants in South Africa', 20 June 1997. Available at: http://www.queensu.ca/samp/sampresources/migrationdocuments/speeches/mgb/200697.htm (accessed 2 May 2011).

Ceuppens, B. and Geschiere, P. (2005) 'Autochthony: Local or Global? New Modes in the Struggle over Citizenship and Belonging in Africa and Europe', *Annual Review of Anthropology* 34: 385–407.

CoRMSA (2008a) *Protecting Refugees, Asylum Seekers and Immigrants in South Africa.* Johannesburg: CoRMSA.

——(2008b) 'Press Release – Xenophobic Attacks "Not a Crisis"?', 15 May 2008. Available at: www.google.co.za/url?sa=t&rct=j&q=&esrc=s&source=web&cd=1&ved=0CDAQFjAA&url=http%3A%2F%2Fwww.cormsa.org.za%2Fwp-content%2Fuploads%2F2008%2F06%2Fcormsa-press-release-xenophobic-attacks-not-a-crisis.doc&ei=Sgo VUe7YKtPK0AWkhoDIBQ&usg=AFQjCNG-DNyTygsvIrS82JSmrND3uhbPqA&bvm=bv.42080656,d.d2k (accessed 12 January 2013).

——(2010a) 'Real Threats of Mass Xenophobic Violence after World Cup'. Available at: www.cormsa.org.za/wp-content/uploads/2009/05/press-statement-real-threats-of-mass-xenophobic-violence-after-world-cup.pdf (accessed 19 July 2010).

——(2010b) 'Human Rights Commission Investigation Report Now on CoRMSA Site'.Available at: http://www.cormsa.org.za/2010/05/17/human-rights-commission-investigation-report-now-on-cormsa-site/ (accessed 8 July 2011).

——(2012) 'The Implications of Moving Refugee Reception Offices to the Border Areas'. Available at: http://d2zmx6mlqh7g3a.cloudfront.net/cdn/farfuture/X3-T5Vr2DVfdwjPw0imvGSu3ryX4bTHpTMPICoBO7FE/mtime:1354261492/files/docs/121126cormsa.pdf (accessed 2 February 2012).

CPS (Center for Policy Studies)(2009) 'Policy Studies Bulletin "Synopsis"',10(3), August 2009. Available at: www.cps.org.za/cps%20pdf/Syn10_3_August2009.pdf (accessed 12 November 2013).

Crush, J. (2000) 'The Dark Side of Democracy: Migration, Xenophobia and Human Rights in South Africa', *International Migration* 38(6): 103–33.

——(2008a) 'South Africa: Policy in the Face of Xenophobia', Cape Town: Southern African Migration Project. Available at: www.migrationinformation.org/Feature/print.cfm?ID=689 (accessed 4 April 2009).

——(2008b) 'The Perfect Storm: The Realities of Xenophobia in Contemporary South Africa', *Migration Policy Series*, 50, Cape Town: SAMP.

Crush, J. and Oucho, J.O. (2001) 'Contra Free Movement: South Africa and the SADC Migration Protocols', *Africa Today* 48(3): 139–58.

Crush, J. and Ramachandran, S. (2010) 'Xenophobia, International Migration and Development', *Journal of Human Development and Capabilities* 2: 209–28.

152 Iriann Freemantle with Jean Pierre Misago

DAC (Department of Arts and Culture and Department of Public Administration and Service Delivery) (2010) 'Delivery Agreement for Outcome 12 (B) of the Medium Term Strategic Framework for 2009–2014'. Available at: www.dac.gov.za.

——(Department of Arts and Culture) (2011a) 'The Face of Social Cohesion. Interview with Dudu Nchoba.' Available at: www.dac.gov.za/newsletter/khariambe_3_6.html (accessed 2 July 2012).

——(2011b) 'Social Cohesion. Bringing Together a Diverse People'. Pretoria Inauguration of the Social Cohesion Campaign. Available at: http://www.dac.gov.za/newsletter/khariambe_3_5.html (accessed 2 August 2012).

Die Welt (2008) 'Nach Gewalt-Welle fürchtet Südafrika um WM', 21 May 2008. Available at: http://www.welt.de/politik/article2018079/Nach-Gewalt-Welle-fuerchtet-Suedafrika-um-WM.html (accessed 9 April 2009).

Dlamini-Zuma, N. (2011) 'Briefing by Minister Dlamini-Zuma regarding Immigration'.

Fierke, K.M. (2007) *Critical Approaches to International Security*. Cambridge: Polity Press.

Freemantle, I. (2012) 'Addressing the Division of Whom? South Africa's "Fault lines" and Trends in Social Cohesion Policy', ACMS policy brief, Johannesburg: African Centre for Migration and Society. Available at: http://www.migration.org.za/sites/default/files/social – cohesion_trends_policy_brief.pdf (accessed 8 February 2013).

Hadland, A. (ed.) (2008) *Violence and Xenophobia in South Africa: Developing Consensus, Moving to Action*. Pretoria: HSRC.

Hammerstad, A. (2012) 'Making the Best Out of Immigration into South Africa', SAIIA policy briefing 58, Johannesburg: SAIIA. Available at: www.saiia.org.za/policy-briefings/making-the-best-out-of-immigration.html (accessed January 2013).

Harris, S. (2008) 'Constructionism in Sociology', in J.A. Holstein and J.F. Gubrium (eds) *Handbook of Constructionist Research*. New York: Guilford Press, pp. 231–47.

Hassim, S., Kupe, T. and Worby, E. (eds) (2008) *Go Home or Die Here: Violence, Xenophobia and the Reinvention of Difference in South Africa*. Johannesburg: Wits University Press.

Hawabibi, L. (2009) 'Explaining Xenophobic Violence: Information Sheet', Pretoria: University of South Africa. Available at: http://www.saiia.org.za/images/stories/pubs/books/aprm_amp_report_sa_20110628.pdf.

HSRC (Human Sciences Research Council) (2008) 'Citizenship, Violence and Xenophobia in South Africa: Perceptions from South African Communities', Democracy and Governance Programme, Pretoria: HSRC.

——(2011) 'Xenophobia. Causes, Responses, Policies', *HSRC Review* 9(2), June 2011. Available at: www.hsrc.ac.za/HSRC_Review_Article-258.phtml (accessed October 2011).

IOL (2008) 'Xenophobia: 'Reintegration Conditions Good', July 25. Available at: www.iol.co.za/news/south-africa/xenophobia-reintegration-conditions-good-1.409844#.URa4LB2TxZo (accessed 2 February 2013).

IRIN (2008) 'South Africa: Burning the Welcome'. Available at: www.irinnews.org/report.aspx?ReportID=78302 (accessed 17 October 2011).

Jackson, S. (2006) 'Sons of Which Soil? The Language and Poltics of Autochthony in Eastern D.R. Congo', *African Studies Review* 49(2): 95–123.

Landau, L. (2010) 'Loving the Alien? Citizenship, Law, and the Future in South Africa's Demonic Society', *African Affairs* 109(435): 213–30.

——(2011) 'Introducing the Demons', in L. Landau (ed.) *Exorcising the Demons Within: Xenophobia, Violence and Statecraft in Contemporary South Africa*. Johannesburg: Wits University Press, pp. 1–25.

Xenophobia, immigration, social cohesion 153

Landau, L. and Segatti, A. with Misago, J.P. (2011) 'Governing Migration and Urbanisation in South African Municipalities. Developing Approaches to Counter Poverty and Social Fragmentation', Pretoria: South African Local Government Association.

Lawyers for Human Rights (2011) 'LHR Calls on the Police to Protect Foreign Nationals and Foreign Owned Businesses in the Pre-Election Intimidation and Attacks in Gauteng Province'. Available at: www.lhr.org.za/news/2011/lhr-calls-police-protect-foreign-nationals-and-foreign-owned-businesses-pre-elections-inti (accessed 1 July 2011).

Le Figaro (2008) 'Violences xénophobes: Prétoria présente ses excuses'. Available at: http://www.lefigaro.fr/actualites/2008/05/23/01001-20080523ARTFIG00611-violences-xenophobes-pretoria-presente-ses-excuses.php (accessed 18 July 2008).

Mail and Guardian (2008a) 'Parties Slam Government over Xenophobic Attacks'. Available at: http://mg.co.za/article/2008-05-19-parties-slam-govt-over-xenophobic-attacks (accessed 7 February 2013).

——(2008b) 'Xenophobia: Mbeki Gives Nod to Army'. Available at: http://mg.co.za/article/2008-05-21-xenophobia-mbeki-gives-nod-to-army (accessed 12 January 2013).

——(2008c) 'Gauteng Refugee Shelters to Close', 30 September 2008. Available at: http://mg.co.za/article/2008-09-30-gauteng-refugee-shelters-to-close (accessed 2 January 2012).

——(2010) 'SACP: It's Crime, Not Xenophobia', 13 July. Available at: http://mg.co.za/article/2010-07-13-sacp-its-crime-not-xenophobia (accessed 11 February 2013).

——(2012) 'Xenophobia Rears Its Head as "War" Declared in Mayfair', 3 September. Available at: http://mg.co.za/article/2012-09-03-xenophobia-rears-its-head-in-mayfair (accessed 5 September 2012).

——(2013) 'Diepsloot: Crime, Xenophobia – or Both?'. Available at: http://mg.co.za/article/2013-05-28-diepsloot-crime-xenophobia-or-both (accessed 1 June 2013).

Masetlha, B.L. (2002) 'Remarks at the Presentation of the Department of Home Affairs on the Migration System in South Africa to the Home Affairs Portfolio Committee' (15 April 2002). Available at: http://www.info.gov.za/speeches/2002/02042002146p1002.htm (accessed 10 May 2012).

Mbeki, T. (2008) 'National Tribute in Remembrance of Xenophobic Attacks Victims. Address of the President of South Africa, Thabo Mbeki at the National Tribute in Remembrance of the Victims of Attacks on Foreign Nationals', Tshwane, 3 July. Available at: www.polity.org.za/article/sa-mbeki-national-tribute-in-remembrance-of-xenophobicattacks-victims-03072008-2008-07-03 (accessed 3 March 2009).

Misago, J.P. (2009) 'Xenophobic Violence in South Africa: Reflections on Causal Factors and Implications', *Synopsis Policy Studies Bulletin CPS* 10, 3, August 2009. Available at: http://www.cps.org.za/cps%20pdf/Syn10_3_August2009.pdf (accessed 12 June 2012).

Misago, J.P. with Landau, L. and Monson, T. (2009) 'Towards Tolerance, Law, and Dignity: Addressing Violence against Foreign Nationals in South Africa', research conducted for IOM by the Forced Migration Studies Programme at the University of the Witwatersrand, Johannesburg: Forced Migration Studies Programme. Available at: http://www.observatori.org/paises/pais_77/documentos/violence_against_foreign_nationals.pdf (accessed 16 September 2010).

Monson, T. (2011) 'Making the Law; Breaking the Law; Taking the Law into Our Own Hands: Sovereignty and Territorial Control in Three South African

154   *Iriann Freemantle with Jean Pierre Misago*

Settlements', in L. Landau (ed) *Exorcising the Demons Within: Xenophobia, Violence and Statecraft in Contemporary South Africa.* Johannesburg: Wits University Press, pp. 151–71.

Monson, T. and Arian, P. (2011) 'Media Memory: A Critical Reconstruction of the May 2008 Violence', in L. Landau (ed.) *Exorcising the Demons Within: Xenophobia, Violence and Statecraft in Contemporary South Africa.* Johannesburg: Wits University Press, pp. 26–55.

Monson, T., Igglesden, V. and Polzer Ngwato, T. (2009) 'Humanitarian Assistance to Internally Displaced Persons in South Africa: Lessons Learned Following Attacks on Foreign Nationals in May 2008', FMSP Research Report, Johannesburg: Forced Migration Studies Programme.

Monson, T. and Misago, J.P. (2009) 'Why History Has Repeated Itself: The Security Risks of Structural Xenophobia', *SA Crime Quarterly* 29, September.

Monson, T., Takabvirwa, K., Anderson, J., Polzer Ngwato, T. and Freemantle, I. (2012) 'Lessons Learned. Promoting Social Cohesion and Countering Violence Against Foreigners and Other "Outsiders": A Study of Social Cohesion Interventions in Fourteen South African Townships', ACMS research report, Johannesburg: African Centre for Migration and Society.

NPC (National Planning Commission of South Africa) (2011a) 'Diagnostic Overview'. Available at: http://www.npconline.co.za.

——(2011b) 'Nation Building Diagnostic'. Available at: http://www.npconline.co.za/MediaLib/Downloads/Home/Tabs/Diagnostic/Nation%20Building%20diagnostic.pdf (accessed 17 July 2012).

——(2011c) 'Vision 2030'. Available at: 'http://www.npconline.co.za/.

Nchoba, D. (2011) 'The Face of Social Cohesion. Interview Dudu Nchoba'. Available at: http://www.dac.gov.za/newsletter/khariambe_3_6.html (accessed 30 July 2011).

Neocosmos, M. (2008) 'The Politics of Fear and the Fear of Politics. Thinking About Xenophobia in South Africa'. Available at: www.courrierdelaplanete.org/86/Neocosmos.pdf (accessed 11 February 2012).

New York Times (2008) 'South Africans Take Out Rage on Immigrants', 20 May. Available at: http://www.nytimes.com/2008/05/20/world/africa/20safrica.html?_r=0 (accessed 14 January 2012).

News 24 (2010) 'Xenophobia Hysteria Dismissed', 15 July. Available at: http://m.news24.com/news24/SouthAfrica/News/Xenophobia-hysteria-dismissed-20100715 (accessed 31 July 2011).

Nieftagodien, N. (2011) 'Xenophobia's Local Genesis: Historical Constructions of Insiders and the Politics of Exclusion in Alexandra Township', in L. Landau (ed.) *Exorcising the Demons Within: Xenophobia, Violence and Statecraft in Contemporary South Africa.* Johannesburg: Wits University Press, pp. 109–34.

Nyar, A. (2010) *What Happened? A Narrative of the May 2008 Xenophobic Violence.* Johannesburg: Gauteng City Region Observatory (GCRO).

PMG (2010) 'Summary of Briefing by the Department of Arts & Culture on Social Cohesion & National Building', 26 May. Available at: http://www.pmg.org.za/report/20100526-social-cohesion-and-nation-building-department-briefing (accessed 2 November 2011).

Polzer, T. (2010) 'Population Movement in and to South Africa', Migration Fact Sheet 1, Johannesburg: Forced Migration Studies Programme. Available at: www.cormsa.

Xenophobia, immigration, social cohesion 155

org.za/wp-content/uploads/2010/07/fmsp-fact-sheet-migration-in-sa-june-2010doc.pdf (accessed 9 January 2011).

Polzer, T. and Segatti, A. (2011) 'From the Defense of Migrants' Rights to New Political Subjectivities: Gauteng Migrants' Organisations After the May 2008 Crisis', in L Landau (ed.) *Exorcising the Demon Within: Xenophobia, Violence, and Statecraft in Contemporary South Africa.* Johannesburg: Wits University Press.

Polzer, T. and Takabvirwa, K. (2010) 'Just Crime? Violence, Xenophobia and Crime: Discourse and Practice', *SA Crime Quarterly* 33.

Potter, J. and Wetherell, M. (1987) *Discourse and Social Psychology. Beyond Attitudes and Behaviour.* London: Sage.

Rosenthal, U. (2003) 'September 11: Public Administration and the Study of Crises and Crisis Management', *Administration & Society* 35: 129–43.

Rosenthal, U., Charles, M.T. and T' Hart, P. (1989) 'The World of Crises and Crisis Management', in U. Rosenthal (ed.) *Coping with Crises: The Management of Disasters, Riots, and Terrorism.* Springfield, IL: Charles C. Thomas.

Roux-Dufort, C. (2007) 'Is Crisis Management (Only) a Management of Exceptions?' *Journal of Contingencies and Crisis Management* 15: 105–14.

SABC (2011) 'Gauteng Given 14 days to Respond to Ekurhuleni Shop Owners' Demands'. Available at: www.sabc.co.za/news/a/c7ba668048edc5179e789f0c644cb173/ Gauteng-given-14-days-to-respond-to-Ekurhuleni-shop-owners-demands–20111103 (accessed 4 November 2011).

SAIIA (South African Institute of International Affairs), CPS (Centre for Policy Studies) and AGMAP (Africa Governance Monitoring and Advocacy Project) (2011) 'Implementing the APRM: Views from Civil Society', Johannesburg: South African Institute of International Affairs. Available at: http://www.saiia. org.za/images/stories/pubs/books/aprm_amp_report_sa_20110628.pdf (accessed 8 July 2011).

Segatti, A. (2011a) 'Mobilisation Against Foreign Traders in South Africa', Migration Issue Brief No. 5, African Centre for Migration and Society, Johannesburg: African Centre for Migration and Society. Available at: www.migration.org.za/sites/default/ files/publications/2011/migration_issue_brief_5_mobilisation_against_foreign_traders. pdf (accessed 7 April 2012).

——(2011b) 'Migration to South Africa: Regional Challenges Versus National Instruments and Interests', in A. Segatti and L. Landau (eds) *Migration to South Africa: Regional Challenges versus National Instruments and Interests: A Regional Development Issue.* Washington, DC: Agence Française de Développement and World Bank.

Sharp, J. (2008) 'Fortress SA: Xenophobic Violence in South Africa', *Anthropology Today* 24(4): 1–3.

Simpson, M. (1994) 'The Experience of Nation-Building: Some Lessons for South Africa', *Journal of Southern African Studies* 20(3): 463–74.

South Africa (2012) 'Cape Town: Southern African Migration Project'. Available at: http://www.genocidewatch.org/images/South_Africa_09_03_30_the_perfect_storm. pdf (accessed 9 August 2012).

Sowetan (2008a) 'Gauteng Premier Mbhazima Shilowa Yesterday Cautioned Politicians Against Imposing Their Opinions on How Police Should Deal with Xenophobic Attacks', 21 May. Available at: www.sowetanlive.co.za/ sowetan/archive/2008/05/21/shilowa-says-no-to-state-of-emergency (accessed 11 January 2013).

156　*Iriann Freemantle with Jean Pierre Misago*

——(2008b) 'Ease Plight of Refugees', 8 August. Available at: http://www.sowe tanlive.co.za/sowetan/archive/2008/08/08/ease-plight-of-refugees (accessed December 2011).

——(2012) 'Miners Turn Anger onto Foreign Traders', 4 October. Available at: http://www.sowetanlive.co.za/news/business/2012/10/04/miners-turn-anger-onto-foreign-traders (accessed December 2012).

Stinson, A.T. (2009) 'National Identity and Nation-Building in Post-Apartheid South Africa', unpublished MA thesis, Rhodes University.

Stone, D. (1989) 'Causal Stories and the Formation of Policy Agendas', *Political Science Quarterly* 104(2) :281–300.

The Presidency of the Republic of South Africa (2008a) 'President Mbeki Approves Request for SANDF Involvement to Stop Attacks on Foreign Nationals', 21 May. Available at: http://web.archive.org/web/20080610181937/http://www.thepresidency.gov.za/show.asp?type=pr&include=president/pr/2008/pr05211746.htm (accessed 15 January 2013).

——(2008b) 'Discussion Document: Towards an Anti-Poverty Strategy for South Africa'. Available at: www.thepresidency.gov.za.

——(2009) 'Medium Term Strategic Framework for 2009–14'. Available at: www.the presidency.gov.za.

——(2010) 'South African Development Indicators 2010'. Available at: http://www. thepresidency.gov.za/pebble.asp?relid=2872, p.25. (accessed 12 August 2011).

——(2011) 'State of the Nation Address by His Excellency Jacob G. Zuma, President of the Republic of South Africa, at the Joint Sitting of Parliament, Cape Town', 10 February. Available at: http://www.info.gov.za/speech/DynamicAction?pageid=461& sid=16154& tid = 27985 (acccessed 17 November 2011).

The South African (2012) 'Home Affairs Shadow Minister Calls for Immigration Crackdown',16 July. Available at: http://www.thesouthafrican.com/news/home-affairs-shadow-minister-calls-for-immigration-crackdown.htm (accessed 18 July 2012).

The Star (2012) 'Battlefield Joburg: Traders Targeted', 13 January. Available at: www. iol.co.za/the-star/battlefield-joburg-traders-targetted-1.1212343?showComments=true (accessed 17 December 2012).

UNDESA (2010) *Trends in International Migrant Stock: The 2009 Revision.* New York: Department of Economic and Social Affairs, Population Division (UNDESA).

UNICEF (2008) 'A Brief Summary of UNICEF's Overall Response to the Emergency'. Available at: http://www.unicef.org/southafrica/resources_4781.html (accessed 17 January 2013).

Valji, N. (2003) 'Creating the Nation: The Rise of Violent Xenophobia in the New South Africa', unpublished Master's thesis, York University. Available at: http://cormsa.org.za/wp-content/uploads/Research/Xeno/riseofviolent.pdf (accessed 12 July 2011).

Wa Kabwe Segatti, A. (2008) 'Reforming South African Immigration Policy in the Postapartheid Period (1990–2006): What It Means and What It Takes', in A. Wa Kabwe Segatti and L. Landau (eds) *Report to the French Development Agency*: *Migration in Post-apartheid South Africa: Challenges and Questions to Policy-Makers.* Available at: http://www.afd.fr/webdav/site/afd/shared/PUBLICATIONS/ RECHERCHE/Archives/Notes-et-documents/38-notes-documents-VA.pdf (accessed 19 March 2011).

Western Cape News (2012) 'Home Affairs in Court for Contempt over Closure of Refugee Reception Office'. Available at: http://westcapenews.com/?p=5910 (accessed 12 December 2012).

Wooffitt, R. (1993) 'Analysing Accounts', in N. Gilbert (ed.) *Researching Social Life.* London: Sage, pp. 287–305.

8 Imagined threats, manufactured crises and 'real' emergencies

The politics of border closure in the face of mass refugee influx

Katy Long

This chapter investigates when, how and why states explicitly close their borders to refugees, and with what consequences. It also considers how the international community has chosen to respond to such crises and what this in turn suggests about the strength of international commitment to asylum as a normative exception to states' right to choose whom to admit into their territory. Focusing on the specific politics which led to three border closures – Turkey/Northern Iraq in 1991, Macedonia/Kosovo in 1999, and Kenya/Somalia from 2007 to 2011 – this chapter argues that these border closures were above all responses to *manufactured* ethno-national crises (for more on these border closures and the responses to them by the United Nations High Commissioner for Refugees (UNHCR), see Long, 2010, 2012).[1] The language of crisis was deliberately invoked not because the imminent entry of a mass refugee flow posed any imminent threat to life within the state, but because it served the interests of governing elites to securitise migration and asylum, and in so doing to construct a 'national' political crisis that could mask sub-national conflicts and discontents.

Labelling those moving across borders as 'refugees' allows a humanitarian response to political crisis. A fundamental tenet of the state sovereignty that underpins modern political order is that states have the right to determine whether non-citizens should be permitted to enter, or permitted to remain. The category of 'refugee', however, carves out an exception to this rule. Refugees make a powerful moral claim for admission; however, the normal paths of migration are restricted, because their survival depends upon crossing the border. As such, they are 'needy outsiders whose claims cannot be met by yielding territory or exporting wealth; they can be met only by taking people in … [the] need is for membership itself, a non-exportable good' (Walzer, 1983: 48).

In the twenty-first century, this appeal is backed by legal protection. The 1951 *Convention on the Status of Refugees*, with 145 state parties, declares that:

> No Contracting State shall expel or return ('refouler') a refugee in any manner whatsoever to the frontiers of territories where his life or freedom

would be threatened on account of his race, religion, nationality, membership of a particular social group or political opinion.

(UN General Assembly, 1951: Art. 33)

A space of exception is carved out by international law. This at once recognises the exceptional claim of refugees – those who have a well-founded fear or persecution on the basis of race, religion, nationality, membership in a particular social group, or political opinion – to seek asylum, and reinforces the 'normal' powers of state sovereignty to exclude other, less deserving claimants (on label-making, see Zetter, 2007).

The very creation of the 'refugee' is therefore an exceptional response to crisis, permitting the partial permeating of otherwise closed borders in the search for safe spaces. Yet in rare instances states *do* close their borders to arriving refugee flows: how are we to understand this?

Clearly, states normally want to retain as much control as possible over who is admitted and when: their interest lies in limiting the numbers who can be called 'refugees'. Often this process of exclusion rests upon refusing the merits of a refugee claim: demanding a standard of 'proof' that allows individuals to be refused asylum without directly questioning the rules that carve out an exception to border control in the abstract (Gibney and Hansen, 2003; see also Fassin and D'Halluin, 2005). In more developed states, the soft powers of visa regimes, transport-carrier fines, extraterritorial processing and bureaucratic paperwork allow an implicit closing of borders: again, the norm of asylum itself is not subject to scrutiny, even as the mobility of those seeking sanctuary is squeezed to ensure that the spaces of asylum offered are not located in the West (see also Jeandesboz and Pallister-Wilkins, Chapter 6 in this volume). The norm of 'refugee' is emphasised and reinforced even as asylum becomes increasingly difficult to locate in practice.

Yet many other states lack the capital, infrastructure or geographical barriers that would allow them to insist the institution of asylum is being protected even as it is also being made more difficult to actually arrive and make a claim. These states – when faced with the imminent entry of refugees – must fall back upon the language and actions of crisis themselves, meeting refugees' crisis-induced migration with claims of imminent (mass) migration-induced crisis, the potential consequences of which would be sufficiently serious to justify removing refugees' exceptional border-crossing rights. The politics of border closure in the face of mass refugee influx are thus the politics of demanding an exception to the exception.

That border closures to prevent refugee entry are justified in terms of national security – a threat to the stability of the 'imagined community' and the embedded political, social and economic hierarchies that depend upon this order – is not, perhaps, surprising. However, this chapter explores not only the architecture of such crisis-building but also the consequences, including the very 'real' humanitarian emergencies that can follow a manufactured crisis. It argues that when faced with a border closure that has resulted in acute

160   *Katy Long*

mass human suffering – as in Northern Iraq or Macedonia – the international community has often chosen to respond to urgent humanitarian demands by creating new exceptional programmes (including in-country safe zones and humanitarian evacuation programmes), rather than by challenging the border closure itself. By electing to focus on the 'real' emergency, the language of humanitarian action therefore masks the politics of border closure, and the role that the nation-state system plays in producing the 'refugee problem' through processes of inclusion, exclusion and rights distribution (see Haddad, 2008). In so doing, the language of migration-induced crisis is reaffirmed, and the reality of crisis-induced migration contained within a depoliticised, humanitarian space of exception.

The rest of this chapter is divided into five sections. The first outlines the contours of crisis and the process of securitisation. The second outlines the crisis-induced migration and the political decision-making that led to the three border closures under scrutiny. The third looks at the humanitarian consequences of these closures. In the fourth section, the international politics of response to these 'real' emergencies are examined. The final section considers what conclusions can be drawn from these cases to inform our wider understanding of the intersection between crisis-induced migration, and the language, construction and consequences of migration-induced crises.

The contours of crisis

Before we can examine the politics of crisis surrounding border closures and responses to border closures, we must first understand the implications of the language of 'crisis'.

As Chapter 1 in this volume reminds us, a crisis is often viewed as a moment when the essential structures of a social system are under threat, from external forces or internal contradictions. Border closures are a *response* to crisis: they result from the identification of an impending migration-induced crisis that legitimises an exceptional action – in this case, a refusal to admit refugees fleeing violent conflict in fear of their lives.

Border closing in the face of mass refugee influx can thus be understood as an act of securitisation.[2] Since the end of the Cold War, the United Nations Security Council has repeatedly recognised refugee flows as a 'threat to international peace and security' (United Nations Security Council, 1991, 1992). This description of international crisis permits extraordinary intervention to *stop* the movement of people. To close a border follows the same logic: the entry of refugees is an existential threat to 'the life of the nation' (economic, social and, above all, political) and so permits extraordinary action – the refusal to honour refugees' exceptional claim to admission. The dilemma then becomes whether humanitarian needs can be met outside this political framework. Border closures in Turkey and Macedonia certainly prompted radical international actions aimed at brokering a humanitarian crisis. But we

The politics of border closure 161

need to consider how the international community[3] chooses which crises to consider, and whether some are 'manufactured' for political purposes. Most importantly, can a potential threat to the integrity of a national community be considered a crisis sufficient to justify the deaths from exposure of Iraqi or Kosovar children that resulted from closing the Turkish and Macedonian borders and delaying humanitarian access?

Biopolitics[4] might offer one lens through which to understand the connections between political and humanitarian crises. Humanitarian crises are obviously 'real' in the sense that they involve an immediate threat to human life. In a humanitarian crisis, it is not only the social, but also the biological that is threatened.

However, the crises that provoked the actions that in turn caused this humanitarian emergency are best understood as political crises. The claim is that the danger posed by refugees threatened *political* stability. Understandings of political stability may often reflect elite power interests, and border closure can be a performance designed to appeal to domestic or international audiences, or to mask sub-national domestic crises (by identifying an external threat) (see also Freemantle and Misago, Chapter 7 in this volume). In this sense, we can refer to 'imagined' threats, because the selection of this 'crisis' may be deliberately intended to focus attention upon a possible external threat rather than an ongoing internal unrest. The 'imagining' of crises may help to block social change and cement elites' power.

This does *not* mean that political crises are never serious, or exist only as the machinations of elites. Even if the arrival at the border of thousands of refugees does not threaten the lives of citizens, it may disrupt political security or social concord. These too are important, our protection against a life that is 'nasty, brutish and short'. As Hannah Arendt's work reminds us, it is through the artifices of political construction that we secure our rights to a 'good life', and are secure against exposure to the 'bare life' suffered by refugees (Arendt, 1967; Agamben, 1998). The securing of rights and freedoms is difficult and achievements should be protected. As a result, closing the border to protect not just citizens, but citizenship itself against the disorders and dangers beyond the border, could be justified in the case of extreme, national crisis. The difficulty lies in determining when a refugee-induced political crisis might really threaten national life, and when border closure is in fact an action calculated to reduce the risk to private interest, not the existence of public good.

Thinking about borders can help us to understand this intersection between political constructions and the more ambiguous realities of everyday life (see Shapiro, 1997; Hyndman, 1999). Quite clearly, connection between the abstract – the line on a map in an office in Geneva – and the concrete, physical reality of a border is often ambiguous. In refugee-producing regions, borders have often been of little real importance to locals on either side prior to the eruption of conflict and the arrival of international actors in the region. Pashtun live on both side of the Afghan/Pakistan border; ethnic Somalis live

162   *Katy Long*

on both sides of the Kenya/Somalia line; the Kurds have often been described as a stateless people, stretching across the borders of the Middle East from Turkey to Syria. As researchers looking at transnational and cross-border livelihood strategies have conclusively shown, borders are often highly porous abstractions that do not reflect lived reality (e.g. Bakewell, 2000; Kaiser, 2010). In the case of Kenya, UNHCR statistics show that the rate of entry of Somali refugees actually rose dramatically following the 2007 border closure (Crisp *et al.*, 1992; Long, 2010: 2–3). So given this disconnect between everyday lives and the politics of border control, do borders – and border closures – really matter?

The answer is that borders matter in part precisely because we are not just human beings, but *citizens*. Our rights and entitlements in international law are dependent upon our attachment to sovereign nation-states. Even though borders are indisputably artificial constructions in terms of origin, they are today embedded with political meaning. Most importantly for our case, to cross a border and leave your country of origin is an essential act through which you become a refugee. Once you have crossed an international border fearing for your life, you are no longer a neglected citizen, nor just a humanitarian subject in need, but a rights-holder with a claim to international protection.[5] Crossing a border to become a refugee is thus a powerful act because it is a powerful exception to the norms of border control that mark the 'permanent crisis of a divided mankind' (Hont, 1994). This helps to explain why crisis-induced migration can be inverted and presented instead in the form of a migration-induced crisis, which in turn may sometimes lead to humanitarian crises resulting as would-be refugees are trapped between persecution and exclusion.

Border closure

The very extent to which borders and mobility across borders can be shaped and manipulated within the normal course of national politics suggests that the rare occasions when borders are in fact explicitly and publicly closed are exceptional events. The neat fixed borders on school maps prove to be already ambiguous political constructions once they are examined. The act of closing a border to refugees – as we have already noted – may be implicit in the ratcheting up of visa controls and extraterritorial processing rather than the physical barring of entry on the border by police or soldiers. Yet it is the very fact that formal, physical border closure in the fact of mass refugee influx is so unusual that suggests it has something important to tell us about the politics of crisis-making. To make sense of this, we first need to understand under what circumstances borders are closed, and with what motivation.

This chapter focuses on the closing of borders to refugees by asylum states. However, it is important to remember that borders can also be used to keep would-be refugees *in*, and to prevent them escaping *out*. During the Cold War, Communist states practised strict exit control, which reduced the

The politics of border closure 163

numbers able to leave Eastern Europe or Indochina to seek asylum (see Dowty, 1987). Today, some authoritarian states – including Uzbekistan, Eritrea and Iran among others – still use exit visa regulations to control citizens' mobility in clear violation of international human rights law.[6]

However, with the end of the Cold War, most exit controls were removed and the political capital attached to the Western performance of 'open borders' was reduced. This led to a new emphasis on border control from *host* communities. Since 1990, borders closed in response to refugee flows include (but are not limited to) the Turkish-Iraqi border (1991), the Zairean-Rwandan border (1994, 1996), the Tanzanian-Burundian border (1995), the Rwandan-Burundian border (1996), the Macedonian-Kosovan border (1999), all of Afghanistan's borders with neighbouring states (2000–2002), the Chadian-Sudanese border (2006), the Jordanian-Iraqi border (2006), the Syrian and Iranian borders with Iraq (2007), the Malawian-Tanzanian border (2007), the Kenyan-Somali border (2007–11), the Egyptian borders with the Gaza Strip and Israel (2007–present), the DRC's border with Zambia (2008), the Saudi Arabian-Yemeni border (2009), the closure by Khazakstan and Uzbekistan of their borders with Kyrgyzstan (2010), and the Syrian-Lebanese border (2011). This list underlines that border closures aimed at preventing mass refugee entry have most often occurred in the post-Cold War period in politically fragile regions where the prospective arrival of refugees can be presented as an imminent (ethno-national) migration-induced crisis. This chapter focuses on three of these closures – the Turkish, Macedonian and Kenyan decisions – in which the politics of manufacturing a migration-induced crisis were intended not only to reassure domestic audiences, but also to provoke international response.[7]

Turkey/Northern Iraq, 1991

In the first three weeks of April 1991, following the failure of a US-encouraged uprising against Saddam Hussein in the aftermath of Iraq's Gulf War defeat, and fearing Iraqi state reprisals, 400,000 mostly Kurdish Iraqis fled Northern Iraq for Turkey. Another 1.3 million fled to Iran. The Turkish state responded to this influx by closing the border, leaving the refugees stranded in a mountainous and inaccessible 'no-man's-land' at the Turkish-Iraq border.

The reasons behind the Turkish decision to close the border were very clear: concern that admitting a large number of persecuted Kurds into the country would fuel its own 'Kurdish problem'. The April 1991 outflow was not an isolated incident, but was rather the latest episode in a long history of regional Kurdish conflict. For both Turkey and Iraq (as well as to a lesser extent Iran and Syria), the 'Kurdish problem' was one that struck at the heart of understandings of state sovereignty and nation-state identity. Kurdish refugee flows thus presented a political and not just a humanitarian problem for the Turkish state. The Kurdish population in Turkey had struggled for decades against Atatürk's imposition of a Turkish national state (and the resultant suppression of the Kurdish language and culture) and by 1978 the

164 *Katy Long*

Kurdish Workers' Party (PKK) had entered into armed struggle. The population gathered on the mountainside were not just refugees – they were *Kurds*, their political identity making humanitarian admission difficult for the host state.

It is important to recognise that the decision to close the border was deliberate and not unexpected. Turkey had already employed border closures to prevent the entry of Iraqi Kurdish refugees into its territory. In July 1974, during the Iraqi Civil War, Turkey had closed its border to the Kurdish rebels and kept it closed through 1975 despite the escalation of Iraqi reprisals against the Kurds, which included the use of napalm and phosphorous against civilians. The political logic driving Turkish policies towards Kurdish refugees was also evident in the fact that Turkey, despite signing the 1967 Protocol to the 1951 Convention, retained the geographic limitation that saw it only confer refugee status on those coming from Europe. Kurdish exiles were accorded only 'temporary guest' status (Human Rights Watch, 1991).

As a result, the notion that Turkey might choose to see a Kurdish exodus from Iraq as threatening national security was not unanticipated. Writing in March 1991 (during the Gulf War, but before the mass influx), UNHCR's Ankara Branch issued a warning that underlined these tensions and spoke directly to the prospects of Kurds being able to claim asylum in Turkey:

> Turkey continues to maintain the European geographical reservation attached to the 1951 Convention, offering only temporary asylum to non-European refugees ... Turkish authorities appear to be worried at the prospect of a mass influx and their willingness to open their borders to such an influx cannot be taken for granted.
>
> (BO Ankara, March 1991, UNHCR Archives, Geneva)

The Turkish reluctance to consider Kurdish admission was also not simply a fear of the state's institutional capacity to cope with sudden mass influx. As UNHCR pointed out in the same report, in 1989, the Turkish state had granted 350,000 Bulgarian Turks permanent settlement. International planning had focused on how to respond to an anticipated mass movement at the Turkish border and to mobilise the aid response: but the expectation was that this would be triggered by the Coalition offensive in Iraq from January 1991, and this early wave did not materialise.

Macedonia/Kosovo, 1999

In April 1999, the Macedonian state formally closed its border with Kosovo in order to prevent the entry of several thousand Kosovar Albanian refugees who were massed at the Blace border crossing. The refugee exodus was a consequence of a 'classic secessionist struggle' between the Serbian state led by Slobodan Milošević and Kosovar separatists (Suhrke *et al.*, 2000: 5). Kosovo had long been a site of national contestation between the Serbian elite – who accorded the area a symbolic importance in Serbian national narratives – and the Albanian majority. By 1995, following the disintegration of Yugoslavia, and the securing of independence by Croatia and Bosnia and Herzegovina, the Kosovo Liberation Army had begun waging an armed struggle for independence from the Serb-dominated successor state.

In 1998, the Rambouillet peace negotiations had seen a proposed agreement laying out terms for Kosovar autonomy within Serbia rejected by the Serbian delegation on 18 March (who objected to the proposed presence of a NATO force within the autonomous region). This rejection – coupled with evidence that the Serbian state had authorised (though not yet fully executed) an ethnic cleansing campaign designed to remove or eliminate the majority Albanian population within Kosovo – caused NATO to take military action against the Serbian state, with air strikes beginning on 24 March 1999.

UN Security Council Resolution 1199, adopted in September 1998, had already noted 'grave concern' at an estimated 230,000 displaced persons as a result of Yugoslav force (UN Security Council, 1998). Yet the air campaign equally prompted an acceleration of Serbian action against Kosovar Albanians, causing an escalation of violence on the ground and large refugee flows that included organised expulsions.

The majority of Kosovar refugees crossed to Albania, but a substantial minority fled to the Macedonian border. Macedonia admitted these refugees for the first few days, until 30–31 March, but from this point onwards deliberately obstructed the refugees' entry. The border closure began with implicit bureaucratic measures: guards first slowed down admission by meticulously checking arrivals' paperwork. However, the border closure escalated and became a formal, explicit closure when 25,000 Kosovar refugees arrived in six trainloads on 1 April and only the first 3,000 were permitted to enter Macedonia. The remainder were left in a field at the Blace border post without access to adequate shelter or food.

The Macedonian border closure was not unexpected. The Macedonian government had publicly announced that in the event of an influx, it would receive only 20,000 refugees from Kosovo. As the post-emergency evaluation also made clear, reports from the UN's Special Envoy predicted a border closure from 1998 onwards and anticipating a border 'delay' was an integral part of UNHCR contingency planning, though the scale of the influx – some 300,000 over the course of the crisis – was not anticipated. Yet as the evaluation reported, 'for years local media and politicians in FYR Macedonia were saying that the border would be closed in the event of a mass refugee flow from Kosovo' (Suhrke et al., 2000: 102). In this sense, the border closure in Macedonia in 1999 was a predictable response to a pre-constructed national crisis.

The circumstances surrounding Macedonia's closure of its Kosovar border bore striking similarity to those surrounding the border closure in Northern Iraq in 1991. Again, the choice to close the border was made deliberately – in this case over a matter of days – framed by the political language of national crisis. Ethnic-national concerns were at the heart of Macedonian reluctance to

166 *Katy Long*

permit the Kosovars to cross the border. Ethnic Albanians constitute the largest ethnic minority in Macedonia (some 20–25 per cent of the total population) and in 1999 Macedonian Albanian political grievances were already a source of considerable political tension and in fact erupted into a brief but violent separatist insurgency two years later.

The Albanian influx therefore posed a political threat to the Macedonian state, who feared that the arrival of the Kosovar Albanians would further radicalise their own, already discontented, Albanian minority. Again, as with the Kurdish Iraqi refugees, the state's decision to close the border was motivated by political and national concerns., These refugees were a collective threat to the integrity of the Macedonian state because they were not just refugees, but *Albanian* refugees, and thus they presented a threat to the foundations of political order. The Macedonian border closure was therefore not prompted by an immediate threat to life: nor was it unforeseen. It was a deliberate political calculation. Prior to the border closure, the majority of Kosovar Albanians were hosted by co-ethnic host families in the border region (Amnesty International, 1999). Though the speed of the arrivals into Macedonia after 24 March undoubtedly required additional international assistance and monitoring, NATO's interests in containing the refugee crisis within the Balkan region to prevent any arrival of refugees in Western Europe certainly meant there was no shortage of funds or logistical capacity (Parker, 1999).

Kenya/Somalia, 2007–11

On 3 January 2007, following the defeat of the Somali Islamic courts that had brought a degree of stability to much of south-central Somalia by Ethiopian-backed forces and the Transitional Federal Government (see Lindley and Hammond, Chapter 3 in this volume), the Kenyan government announced the closure of its long and porous border with Somalia. The border remains officially closed, though since the East African famine in 2011 (and its own invasion of south-central Somalia in October of that year), the Kenyan government's statements on the border have been at times ambiguous, repeatedly promising an imminent formal reopening (see e.g. *Daily Nation*, 2011).

Many aspects of the Kenyan state's decision to close its border echo the earlier cases of Turkey and Macedonia in the construction and performance of a border closure for both a domestic audience and an international one. Border closure could be used both to reinforce a fractured Kenyan national narrative by diverting attention away from Kenya's own sub-state economic and ethnic crises, and to appeal to the international community. A further political concern was the complex relationship of the Kenyan state with its own substantial Somali minority, a population concentrated in the marginal North Eastern Province bordering Somalia (see Lochery, 2012).

The January 2007 border closure was again not unexpected. Kenya had previously closed its border with Somalia on at least two occasions in order to prevent asylum seekers entering Kenya. In July 1999, Kenyan President

Daniel Arap Moi gave a public speech linking refugees to crime and illicit arms proliferation, followed by the government closing its border with Somalia. In 2001, the government again closed its border with Somalia on the grounds that rising numbers of refugees were responsible for increasing levels of violent crime. The border closure in 2007 therefore fit a broader pattern of the Kenyan state's construction of a 'Somali problem'.

Kenya built its 2007 case for border closure in a new language drawing on the securitisation discourses of the War on Terror. This in part reflected the 'implicit' border-closing tactics employed by developed states. Foreign Minister Raphael Tutu argued that 'there is no evidence that anybody who is not a combatant is in danger ... We are not able to ascertain whether these people are genuine refugees or fighters and therefore it's best that they remain in Somalia' (Bosire, 2007). Ministers complained too at the threat that the large refugee camps posed to Kenya: 'Europe and America do not give us enough aid to support these refugees' (ibid.).

Yet the Kenyan border closure was also very different from the Turkish or Macedonian cases. First – unlike these other two, short acute crises – this has proven to be a long border closure, stretching through six years. Second, the border closure – though 'official' – has had limited if any effect on the numbers actually crossing the border to seek assistance in Kenya's refugee camps. In fact, the rate of arrivals actually increased in the weeks following the announcement of the border closure (Long, 2010: 52). Third, it was actually the arrival of a much more severe crisis – the 'real' emergency of the East African famine of 2011 – that prompted a shift by at least some in the Kenyan government to adopt a much more conciliatory language when talking about the border and Somali mobility (Opiyo, 2011).

Kenya's border closure therefore poses different questions about the processes involved in crisis-making, and state responses to it. The border closure existed at the level of political performance – domestic and international – but it did not reflect the crossings of everyday reality. The border closure did nothing to 'solve' the national crisis that the refugee influx was claimed to present, because Somalis continued to arrive. Instead, the event can help to shed light on the consequences of an 'imagined' border closure – existing only on paper but not as a physical reality for the public discourse surrounding migration-induced crises.

Real emergencies

This prompts a new question: what are the consequences that follow from a formal, explicit border closure locking would-be refugees out? The evidence would suggest that, when the declaration of a border closure is followed by physical enforcement, the involuntary immobility that results can become a 'real' humanitarian emergency, placing lives at risk. Border posts are often in remote, inhospitable areas (as in Northern Iraq); if the border closure is being enforced, there is likely to be a significant military and police presence. These

168   *Katy Long*

factors are likely to obstruct the delivery of humanitarian assistance and exacerbate humanitarian needs, not least because of the additional risks associated with a militarised environment. In the case of both the Turkish and the Macedonian border closures, there is evidence that the construction of and response to a migration-induced crisis resulted in a new, very real, humanitarian emergency.

In the case of Northern Iraq, there was an undoubted humanitarian crisis. By 3 April 1991, more than 200,000 Kurdish refugees were already massed in appalling conditions. On 7 April, as the numbers trapped grew, the Turkish Foreign Ministry announced that 1,500 refugees had died from exposure in the past three days. Later research would calculate that at least an additional 6,200 people died because of the border closure, two-thirds of them children under 5 (CDC, 1991).

Writing at the end of that year, Bill Frelick graphically depicted refugees 'left to fend for themselves clinging to the sides of mountains ... a picture of misery and death that briefly riveted the world's attention and stirred its conscience' (Frelick, 1992). UNHCR staff talked of the enormity of the crisis: 'It is a situation almost beyond imagination and certainly beyond management ... never before has there been a refugee situation that has developed to this magnitude in this space of time' (*The Observer*, 1991). The immediate task was keeping the Kurdish refugees alive: Médecins Sans Frontières estimated that hundreds were dying on the mountainsides each night from exposure. The border closure created conditions in which aid was almost impossible to deliver: many of the camps were inaccessible to road vehicles, leaving aid delivery dependent upon US helicopter drops. The airdrops resulted in further deaths as crates fell onto refugees. In addition, nervous Turkish soldiers corralled the refugees, fatally shooting some when they crossed into Turkish territory to retrieve aid (Gurdilek, 1991). By mid-April, the Kurdish population 'perched among the crags in a deadly trap set by international politics' were undoubtedly facing a severe crisis resulting from their *im*mobility (Reeves, 1991). A constructed crisis had produced a very real and immediate *humanitarian* emergency.

In the case of the Kosovar would-be refugees, the emergency was smaller in scale but still acute in the sense that it presented an immediate threat to the Kosovars' lives. In less than a week after the border closure, observers reported 25,000 Kosovar refugees massed at Blace border crossing in a muddy field, with the suffering of those in flight amplified because border security operations were preventing the flow of aid to the Kosovars:

> Caught in no-man's-land, expelled by Serb forces but refused entry by Macedonia. International observers report armed Macedonian troops encircling the bewildered refugees have beaten them to keep order. The government has restricted the flow of humanitarian assistance. Many are still without any shelter. There are no sanitation facilities. The rain has extinguished small campfires, adding to the misery. According to the

International Red Cross, at least 11 people died overnight, including four children.

(Garrels, 1999)

International humanitarian actors were denied access to the Kosovar population by Macedonian troops: a few Macedonian Albanians were able to cross the borderline, but with extremely limited resources the distribution of bread was chaotic, so that journalists reported how a worker from an Albanian charity 'wept with frustration as he ran out of bread within a minute. "The UN says they have plenty of supplies, so where are they? Refugees should not be made to feel like animals"' (McGrory, 1999a).

This description of the Kosovar plight underlines the way in which humanitarian crises, in stripping political agency, can reduce populations to 'bare life'. By 4 April 1999, it was clear that 'the Macedonian authorities [were] exacerbating the humanitarian crisis in order to avert a political one' (Garrels, 1999).

In the cases of Northern Iraq and Macedonia, then, the border closure – enforced by the hard physical presence of state authorities – turned a political crisis into a humanitarian emergency. Obstructing crisis-induced migration had amplified the effects of crisis and created new problems, particularly in relation to the delivery of humanitarian aid in border regions. However, the Kenyan case suggests that this border closure had far less impact on the actual dynamics of crisis-induced migration, because declared intent did not translate to physical reality.

As already noted, border closure did not stem the flow of Somali refugees to Kenya: in fact, the numbers increased in the immediate weeks following the government's public statements. This was in part because the border is extremely porous – its length (682 kilometres) – running through relatively flat, sparsely populated terrain allowed many Somalis to circumvent thinly distributed border patrols, while an informal border economy allowed others to pay and pass. Yet the fact that there was no wide-scale humanitarian crisis resulting directly from the border closure does not mean – as is sometimes suggested – that it had no humanitarian impact, or that its effects were felt in the political realm only.

As Human Rights Watch reports in 2010 made clear, the corrosive effect of the official border was to expose Somalis to greater risk and reduce humanitarian capacities to protect as a result of the closure of the UNHCR's border outposts. In particular, because would-be refugees were left to cross the border as illegal migrants, they were susceptible to increased harassment and exploitation by police and border guards en route, and were more dependent on smugglers and other informal agents:

Making no distinction between women, children, and men, police often use violence, unlawful detention in appalling overcrowded conditions, and threats of deportation to extort money from them. Some police officers

170   *Katy Long*

rape women near the border. During the first ten weeks of 2010, hundreds, if not thousands, of Somali asylum seekers unable to pay were unlawfully sent back to Somalia.

(Human Rights Watch, 2010)

Thus, while Kenya's border closure did not prevent the physical entry of Somalis, and therefore did not create conditions for an immediate and massive emergency resulting from this involuntary immobility, the border closure – a constructed crisis – did exacerbate conditions of humanitarian suffering and placed refugees at risk of significant bodily harm. Even porous border closures can have real human consequences.

Responding to crisis

Border closures, then, are the products of politically manufactured crisis – responses to threats to the national community as perceived by dominant political actors. Yet they can create humanitarian emergency – placing human lives at risk. To understand how crisis-induced migration can be reimagined as migration-induced crisis, and in turn create new crises of immobility, we need to consider not just how the border closures themselves were enacted. We also need to consider also how and why the international community responded to border closure, and what this reveals about the types of crisis that prompt or permit action and the ways in which such exceptional crises are legitimised.

As evidence from both Northern Iraq and Macedonia shows, the urgency of humanitarian needs resulting from the border closure permitted the development of extraordinary responses to a *humanitarian emergency*, while at the same time largely ignoring the reason for the restricted humanitarian access: the border closure. In this way, claims of the political crisis that a prospective mass influx of refugees would present to nation-state order were largely allowed to remain unchallenged, while the international community focused upon addressing humanitarian needs outside a political framework.

Turkey/Northern Iraq, 1991

As Turkey closed its border to the Kurds fleeing Iraq in April 1991, turning crisis-induced migration into a humanitarian emergency, the humanitarian community's initial response was to engage in advocacy in order to persuade the Turkish authorities that humanitarian need should trump political strategy.

Sadako Ogata, the new UN High Commissioner for Refugees (who had taken up her post only a month before the Gulf crisis began), wrote to the Turkish government, urging it to continue to allow exceptional access to these 'victims of internal strife' (letter to Turkish government, April 1991, UNHCR Archives, Geneva). However, within a few days, the strategic concerns of states meant that the would-be refugees' humanitarian needs were increasingly

The politics of border closure   171

focused upon without reference to the border closure as a *cause* of crisis: instead, media reports and UNHCR briefing papers focused on the Iraqi Army's reprisals for the failed uprising as the root cause prompting the Kurds' initial flight.

This selective framing of the crisis served a number of Allied strategic aims. It focused attention back on the Saddam regime as the *cause* of crisis-induced migration; it prevented Turkey – a key supply and logistics hub for the Allied operations – becoming the focus of criticism and, at a more abstract level, it shifted responsibility for this migration-induced crisis back onto the Iraqi state, reinforcing the norms of 'good' state sovereignty and actually reducing the obligations of 'good' states towards strangers in need. In Bill Frelick's words, 'Turkey, the good ally, was essentially let off the hook with the creation of a "safe haven zone" inside Iraq' (Frelick, 1992: 26).

Crucially, in reacting to the humanitarian crisis – the undeniable fact of thousands of human lives at risk on an inaccessible mountainside – international actors quickly lost sight of the border closure. As a UNHCR report from Ankara at the time made clear, 'Ambassadors did not speak out in favour of opening Turkey's border to refugees. The absence of such statements was notable' (BO Ankara, 7 April 1991, UNHCR Archives, Geneva). Support grew for a 'cross-border' operation, in which assistance would be delivered to the Kurdish population through their return to Iraqi territory. On 16 April, US President George Bush announced a plan for Coalition forces that had been based at the Turkish border to extend their presence into Northern Iraq, constructing camps within a safe zone that would allow the Kurdish population to return to Iraq and the international community to provide relief *in situ*.

The political power of interested Western states can be seen in the almost total absence of public or private discussion of the border closure by states controlling the relief operations. The media and US officials described a 'humanitarian catastrophe', but did not expand on the reasons why a cross-border relief effort was necessary. Operation Provide Comfort – which established safe zones within Iraq – was enacted through United Nations Security Council Resolution 688, which did not mention the border closure. It was now the refugee flows themselves that were presented as the threat.

Yet it was clear to the international community that this safe-zone operation undermined the fundamental principles underpinning asylum: 'cross-border operations must be seen as the antithesis of the first principle of admission. Programmes designed to keep people in their country of origin are also programmes designed to keep them out of a country of asylum' (UNHCR Turkey, 5 April 1991, UNHCR Archives, Geneva). However, what is notable is that it was the 'humanitarian' argument that provided a basis for legitimising the extraordinary in-country intervention: 'should UNHCR prevent, or seek to prevent, assistance from reaching desperate people?' (Urgent Communiqué, Branch Office Ankara, 7 April 1991, UNHCR Archives, Geneva). In effect, the 'reality' of the humanitarian crisis on the border had eclipsed the act of border closing, so that exceptional acts of intervention could be justified while simultaneously reinforcing the idea – through a lack of sustained public or

172   *Katy Long*

private critique – that states could close borders in the construction of political crises.

The 'safe zone' solution did provide immediate humanitarian protection to the Kurds. Some officials have argued – flirting with the dangerous possibilities offered by counterfactual histories – that in forcing the creation of a new humanitarian space within Iraq, the border closure actually prevented the emergence of a new protracted refugee situation, trapped permanently within the limited freedoms offered in asylum space (interview with senior UNHCR official, June 2010). There is also evidence that events in Northern Iraq helped to build the case for the protection of internally displaced persons (IDPs) (see Long, 2012).

Yet this protection was dependent upon massive and continued military investment in the safe zone, resulting from its political and strategic importance. As the UNHCR remarked, 'people did not return because it is safe in their country of origin: they returned because they were protected from the government of their country of origin' (Confidential Planning Document, Branch Office Ankara, *Review of Developments in Turkey*, 5 June 1991, UNHCR Archives, Geneva). The response to the Turkish border closure both addressed the immediate humanitarian emergency and resolved the political crisis that had prompted the border closure by providing an acceptable alternative to admission. Yet in failing to link the two events – in presenting the causes of flight as primarily responsible for the emergency on the mountainsides – the border closure itself was legitimised.

Macedonia/Kosovo, 1999

In May 1998, Zvonimir Jankuloski, a Macedonian human rights activist, had argued that any border closure would be justified to protect the 'fragile peace in Macedonia'. He argued that such a border closure should be met by co-ordinated international action and the evacuation of Kosovan refugees, because forcing Macedonia to host the refugees 'could increase internal ethnic tensions and undermine its peace and stability' (Jankuloski, 1998: 33). Nearly a year before the mass Kosovan refugee flight actually materialised, then, the Macedonian government was mapping out its solution to this 'crisis', and observers were suggesting that a programme of temporary evacuation using Macedonia as a transit zone only could be carried out 'with the help of UN or NATO troops' (ibid.: 34).

It is therefore perhaps not surprising that the Macedonian border crisis – neither unexpected nor unplanned for – was extraordinarily swift in reaching a resolution. Less than a week after Macedonia had begun to slow down entries from Kosovo through a 'soft' border closure at the end of March 1999, a plan allowing for the lifting of the border closure and the humanitarian evacuation of Kosovan refugees to third countries was brokered by NATO. By 6 April, Blace field – the scene of such misery just one week previously – was empty. By mid-June, Kosovars were engaged in a massive and rapid

The politics of border closure 173

spontaneous *repatriation*, as NATO drove Milošević's army from Kosovo. The Humanitarian Evacuation and Humanitarian Transfer Programmes (HEP and HTP) saw around 90,000 refugees transferred from Macedonia to third countries. Notably, Turkey's offer of 25,000 places was a key factor (alongside Norway's offer of 6,000 places) in persuading Macedonia to open its border on 3 April (see Long, 2010).

The entire Kosovo refugee crisis lasted less than three months. Given the length of most refugee crises – with three-quarters of registered refugees spending five years or more in exile – it is important to understand how the processes of crisis-making and crisis response in Macedonia allowed the international community to react so quickly to the Kosovo refugee crisis. The answer again lies in the way in which NATO states' political interests lay in publicly addressing the Kosovan crisis, not only because of their interest in securing NATO use of Macedonian airspace, but perhaps more importantly because the border closure created a visible humanitarian emergency for the 'media circus' at Blace. The politics of humanitarian intervention that had led to NATO airstrikes now demanded more humanitarian action.

The Kosovars' crisis-induced migration had at the very least been accelerated by NATO's military engagement with Serbia. Yet – unlike 1991 in Turkey – the Macedonians were also subject to far more public criticism regarding their decision not to allow the Kosovars to cross and instead to try and leverage an alternative form of response to a migration-induced crisis. NGO workers spoke of the Macedonian authorities 'blackmailing the West ... using the refugees as ransom to get millions in Western aid' (McGrory, 1999b). There was far more explicit recognition that – in choosing to close the border and reduce access to asylum – Macedonia was deliberately manufacturing a refugee crisis for its own political ends.

However, the logic behind the Macedonian decision was not seriously tested because Western European leaders were also keen to prevent the Kosovar crisis from resulting in 'a tide of refugees spreading across Western Europe' (Binyon, 1999). The spectre of a hundred thousand Kosovars on Europe's doorstep, presenting new crises for each European Union state and their national social contracts, not only explains the rapidity of NATO action but also explains why such action focused on Milošević's crime in forcing the Kosovars out of Kosovo, rather than the political stratagems of Macedonia. They were remarkably similar to the crises that other polities were also constructing to appease domestic political audiences and justify an exceptional *political* collaboration in the name of *humanitarianism*.

It is important to note that, as in Iraq, the humanitarian community itself did not negotiate the exceptional response which allowed admission to Macedonia to be made conditional upon further relocation to a third country. It was the US – leading NATO – that insisted upon a solution that addressed both the humanitarian crisis on the border and the political crisis framing the Macedonian response. The premise of the border closure was effectively accepted: the focus was not on scrutiny but on facilitating an extraordinary

174   *Katy Long*

humanitarian operation designed to deal with 'the immediate crisis at Blace'. As a result, Macedonia was able to renege on its commitments to preserving the exceptional space of asylum as both a political and humanitarian safety valve, intended to balance the demands of sovereignty against the need for sanctuary. Defenders of the Humanitarian Evacuation Programme (HEP) argue that '[if] asylum became conditioned on other actions, [that] was a price that had to be paid even if it created problems later' (email correspondence with Nicholas Morris, UNHCR Special Envoy for the Balkans, 1998–99, April 2010). What is clear is that, as in Northern Iraq, it was the shaping of a *humanitarian* crisis – one in which human life was at risk and which could be viewed in terms of imminent suffering – that both allowed the brokering of an exceptional collaborative action to redistribute the refugee population across some dozen developed states, and justified the normative price. In creating and responding to a 'real' emergency, the politics of constructed crisis – that justified the border closure itself – could be largely forgotten.

Kenya/Somalia, 2007–2011

The Kenyan government's decision to announce the closing of the border with Somalia in order to prevent the further entry of refugees was never fully implemented on the ground. It was, above all, designed to counteract domestic political pressures and divisions by imposing a national narrative of crisis upon the movement of Somalis across the border. There was also an explicit call from the Kenyan government for the international community to engage in burden-sharing, particularly by helping to establish safe zones in south-central Somalia to allow humanitarian needs to be met without requiring Kenya to offer political asylum (see p. 000). Other concerns included the need for assistance to help screen arriving refugees and avoid Islamist militants infiltrating the refugee camps.

Yet because the border closure existed largely as a rhetorical flourish, a political and not a physical act, its impact was also limited and so too was the international response in its wake. Some 140,000 Somali refugees registered at Dadaab between January 2007 and mid-March 2010; at least as many were estimated to have travelled towards Nairobi in the same period. In the immediate wake of the border closure, UNHCR did condemn Kenya's actions, again invoking the humanitarian defence against political action:

> Governments have a responsibility to ensure border security in such situations ... But Kenya also has a humanitarian obligation to allow civilians at risk to seek asylum on its territory. Most of those in Liboi are women and children and they should not be sent back to a very uncertain situation. To do so would be a transgression of the principle of non-refoulement.
>
> (*Daily Nation*, 2007)

The politics of border closure 175

However, what followed was silence. On a visit to Dadaab in August 2009, High Commissioner Gueterres did not mention the closed border, although in 2010 UNHCR did issue a statement urging all parties to respect the norm of non-refoulement and not to return any Somali refugee to south-central Somalia against their wishes. In fact, the border closure largely faded into the background, so that many observers and experts express uncertainty about when and for how long the Kenya/Somali border has been officially, explicitly closed.

How can we explain this inaction? At the physical level of direct action, the lack of an international response is not, perhaps, surprising: because the border closure itself existed largely in the political and not the physical realm, creating a climate for abuse, extortion and pushbacks at border crossings rather than sealing the border, therefore it did not in itself prompt a humanitarian crisis,[8] and demanded no immediate action. Given that it was ultimately the 2011 famine that prompted serious discussion and promises that the border would be reopened – prompted by clear evidence of undoubted humanitarian crisis and the pressure of international attention (IRIN, 2011) – the conclusion must be that without the pressure of immediate humanitarian emergency, the international community is unlikely to take extraordinary actions to demand the observance of asylum norms.

What is perhaps more surprising is that – while the border closure did exist in political terms – there was relatively little serious attempt to condemn it through public statements or other forms of political discourse. A political imagining of migration-induced crisis was not met with political speeches warning of the humanitarian dangers that could result from artificially restricting crisis-induced migration. Two possible explanations for this silence can be advanced. First, that because there was no 'real' humanitarian crisis resulting from the official closure, UNHCR and other actors made a strategic decision not to contest the political border closure, in the hope this would keep physical space *de facto* open, and not encourage the Kenyan authorities to tighten restrictions. However, a second possible explanation is that states' interests were clearly not served by strongly and publicly critiquing Kenya's asylum policies when they share a common interest in strengthening borders and narrowly circumscribing the exceptional rights of the asylum seeker to cross into sovereign space. The construction of a constant asylum crisis – the notion that nation-states are stretched almost beyond endurance by the movement of refugee flows across the borders – is extremely useful. Counterintuitively, it actually reinforces the status quo of the international system.

Since October 2011, the story of Kenyan border closure has arguably evolved into border incursion, with the invasion of south-central Somalia by the Kenyan army followed by repeated calls for early repatriation of Somali refugees following the end of famine. With the decision in December 2012 to call for the encampment of all Somali refugees in Kenya – viewed by many experts as a prelude to pursuing their return to a still fragile Somalia – Kenya's assault on the ability of crisis-induced migrants to reach sanctuary has moved on

176   *Katy Long*

from the politics of crisis-making to the politics of crisis-solving. The aim now is to persuade both the international community and Somalis that there is no longer a crisis or emergency, and therefore there is no longer a need to claim refuge in Kenya (Refugees International, 2013).

Conclusion

Turkey, Macedonia and Kenya are not the only states to have chosen to explicitly close their borders in the face of prospective mass refugee influx. Yet examining these cases, stretched across two decades and three continents, and looking not only for the context-specific but the common political meanings across all three, can help us to understand crisis-making and crisis response. The category of 'refugee' is itself a label of exception, designed to cut across the politics of sovereignty and carve out a space of humanitarian sanctuary. Considering why states may choose to withdraw this protection – and why they may choose to use such a blunt tool as physically closing their border – helps us to understand the juxtaposition of the humanitarian and the political.

In all three cases, the border was closed because of the alleged or perceived risk that allowing the refugees to enter would present to *national* security. The achievements of national political citizenship were seen by the state to be at risk due to the imminent arrival of refugees who were not viewed only as suffering men, women and children. These would-be refugees were understood as collective groupings Kurds, Kosovars, Somalis: ethnic, politicised identities that were perceived as threatening the state elites' national imaginings of Turkey, Macedonia and Kenya respectively. The border closures were therefore carefully constructed, considered responses to the political framing of the nation-state. There was an alternative – to allow the refugees in and to permit international humanitarian assistance to be delivered within state territory. While this is not to suggest that there was no basis for the claims that admitting refugees would increase political tension and highlight sub-national crises within the states, a choice was made to secure the political peace at the price of increased risk to refugees left in danger at the border.

In responding to their political crises, Turkey and Macedonia created new humanitarian emergencies. That Kenya did not was a reflection of the limited implementation of its border closure, though the humanitarian consequences of increased exploitation and exposure to risk should not be underestimated.

In all three cases, crisis-induced migration clashed with migration-induced crisis: it was the resulting *immobility* that led to humanitarian emergency and rising death tolls. It was this 'real' crisis that resulted in an exceptional humanitarian response: in seeing the emergency as 'beyond politics', safe zones and Humanitarian Evacuation could therefore be sanctioned with little – if any – reference to the border closure itself, only to the destabilising impact of mass crisis-induced migration upon 'international peace and security'. The language of humanitarian response helps to mask the political construction of crisis, focusing on consequences rather than structural causes.

The politics of border closure   177

Refugee protection relies above all on the freedom of those seeking sanctuary to cross borders. While the international refugee regime sets out states' obligations in the 1951 *Convention on the Status of Refugees*, including prohibition against refoulement, in political terms, these norms rely upon state compliance. Exceptions to the exception – migration-induced crises that are claimed to override the needs of crisis-induced migrants – thus act to reinforce the powers of the nation-state system against the claims of refugees. Their tacit acceptance by a broader host of international actors tied into this system avoids the need to tackle the extent to which the nation-state distribution of resources, and control of movement, have created structures that will inevitably produce refugees (Haddad, 2008). In choosing to connect the humanitarian emergencies that follow border closures to states of origins' failures to protect, but not to would-be host states' actions in failing to admit refugees, nation-state responsibility is reinforced and the power of a claim to universal protection diminished. This underlines both why it is so important for international NGOs and agencies like UNHCR to speak loudly against such practices, and why – given the extent to which they themselves are embedded within the state-based international system – they are often slow to do so.

The lessons of Turkey and Macedonia – and of Kenya – resonate with the politics of migration crises today, and the emphasis on both closing borders and responding to *humanitarian* need. Twenty years after the Northern Iraqi crisis, the Syrian refugee emergency is posing new questions about the intersection between humanitarian refugee admission and the state's political capacity. France's decision to close its border temporarily to incoming Italian trains in the wake of a Tunisian 'mass influx' on 17 April 2011, citing 'public order concerns', has already led to new proposals to allow the re-imposition of national border controls within the Schengen Area that may fundamentally alter the politics of movement within the EU (BBC, 2011; *The Guardian*, 2011).

Crisis-making around borders thus ultimately reinforces the status quo, because responses to these political decisions are characterised as *humanitarian* actions, excising politics, and in doing so tacitly condoning rather than explicitly condemning the original border closure. Furthermore, such constructed crises are likely to reduce the capacity of those migrating away from crisis to find safety through such movement, because states', NATO's and United Nations' responses have tended to represent migration itself as the threat, rather than an opportunity to escape the worst excesses of conflict and crisis. While no one would suggest that addressing the crises that cause people to flee is not vital, focusing on peacebuilding and repatriation while allowing borders remain closed has permitted too many states to replace protection with containment.

This serves the interests of states, whose migration-induced crises are intended to preserve the imaginings of fixed political community and a neat bordered world. It does not serve the interests of individuals trapped on the border to offer not asylum but only humanitarian assistance and rescue. For whatever the exceptional operations that are negotiated in response to border

178   *Katy Long*

crises, these ad-hoc rescues can never be more valuable to the vulnerable than the norms of universal protection that such border closures undermine in the first place.

Notes

1 This chapter draws in part on research carried out in UNHCR's Archives and interviews conducted in Geneva in 2010 for a project on border closures commissioned by UNHCR's Policy Development and Evaluation Service, in response to a request from High Commissioner Antonio Guterres, who wished to know what policy options might be available for him to pursue when states refused entry to large-scale refugee populations. See Long (2010), published online at: http://www.unhcr.org/4c207bd59.html.
2 Securitisation is a concept in International Relations theory that is generally associated with the Copenhagen School, focusing attention not on the material nature of a threat, but on the processes through which an issue can be transformed by an actor into a matter of security, thus legitimating an exceptional response.
3 In this chapter, I use 'the international community' to refer to a collective group of powerful actors that broadly share a liberal-democratic political outlook. These include the United Nations, Humanitarian Agencies, NATO and a number of individual Western states, most notably the USA. The use of this term does not mean that these actors share a homogeneous outlook, or that their interests and actions are always shared.
4 Biopolitics is generally associated with Foucault's concept of biopower, and centres on the exercise of political power through control of every aspect of human life, including the physical.
5 As this chapter will discuss, the place of the border in determining humanitarian response and legal rights of the displaced is shifting. The Kampala Convention on Internal Displacement (which entered into force in December 2012) has seen the rights of internally displaced persons (IDP) protected (at least in theory) in international law. However, in general, the act of border-crossing is still an important one in being recognised by the international community as a person of concern.
6 The International Covenant on Civil and Political Rights states that 'Everyone shall be free to leave any country, including his own' (UN General Assembly, 1966: Art. 12).
7 The following sections draw on UNHCR archival research carried out while working as a consultant for UNHCR in 2010 and published as Long (2010).
8 This is not to suggest that Somali refugees were not in need of humanitarian assistance: but rather that the humanitarian impact of the border closure itself – despite the resulting increase in corruption and exploitation – was relatively limited, especially in terms of numbers affected.

References

Agamben, G. (1998) *Homo Sacer: Sovereign Power and Bare Life.* Stanford, CA: Stanford University Press.
Amnesty International (1999) *The Protection of Kosovo Albanian Refugees.* EUR 65/03/99, 19 May. Amnesty International.
Arendt, H. (1967) *The Origins of Totalitarianism*, 2nd edn. New York: Harvest.
Bakewell, O. (2000) 'Repatriation and Self-Settled Refugees in Zambia: Bringing Solutions to the Wrong Problems', *Journal of Refugee Studies* 13(4): 356–73.

The politics of border closure   179

BBC (2011) 'France Blocks Italian Trains Carrying Migrants', 17 April.

Binyon, M. (1999) 'West Is Braced for Wave of Asylum-Seekers', *The Times,* 1 April.

Bosire, B. (2007) 'Kenya Deports Hundreds of Somali Refugees Fleeing Tension at Home', *Agence France-Presse*, 3 January.

CDC (Centre for Disease Control and Prevention) (1991) 'International Notes Public Health Consequences of Acute Displacement of Iraqi Citizens – March–May 1991', *Morbidity and Mortality Weekly Report* 40(26): 443–6.

Crisp, J., Martin, L. and Prattley, W. (1992) *Review of UNHCR Emergency Preparedness and Response in the Persian Gulf Crisis.* UNHCR, UNHCR/GULF/EVAL/12, Geneva: UNHCR.

Daily Nation (2007) 'UN Protests as Kenya Sends Back Somali Refugees', 4 January 2007.

——(2011) 'Ojodeh, Raila Differ Over Border Reopening', 20 July.

Dowty, A. (1987) *Closed Borders: The Contemporary Assault on Freedom of Movement.* New Haven, CT: Yale University Press.

Fassin, D. and D'Halluin, E. (2005) 'The Truth from the Body: Medical Certificates as Ultimate Evidence for Asylum Seekers', *American Anthropologist* 107(4): 597–608.

Frelick, B. (1992) 'The False Promise of Operation Provide Comfort: Protecting Refugees or Protection of State Power?' *Middle East Report* No. 176.

Garrels, A. (1999) 'Analysis: Tens of Thousands of Ethnic Albanian Refugees Being Denied Access to Bordering Countries and Humanitarian Aid', *Weekend: All Things Considered* 3 April.

Gibney, M. and Hansen, R. (2003) 'Asylum Policy in the West: Past Trends, Future Possibilities', World Institute for Development Economics (UNU-WIDER), WIDER Discussion Paper 2003/68.

Gurdilek, R. (1991) 'Kurdish Refugees Increasingly Desperate as Relief Aid Trickles in', *Associated Press*, 11 April.

Haddad, E. (2008) *The Refugee in International Society: Between Sovereigns.* Cambridge: Cambridge University Press.

Hont, I. (1994) 'The Permanent Crisis of a Divided Mankind: Contemporary Crisis of the Nation State in Historical Perspective', *Political Studies* 42(s1): 166–231.

Human Rights Watch (1991) 'Whatever Happened to the Iraqi Kurds?', 11 March. Available at: http://www.hrw.org/reports/1991/IRAQ913.htm.

——(2010) 'Welcome to Kenya: Police Abuse of Somali Refugees'. Available at: http://www.hrw.org/node/90852.

Hyndman, J. (1999) 'A Post-Cold War Geography of Forced Migration in Kenya and Somalia', *The Professional Geographer* 51(1): 104–14.

IRIN (2011) 'Kenya-Somalia: Border Town Feels the Refugee Pressure', 29 August.

Jankuloski, Z. (1998) 'Why Macedonia Matters: Spill-Over of the Refugee Crisis from Kosovo to Macedonia', in RSC Working Paper No.1, *The Kosovo Crisis*, Refugee Studies Programme, Queen Elizabeth House, University of Oxford, pp. 28–34.

Kaiser, T. (2010) 'Dispersal, Division and Diversification: Durable Solutions and Sudanese Refugees in Uganda', *Journal of Eastern African Studies* 4(1): 44–60.

Lochery, E. (2012) 'Rendering Difference Visible: The Kenyan State and Its Somali Citizens', *African Affairs* 111(445): 615–39.

Long, K. (2010) *'No Entry!' A Review of UNHCR's Response to Border Closures in Situations of Mass Refugee Influx.* Geneva: UNHCR.

180 *Katy Long*

——(2012) 'In Search of Sanctuary: Border Closures, "Safe" Zones and Refugee Protection', *Journal of Refugee Studies*. DOI: org/10.1093/jrs/fes050.

McGrory, D. (1999a) 'Crumbs Give Little Comfort: Balkans War-Aid Quagmire', *The Times*, 3 April.

——(1999b) 'British Aid Workers Warned to Expect Skopje Hostility', *The Times*, 5 April.

Opiyo, D. (2011) 'Kenya: Ojodeh, Raila Differ Over Border Reopening', *The Daily Nation*, 20 July.

Parker, G. (1999) 'Kosovo Crisis: Blair Doctrine to Tackle Brutal Regimes', *The Financial Times,* 23 April.

Reeves, P. (1991) 'Dying Continues as West Tries to Step Up Aid to Refugees', *The Independent,* 12 April.

Refugees International (2013) 'Kenya: Government Directive Leads to Severe Abuses and Forced Returns', 26 February.

Shapiro, M. (1997) *Violent Cartographies: Mapping Cultures of War.* Minneapolis, MN: University of Minnesota Press.

Suhrke, A., Barutciski, M., Sandison, P. and Garlock, R. (2000) *The Kosovo Refugee Crisis: An Independent Evaluation of UNHCR's Emergency Preparedness and Response.* Geneva: Refugee Studies Centre, UNHCR.

The Guardian (2011) 'EU Executive Considers Reimposing Border Controls', 1 May.

The Observer (1991) 'Kurdish Tragedy – the Mountainsides of Hell', 14 April.

UN General Assembly (1951) 'Convention Relating to the Status of Refugees', United Nations, Treaty Series. Vol. 189, p. 137.

——(1966) 'International Covenant on Civil and Political Rights', United Nations, Treaty Series, Vol. 999, p. 171.

United Nations Archives. Geneva: UN.

UN Security Council (1991) 'Resolution 688 (1991) Adopted by the Security Council at its 2982nd meeting on 5 April 1991', S/RES/688.

——(1992) 'Resolution 794 (1992) Adopted by the Security Council at its 2982nd Meeting on 5 April 1991', S/RES/688.

——(1998) 'Resolution 1199 (1998) Adopted by the Security Council at its 3930th Meeting, on 23 September 1998', S/RES/1199.

Walzer, M. (1983) *Spheres of Justice.* Oxford: Martin Robertson.

Zetter, R. (2007) 'More Labels, Fewer Refugees: Remaking the Refugee Label in an Era of Globalization', *Journal of Refugee Studies* 20(2): 172–92.

9 Crisis? Which crisis?

Families and forced migration

Tania Kaiser

This chapter considers the relationship between families and forced migration, setting out to unpack some of the common perceptions about the priorities and responses of refugees in contexts of socio-political upheaval. It draws on ethnographic work carried out with Sudanese refugees in Uganda over a long period, and questions assumptions relating to the constitution and character of crises for refugees and those who work with them.

Refugee situations are generally framed by definition as crisis situations. This is self-evidently accurate at one level; facing persecution, conflict, and violence may be continuous with other socio-political experiences, but cannot be described as run of the mill. However, as refugee situations are now more often than not protracted (Lindley, 2011; Long, 2011), the idea of crisis has to be unpacked if we are to understand how exilic processes unfold and are understood by diverse actors. It may be helpful to conceptualise specific crises as pivotal points along forced migration trajectories, and these may have meaning and resonance for different actors at different times. In the case of the Sudanese, some adults during the 1990s and 2000s experienced their third long period of exile in Uganda since the 1950s. What does 'crisis' mean for such people as individuals, and as members of families?

Institutional and humanitarian responses to forced migrants are usually organised around the idea of a crisis or emergency response in the early stages. As time passes, and refugee situations become protracted, what changes in terms of support offered or options available from the perspective of the family? Opportunities for family reunification (officially or informally) probably increase, residence patterns in camps and settlements may change, the amount and type of assistance provided and livelihood opportunities and expectations are also likely to change. Since the amount of and levels of services and support provided are likely to decline as exile becomes protracted, one could argue that families need to act fairly quickly to mobilise opportunities while these are still available in the post-emergency early stages (in Kiryandongo, this meant during the mid-1990s).

Displacement is usually regarded as a serious challenge to family life, and there is a strong focus on the need to preserve family integrity by means of physical re-unification. This is not always easily achieved due to political as

182   *Tania Kaiser*

well as logistical constraints (Sample, 2007; Staver, 2008; ICRC, 2011). The United Nations High Commissioner for Refugees (UNHCR) *Handbook on Emergencies* indicates the parameters of the organisation's thinking on this question in emergency situations: 'The failure to protect family unity not only results in physical and emotional suffering, but subsequent efforts to reunite families are costly and difficult, and delays in family reunification will impede durable solutions' (UNHCR, 2007: 193).

There is recognition of the pain and distress which may be caused to family members if they are separated in the course of flight and humanitarian response. Perhaps inevitably, this insight is directly tied to the bureaucratic and administrative consequences for responding organisations, if they do not deal with the 'problem' of family separation in a timely manner. The handbook makes particular reference to the need to re-unite children with family members, and considers the implications for protection of failures in this respect. Otherwise, 'the family' is addressed in the handbook mainly with respect to registration and population size estimation techniques. Notably, it is hard to find any questioning about what 'family' might mean or how it operates in the context of conflict or flight.[1]

Because work to meet the immediate needs of forced migrants requires a clear unit of analysis and administration, the 'household' or 'family' has often been treated by the humanitarian sector as more or less synonymous (ibid.: 232), and fairly uniform across divergent socio-political contexts.[2] In practice, this may lead to an over-reliance on an uncomplicated and insufficiently nuanced understanding of what a family is understood to mean in different contexts, and by different actors. It may not be the case that people living together in a refugee household are, strictly speaking, family. They may nevertheless perform mutually supportive and meaningful activities together and for each other. Equally, significant family relationships may go well beyond the narrow definition of the nuclear family, still frequently used as a notional yardstick against which deviant variations may be measured in situations of flux.

For all of these reasons, a literal and technical reunification process alone is unlikely to be enough to address the changing needs and priorities of refugee and internally displaced 'families'. This chapter considers how the family and notions of family unity are variously constructed in situations of forced migration, and how challenges and opportunities associated with these categories are engaged by forced migrants.

While it is recognised that displacement itself can provoke crises of various kinds for families, we should not be too quick to assume that we understand the nature and scope of these on the basis of the relatively limited existing evidence base. In addition, it seems likely that rather subtle social processes come into play in situations of forced migration whereby conceptualisations and definitions of family and family members vary depending on the actor and the context, and that these may also be engaged or mobilised at different levels or scale at different times. A point of departure, therefore, is the need to ask what kinds of crisis are faced by what kinds of families in the context of forced migration, to ask how these relate to each other, and to recognise that the way they are understood may also change over time. A number of ethnographic examples from Uganda will be discussed, each offering insights into a different aspect of the way in which crises of various kinds are constructed, interpreted and managed by refugees and others.

An inevitable consequence of this analysis will be recognition of the material difficulties and practical challenges faced by families in the context of forced migration, whether related to their dispersal and attempts to reunify, to consequent livelihood-related problems or other limitations of collective refugee-hood. Crucially, both these difficulties and the ways in which refugees respond to them are continuous with other dimensions of their social, political and economic lives. To this extent, and in recognition of the central role that family and clan relationships play in all aspects of everyday life in many parts of Sub-Saharan Africa, we can legitimately argue that in this context a crisis of any kind is properly viewed as a crisis of and for the family, since it is through this lens that it will be experienced, understood and responded to by individuals and groups.

One of our guiding questions in this chapter, then, refers to the relationship between the idea of family and crisis. While the challenges faced by refugee families may be numerous, might it also be the case that family structures and relations also hold the key to some of the responses that refugees are able to mount to them?

Drawing on long-term ethnographic research among Sudanese Acholi refugees in Uganda (1996–2012), the chapter therefore considers the choices made about how best to deploy individuals within extended families to the advantage of the majority in this context. It argues that further migration for some family members often offers the best option with respect to the achievement of educational or employment opportunities, and that, following recent insights seeking to overturn the sedentarist model (Cresswell, 2006; Monsutti, 2010), it should not be assumed that families will seek to stay together at all costs during experiences of exile and the search for durable solutions.

The rest of the chapter is organised as follows. First, I briefly introduce the Sudanese Acholi refugees in Uganda, whose experience is the basis of the current research and work, and address some empirical and methodological issues. Next, I outline the way that families have tended to be constructed in international and refugee law, before thinking through issues arising from the idea of crisis in refugee situations. The rest of the chapter is devoted to consideration of some of the implications of the relationship between ideas of family and crisis, in the light of ethnographic material from the Sudanese case. It argues that in this case the family is a shifting and mutable category which is re-interpreted variously to meet the changing needs of refugee groups as they face the initial crisis of displacement and subsequent challenges in exile.

184   *Tania Kaiser*

Sudanese refugees in Uganda: two decades in exile

This chapter draws on research engagement with Sudanese Acholi and other groups who have spent 20 or more years in exile in Uganda from the late 1980s. For many of the people who were forced to flee across the border when the Sudanese People's Liberation Army (SPLA) clashed with the Government of Sudan forces and took the village centre of Parajok in 1989, this was their second or third experience of exile. The process of becoming and being refugees was punctuated by crises of physical security and livelihood. Flight from Parajok was difficult and dangerous, with some families separated en route, and not reunited for many years. Initially accommodated in refugee camps close to the Uganda–Sudan border, refugees found that they were exposed to further violence from fighting between the Uganda People's Defence Force (UPDF, the national army) and the insurgent Lord's Resistance Army (LRA). In 1992, most of this group were relocated, with the majority moving to live at a newly established refugee settlement at Kiryandongo. Exile became protracted and life in the settlement went through a number of phases with respect to the degree of involvement of international and local aid actors (Kaiser, forthcoming). The Government of Uganda (GoU) remained strongly present throughout (Kaiser, 2006). Most of the field research on which this chapter is based was conducted in the Kiryandongo Refugee Settlement in Masindi District, Uganda. Initial ethnographic research, carried out in 1996–97, has been followed up with additional linked studies for which field research was conducted in 2002, 2006, 2008 and 2012.[3]

After the signing of the Comprehensive Peace Agreement in Sudan in 2005, Sudanese refugees in neighbouring countries were soon being encouraged to sign up for voluntary repatriation, and over the succeeding years many did so and returned to Sudan. In July 2011, after a vote on secession the previous year, the new state of South Sudan was born. If one includes the larger numbers of internally displaced people returning to the south from areas around Khartoum and elsewhere, several millions of people 'came home' between 2005 and 2012 (UNHCR, 2013). Their experiences of exile were diverse, and fault lines remain visible between groups whose perception is that they have not yet benefited from the peace dividend which was to repay them for the suffering of their exile.

Most of the refugee population came from very underdeveloped rural areas in southern Sudan. Refugees reported having lived very different lives there, with extended families living much more collaboratively, with communal eating and working a much more common feature of life than later became the case. The dearth of available social services, including secondary schools, meant that movement in and out of the village was routine for some sections of the population, but very uncommon for subsistence farmers and the less well educated or connected members of the community. Labour migration was also practised by some residents, and many people had previous experience of forced migration, from as early as the late 1950s. While most also spent the majority of this period of exile in Uganda in a rural refugee settlement, not all have straightforwardly repatriated to 'the village' since 2005. Just as their experiences of exile have been varied and increasingly incorporated encounters with wider Ugandan society (via education, employment, family networks, business activities, etc.), so have their post-independence strategies been highly varied and differentiated.

Research approach and field methods

This research has become a *de facto* longitudinal study, in the sense that it has focused on similar themes for related groups of people over a very long period of time. What unifies the successive and linked studies is a general interest in the ways in which refugee groups have constructed and understood their own changing situations over time, and offered an active response to them. As such, the ethnographic research approach and set of methodologies have been an invaluable tool in helping to understand the perspective of refugees in these communities. Over many years I have carried out variously, participant observation (initially by living and working in the settlement as a school teacher), structured, semi-structured and informal interviews, focus groups and other qualitative research strategies, including the use of photographs, and a focus on material and cultural forms. In recent years, it has also been possible and necessary to diversify to include the use of technologies such as mobile phones, Facebook, and so on, especially with respect to refugees who have moved out of the settlement and settled in urban centres in East Africa, or moved to third countries in other parts of the world.

It should be noted that I have never set out explicitly to study 'the family', though this is, of course, a staple of anthropological work, with its interest in kinship and alliance groups, social relations, and so on. Over the years, a number of issues and insights have emerged from conversations and formal research activities on topics connected to family membership, structure and management. For this reason, among others, I feel quite strongly that we need to locate family issues in relation to the wider socio-political economy of situations of forced migration. People who become forced migrants are subject to a number of internal and external pressures, including the ways in which they are received by refugee hosting states and international and national aid providers. The ways in which, and extent to which these actors consciously or unconsciously frame families as a subject of their response, also have important consequences for how policies and programmes are structured and delivered. In this sense, it is crucial that we understand the extent to which different actors understand family structures, the pressures families face and the ways that forced migrants respond in these terms.

The family in international and refugee law and practice

At the level of international law, the defence of the idea of the integrity of the family is clear. As the Universal Declaration of Human Rights of 1948

186   *Tania Kaiser*

(UDHR48, Art. 16(3)) states, 'The family is the natural and fundamental group unit of society and is entitled to protection by society and the State.' As Jastram specifies, 'A family's right to live together is protected by international human rights and humanitarian law. There is universal consensus that, as the fundamental unit of society, the family is entitled to respect, protection, assistance, and support' (Jastram, 2003). As might therefore be expected, UNHCR reflects international law by asserting and defending the right to a family life, and to family unity and integrity.

> It is a generally agreed fact that the family is the fundamental unit of society entitled to protection by society and the State. Following separation caused by forced displacement such as from persecution and war, family reunification is often the only way to ensure respect for a refugee's right to family unity. Separation of family members during forced displacement and flight can have devastating consequences on peoples' well-being and ability to rebuild their lives.
>
> (UNHCR, 2012)

But how can we universally define the family? Fourlanos suggests that there is no international legal definition of the family, because 'a universally accepted concept of family can hardly be said to exist' (1986: 88). This makes generalising across cases inevitably complicated. The social unit defined as 'family' may not be the same in different places, for different peoples and at different times. Despite this, there exists an emphasis in much of the legal writing on the category of the nuclear family (or some version of it). This constructed version of family is also visible and influential in the way that humanitarian actors understand and engage with the category. Despite some interest in understanding the socio-cultural systems and practices of refugee groups by specific aid actors, it remains the case that at the level of policy and the delivery of programmes, the family is imagined first and foremost as consisting of a set of parents and their children, in short, a nuclear family. For UNHCR, the implications between different possible definitions are significant:

> [I]n some jurisdictions and cultures the term 'family' is interpreted relatively broadly to include extended relatives, spouses in polygamous marriages, same sex or common law couples, but in others, the term is restricted to 'nuclear' family members, spouses and minor children. Almost all national and international authorities have accepted that the members of the nuclear family, that is, the spouse and dependent children are included in the concept of 'family'.
>
> (UNHCR, 2008: 2)

UNHCR's concern for the integrity of family life is predominantly expressed via a commitment to activities relating to family reunification in both the developed and developing world (UNHCR, 2011). It is noted by them that

Crisis? Families and forced migration   187

family unity contributes to other desirable outcomes such as positive integration experiences, though some scholars have pointed to tensions between individual's rights in this respect and the interests of states in controlling immigration (Cholewinski, 2002). The contemporary politics of immigration control to developed states is such that the principle of family unity is now frequently undermined by governments in the race to convince the general public that they are tightening immigration windows. In consequence, families are deliberately divided, with the children of parents of different nationality at risk of exclusion from the home country of one of them (Grove White, 2013).

Beyond the work that it does encouraging and supporting family reunification, UNHCR policy explicitly addresses the implications of its other legal and political decisions in terms of their consequences for family unity. For example, the organisation recently published a note specifying that family unity should not be incidentally undermined in contexts where the cessation clause is declared and a refugee situation is legally brought to an end on the basis that solutions are now available to forced migrants (UNHCR, 2011).

Bureaucratic and legalistic responses to the experiences of refugee families are framed by the highly securitised discourse around immigration and asylum in the developed world. In this context, the separation of families as a result of forced migration, and the practical steps which can be taken at the legal and operational level to reunite them, are the prime policy and political issue. One of the most obvious ways that this is expressed in policy is in relation to the adjudication of asylum claims by refugee children where the child protection norms require that their 'best interests' are the overriding concern. This can mean that children's asylum claims are initially favourably received by States, but does not guarantee that their protection will extend into adulthood. Much of the fairly limited existing literature on forced migration and 'family' issues specifically focuses on the experience and needs of refugee children (UNHCR, 2007, 2012). Their position in social and familial units is much less considered.

Crisis and forced migration: perspectives from the Acholi case

To begin with, there is the fact of refugee-hood; a political and security crisis of some sort has usually precipitated flight in the context of conflict-induced forced migration. Then there is the question of what, in the context of now protracted exile in a refugee settlement, constitutes or 'counts' as a crisis, in the eyes of refugee groups and other actors. We may expect to see differences in the way that refugees and humanitarian, political and institutional actors construct or understand 'crisis'. Arguably, for institutional actors, crisis tends to relate to logistical or externally driven (including funding-related) crises, while for refugees they may refer more widely and variously to security, political, livelihood and social phenomena. Here we focus more on the latter, arguably less-discussed aspects.

If we begin with the idea that people – who are embedded in families, clans and communities of kin – have always moved to a varying degree, then we

188   *Tania Kaiser*

need to recognise that crisis-induced migrations are likely to be continuous with these movements to some extent. They are likely to be oriented in similar directions where this is possible, and to be supported by existing networks of kin and opportunity (see also Monsutti, 2010 and Lubkemann, 2008). It therefore makes sense to tease out the consequences for families of crisis migration with explicit reference to both their non-mobile crisis responses and self-protection and their non-crisis migration histories and activities. As Monsutti notes, 'escape from violence is not necessarily incompatible with a real migratory strategy' (2010: 61), but rather,

> [M]igration is no longer seen as a mere passage from one location to another, but instead as a complex phenomenon characterized by recurrent and multi-directional movements during which a variety of links are woven. For example, the dispersal of family groups can be the result of a strategy aimed at diversifying resources and minimizing risks: it does not always lead to a weakening of social ties.
>
> (ibid.: 46)

In the context of forced migration, one is more or less obliged to think in terms of people being faced with multiple, overlapping or interlocking crises, all of which will bear on the family in the sense that the family is the social, affective and perhaps even aesthetic lens through which everything else is read. We therefore need to include in our consideration different types of crisis; social, security, political which may also evidently interact with each other. One critical crisis modality is the physical risks and assaults experienced by forced migrants, and the ways that they manage and respond to these. In the case of northern Uganda, Sudanese refugees were accommodated in a number of refugee camps and settlements, more or less in the line of fire by Ugandan rebel groups including the Lord's Resistance Army over many years. Navigating the violent politics of the host country can mean many things for refugees. It may mean that they are unable to reunify with family members trapped in insecure locations, or that aid will not be able to reach them, or that their own entre-preneurial activities may be constrained, or that violence will meet them in their ostensibly secure places of refuge. On numerous occasions refugees in Ugandan settlements have been targeted and killed by Uganda rebels. Several Sudanese refugees were abducted by the LRA, some managing to escape and return to their families. When the place of refuge is insecure, everything else is affected by this. Some of the inhabitants of Kiryandongo had taken the initiative to informally relocate there after exposure to danger in other camps and settlements.[4] This might have been the risk or experience of armed attack by a Ugandan rebel groups, or even the risk of forcible conscription by southern Sudanese militias. In general, relocation from one refugee settlement to another was prohibited by the Government of Uganda, and supported by the UNHCR only if a formal (and bureaucratically difficult) application process had been attempted and approved. Failing official recognition, some individuals remained registered for long periods at camps in insecure locations, and were left to decide privately each month whether their need for their food ration outweighed the risks of travelling across rebel-affected areas to collect it. People with extended family members settled closer to the Uganda–Sudan border worried constantly about their security. In the worst cases, the death of relatives at the border led to the arrival of new dependants at Kiryandongo households.

Is migration itself by definition a crisis for families? Given histories of labour and other forms of migration for education, training, or to access services, and the prolonged experience of conflict and forced migration and family dispersal for many, it is almost certainly too simplistic to view separation in and of itself as necessarily problematic (Lubkemann, 2008). One thing that seems to be clear in this case is that the fact of family separation in and of itself does not appear to have been defined as a crisis when this arises as part of the forced migration experience for Acholi people. Specific challenges are faced by dependants separated from care-givers, or where people whose emotional well-being depends on their remaining with family members (or other significant people). More generally, as long as important social and cultural roles and practices are preserved and remain meaningful, the physical presence of all family members may not be a pre-requisite. There are a number of ways that this scenario can be attained: by the remote or removed management of social requirements and relations, by the substitution of social actors for each other, by the modification of important social conventions to accommodate the absence (temporary or permanent) of key social, political or ritual actors. In sum, it may be more important for many Acholi that family relations and processes are carried out properly or well in their terms (*maber*), than that people who have been dispersed are reunited.

There are at least two aspects which we need to bear in mind: first, that there may be events or processes which are directly understood by Acholi refugees and returnees as a challenge to preferred family relations. These may not be directly caused by forced migration. For example, inter-generational tensions existed for many years in the settlement, between elders who felt that the younger generations failed to obey them as they ought to in the observation of marriage arrangements, and youths who railed against such constraints. These were described as signs of socio-cultural crisis and viewed as unwelcome social changes by the elder generation, but may not have been significantly different to experiences of rapidly changing local populations. Second, that crises of any kind identified and experienced by Acholi refugees are inevitably read and mediated by the clan-(*kaka*)-based social relations through which people identify themselves. However, not all families are the same, and not everyone within single clan groups agree on everything. We should expect to see variation within the family, and be aware of differences of perspectives based on age, gender and other forms of differentiation (Kaiser, forthcoming).

The remaining sections delve more deeply into the ethnographic material, to explore some important contexts in which family and ideas of crisis intersected in the case of the Sudanese Acholi at Kiryandongo in the 1990s and 2000s.

190   *Tania Kaiser*

It discusses in turn questions of definition and inclusion, the challenges presented by resettlement processes, and the creative ways found by refugee families to advance their developmental goals. This discussion is informed by ethnographic insights generated from the case of the Sudanese Acholi whose case is not represented here as 'typical' of refugee experience. However, the hope is that as they share with many other groups similar systems of descent, social organisation and cultural practices, their experiences may shed light on those of other people in similar circumstances.

How do Acholi families interact with crisis and forced migration?

For Acholi extended families or clans, as for many other groups, the family is a crucial reference point in all areas of life. One's status, reputation and network are heavily dependent on one's family, and social and other forms of capital also flow from membership of a well-positioned clan. Historically, and certainly in the pre-colonial period, the Acholi identified themselves as a group which practised decentralised political authority, and which consisted of both Royal and Commoner clans. In the pre-flight period in Sudan, refugees reported that their lives were organised around communal living and working to a relatively great extent. To this extent, it was predictable that extended families spent much of their time together, and that children were socialised into clan and social norms around the '*wang-o*' or fireplace. Displacement inevitably caused significant change, not least in these fundamental terms. Not all community members were able or willing to leave, and some departed for Kenya (in some cases, following former labour migration routes), or to Juba in the first instance. For the groups who arrived in Uganda in the late 1980s and early 1990s, the relative chaos and insecurity of journeys meant that families did not necessarily arrive together, and were not always allocated to the same refugee settlements. When some initial re-configurations had taken place and plots were allocated, they were distributed to 'households' comprising a (usually male) head, and a number of dependent adults and children. The opportunity for extended families to be co-resident was a matter of chance, depending on where plots were allocated in settlements. It became clear over time that some households had been constituted which included people who were not natural co-residents in this more dispersed model, and that some people had been separated from the people from whom they might have received more support.

One of the most obvious points of contention, if the family is conceptualised as a source of protection, security and mutual support, is which individuals are defined as members, and which are not. It might be supposed that the benefits of membership of a strong and supportive family structure, especially in the uncertain context of protracted exile, would be an inducement for individuals to claim their membership fairly forcefully. In this case, we should be mindful of which authorities within extended families or clan grouping (which in the case of the Acholi are patrilineal and patrilocal) have the power to accept or reject such claims.

Crisis? Families and forced migration 191

In the case of the Sudanese Acholi in exile in Uganda, family membership was as much about responsibility as it was about accessing benefits, and the range of activities influenced by clan membership was extensive. In the settlement context, routine communal agricultural activity was less practicable, with clan members living as much as several kilometres away from each other. However, sharing activities still took place despite physical constraints, albeit in modified forms. Clan members subdivided plots and exchanged pieces of land between them, to exploit ecological advantages, but also to spread risk against poor weather or crop infestations. It was often possible for individual elderly, young or sick people to be relocated unofficially within settlements, even though full-scale removal so that all family members could live together was ruled out by the prior occupation of nearby plots.

For much of the period of the settlement at Kiryandongo, not only were residential and agricultural plots allocated on the basis of membership of nuclear families, but food rations were also filtered through a 'head of household'. This patriarchal figure was generally male, might be polygamous, and at certain points was also called on to register (or not) for repatriation, and make other similarly important decisions on behalf of the household, which was broadly understood to mean 'the family'. In practice, of course, households were often constituted by a mixture of closely related and loosely related individuals, all of whom acted 'as if' they were members of a nuclear-type family structure for the benefit of the assistance providers and institutional actors. For the aid actors, it was presumably easier to work with these imposed and imagined social categories than it was to decipher and work with the more fluid and difficult to capture reality.

As Sample notes, 'As a result of high mortality, family groupings are very often not "nuclear". The refugee experience causes many families of choice or circumstance to be formed' (2007: 51). Some of the ways that this may happen are via mechanisms of fictive kinship in which individuals play the appropriate social roles of the family member whose part they are playing. An adopted son, for example, will show respect and deference to his adoptive father, and offer his labour in support of the head of household's economic projects for as long as he remains a 'family member'. In return, his adoptive father may be willing to try to provide him with the bride wealth he will need if he is to marry according to customary practice.

Inevitably, the search for adequate livelihoods frames much of the experience of exile in protracted situations like the Ugandan one. For the Sudanese, much of their time was spent searching for income-generating opportunities, protecting assets and farming. Over the long period of the Kiryandongo Settlement's existence, refugees received food rations or had them withdrawn, depending on local political and economic conditions. Budgeting to meet the full needs of refugee family members was extremely difficult for many, for reasons which I have set out elsewhere (Kaiser, 2007). Households sought to provide adequate food for their members, to share with needy neighbours and kin, as well as to access health and educational services when necessary.

192   *Tania Kaiser*

When economic conditions became particularly challenging within a given household, those individuals with weakest claim to family membership were most vulnerable.

For example, while it was commonly accepted that a wife should be able to benefit from the protection and support of her husband, her claim on him might be weaker if the marriage is not an official one, if she has no children by the man, or if there are other, more senior wives present in the household. In Uganda, reference is frequently made to the institution of 'refugee marriage', which may not be expected to outlast the refugee situation, but which may be the least worst option available to a single woman in the difficult conditions of exile. There will be variations on the extent to which women in such relationships can expect them to meet all of their needs. I was aware of a number of women whose 'refugee husbands' were not willing to also support children of previous relationships, or pay their school fees.

The ideal version of marriage arrangements involves the payment of cash or goods by the family of the man to the family of the woman (who will necessarily belong to a different clan), so the extent to which payment has been begun or completed will have an impact on how families are defined and enacted. The clan of an Acholi woman whose husband has not paid bride wealth for her will claim possession of her children, for example, while after payment they would count as members of his clan. Specific crises may emerge out of these kinds of scenarios, for example, if the wife dies before payments are completed, it may be unclear which clan will be able to secure the children. Acholi elders, and possibly official community leaders, may be called in to negotiate outcomes in such cases. They will also act in cases of other disputes within or between clan groups. Refugee settlements are often rather tense places, where dissatisfaction and resentment may characterise social relations within and between groups. This may emerge from local disagreements, fights about women, or from political disagreements relating to conflict dynamics in Sudan. It has been noted in a number of other refugee settings that incidences of witchcraft accusations are often seen to increase, and this itself can be seen as a sign of internal, perhaps existential crisis (Powles and Deakin, 2012). In 1996, refugees from the Achol-pii settlement in northern Uganda were abruptly settled at Kiryandongo, following catastrophic attacks on their settlement by the LRA. The additional pressure on resources and competition for position and authority led to some serious tensions between groups as the honeymoon period of solidarity and brotherhood waned. In this phase it was noticeably the case that accusations of poisoning, traditionally associated with the activities of malign spirits among the Acholi, dramatically increased.

A final point in this section is to note that family membership is performed very publicly in some socio-ritual activities in camp settings. In Kiryandongo, for instance, clan members tend to be seated together at funeral or wedding parties, and family members listed on a single ration card will be required by assistance providers to present themselves all together at registration and verification exercises.

Resettlement

Third country resettlement is used by UNHCR and refugee hosting states as a protection tool for a small minority of refugees who cannot be assured of safety in their first country of exile. Its high profile is due at least partly to the fact that it assumes an almost mythical status among some refugee groups, some of whom regard it as the over-riding goal to which they aspire while in exile (see Omata, 2012; Horst, 2006).

A number of administrative and bureaucratic mechanisms exist to manage and deliver resettlement programmes. Individuals may be resettled alone or with some family members, on the basis of their immediate and pressing security problems. They can be resettled as members of groups which have been defined as having priority status by one of the major resettlement countries (which include the USA, Canada, Australia, several of the Scandinavian countries, the UK and others). Alternatively, others join already resettled family members in third countries under a number of family re-unification schemes, whose parameters vary from country to country.

The practical or administrative process is highly dramatic for those involved, and is characterised by a series of critical decision-making stages, which affect the eventual outcome of applications. On paper the process sounds methodical and straightforward; applicants apply to UNHCR (or sometimes the IOM), for a resettlement place. Decisions are made on the basis of protection needs and the availability of places on specific national programmes (most of which have an annual quota). Once approved by a host country, applicants are security vetted and required to have medical tests. They need to acquire travel documents and wait for information about when and how they will travel.

In practice, for what are sometimes semi-literate refugees with poor understandings of the politics and bureaucratic process of international organisations and little access to objective information, the process can be incredibly opaque. Refugees often have to rely on other refugees and on the rumour mill, to have much sense of what the process is or should be, and may find it difficult, expensive and stressful to follow their own applications. They often languish for long periods, waiting for news, only to be summoned with virtually no notice to capital cities to undergo tests or vetting. Each of these stages may be long anticipated by refugees who have invested meagre resources in the process and for whom each letter, call or summons represents a crisis at some level. Depending on the resettlement route available, some individuals and families are obliged to make substantial investments against their hoped migration. Typical expenses, over and above local travel expenses when they are summoned for screening meetings, are the administrative costs associated with the paper application (including costly passport photographs), one or more kind of medical screening, travel documents and international flights for those reunifying with previously migrated family.

In the context of thinking about the way in which forced migration can be conceptualised and understood as a series of crises of varying kinds, it is not

194   *Tania Kaiser*

hard to see the road to resettlement as continuous with prior crises of politics and the family. Resettlement most directly affects the individuals concerned, but the social and political ripples extend widely across extended families and social groups. Not only do a wide range of people contribute to the application process in diverse ways (contributing to expenses, providing information and guidance, taking care of local responsibilities), but the consequences of an individual's resettlement can be momentous for family members in different locations. In addition to this, if and when resettlement is actually achieved, it engages the crossing of space and social systems and can be seen as entailing the fracturing and renegotiation of family relationships. A number of issues arise, some definitional, other practical.

Most obviously, resettlement may be hard won, but it also necessarily leads to painful separation for family members who have already suffered displacement and exile together. When individuals are resettled on the basis of a specific protection concern, family members are sorry to see them leave but also see them as having been delivered from political persecution, conscription by the military or other threats. When migration is seen more as a lifestyle choice or a step towards self-development, feelings can be more mixed. This may be most acute when older family members see younger family members leave, often taking children with them, due to their own fears that they may never see them again. Further, the elderly may feel the risk of the erosion of culture and social practices to which they are deeply attached, with the departure of younger family members. They themselves frequently refuse to resettle even when the opportunity exists, feeling that they are now too old to avail themselves of the obvious educational and professional opportunities on offer. Younger refugees are frequently summoned to meet elders from their communities prior to their departure, and cautioned against abandoning shared values and practices. They are often exhorted not to forget family members left behind, and the pressure to remit from third countries is never far away (Omata, 2011). While Acholi respondents in the settlement acknowledged the challenges faced by their resettled kin in getting established in their new homes, they also felt a sense of entitlement to support as they remained behind.

A number of pressing issues emerge in relation to the conceptualisation, definition and management of 'the family' when an individual is offered a resettlement place to a faraway developed country. One of the first structural issues is how 'family' is defined by the receiving state. As indicated above, applicants encounter a number of bureaucratic actors along the road to resettlement. In the Ugandan context, these are the UNHCR, the IOM and representatives from the receiving country. The administrative framework employed is not particularly sensitive or friendly to the idea that 'the family' might constitute something other than a nuclear family with immediate close relatives in this context. To some extent, inclusion and exclusion as 'family' member have to be redefined to meet the bureaucratic requirements of the new state. How people are moved from category to category to construct this simple and 'legible' family which is intelligible to the relevant authorities can

Crisis? Families and forced migration 195

be a complicated process (Scott, 1998). The story of James Opio and his family exemplifies the effort and complication that this entails.[5]

James was a relatively well-established businessman in Kiryandongo in the early 2000s, when his long-submitted resettlement application started to move. An entrepreneur in the settlement, he supported his three wives and numerous children by running a successful pharmacy shop, and was a well-known figure in the settlement. He expressed regret that he had never completed his education because of the war in Sudan, but hoped that his children would have better chances in this respect than he himself. When his resettlement application was successful and he was offered a place on the Canadian resettlement scheme, he was initially thrilled about the prospects and opportunities this offered his family. As time passed, and the reality of the offer started to sink in, he had serious misgivings about leaving his business, extended family and friends and the life he knew, for an uncertain future. Unlike many refugees, he saw that life in Canada was unlikely to be easy for a poor English speaker with no formal education to speak of. His family, however, urged him not to pass up the opportunity which so many others were fighting for.

Practical and social obstacles remained. The resettlement offer referred to James, his wife, and their children and other close dependants. At the time the offer was made, James was in dispute with his third wife, who refused to travel with him. This left two wives to plan for, in a process in which polygamy was not accepted. The only option was to name the second wife a dependent sister, and to claim all the children of the two marriages as the product of the union with the first (and, now on paper, only) wife. This need to dissemble and to subsequently perform the deceit under the scrutiny of the social service support staff in Canada led to serious tensions within the family. The plight of the third wife was also a burden, as James remained financially responsible for her and was under moral and family pressure to meet his responsibilities to her adequately and in a timely manner. His own feelings about leaving his children of this third marriage may be imagined to have been very painful, as he was an active and doting father. Nevertheless, despite all his reservations and the contorted way in which the bureaucracy had to be navigated, he felt ultimately that by going to Canada he could offer more to all his children by way of support and opportunities, than by remaining in Uganda.

We can see the ingenuity and flexibility which was practised by this family, while also recognising that it did, in some ways, leave the family needing to redefine itself internally, as well as in relation to institutional actors. This aspect only increased as time passed after the family moved to Canada, with James delighted by his children's academic progress there, but also alarmed by the changes that he could see taking place within the family as a result. His own status in Canadian society was relatively low, since he could only hope to access rather menial jobs, and he felt strongly as the years passed that his children's respect for him was not what he hoped for. He looked back on the social, familial and community sanctions which would have supported his position as a respected father and elder had he stayed in Uganda, and

196 *Tania Kaiser*

regretted at least some of the differences that he saw and experienced on a daily basis.

Perhaps the hardest blow, for James, was the discovery when peace finally came to Sudan in 2005, and some of his family in the Ugandan camps registered for voluntary repatriation to their country, that his now rather integrated teenage children in Canada had no interest at all in returning. On the contrary, he reported that they viewed Sudan and Africa as a whole as dangerous, poverty-stricken and unappealing as a destination. James' substantial effort to find opportunities and security for his family had been successful to a large extent, but had also led to the alienation of the younger generation from his homeland and culture.

Families responding, and providing solutions to the livelihood challenges and opportunities of exile

In the context of protracted exile, it should be expected that for refugees, one of the major ways that they experience forced migration is as a crisis of livelihood opportunities, as a crisis of their personal development. For the Sudanese in Uganda, after the initial phase of settlement life in which most people received humanitarian support in the form of food aid and other inputs, livelihood activities were diverse and usually employed in combination. Where people could access business opportunities or paid employment from the settlement they did, but agricultural activity remained the main source of income over the years for most. As exile lengthened, it became more and more common for refugee individuals to move out of formal settlements and become involved in various ways with economic projects in local markets, or further afield in urban centres. By the early 2000s, the Government of Uganda had shifted its position to allow those refugees who could support themselves, to do so in urban areas without returning them to settlements. It was very common for extended families to retain a household base in refugee settlements like Kiryandongo, however, so that they remained part of the registered refugee population, and so that schooling children or those who were mainly occupied with farming could benefit from settlement resources of these kinds. This tendency for refugees to scatter themselves beyond the settlement became even more marked after the signing of the 2005 Comprehensive Peace Agreement in Sudan, and the search for durable solutions started to look increasingly like one that would end in multi-local outcomes for many refugee families (Kaiser, 2010).

The way that family structures and networks were employed during this period can be seen as a series of pragmatic solutions to some of the logistical, practical and developmental challenges provoked by long-term exile. The failures of the well-documented 'Self-Reliance Strategy' in Uganda meant that as the length of their exile became protracted, refugees never became sufficiently secure to be able to meet their immediate needs. Nuclear families allocated plots in the early 1990s had significantly increased in size as the years passed,

Crisis? Families and forced migration 197

but no further agricultural land was made available to them even as soil became exhausted and yields declined. The kinds of income-generating activities available from the settlement itself were limited and limiting: running a small shop, bar or kiosk or other small business; doing day labour, running a video hall, offering bicycle taxi rides, brick making, carpentry, and so on. Slightly more lucrative was the illegal burning of charcoal, or engaging in business at a greater scale, but this required capital and contacts. Extended families therefore creatively distributed members where possible outside the settlement, in ways which contributed to the likelihood of family security in physical and livelihood terms. This also offered the possibility of fulfilling some of the ambitions or aspirations of individual family members, but not everyone's desires could be accommodated. In some cases this literally meant a clan elder making decisions on how best to deploy individuals so that a range of positive outcomes were achieved across the family, including the generation of income, the maintenance of ties and claims on property in South Sudan, the education and training needs of younger family members, and so on. Families could attempt to minimise the risk of sudden reversals by having members in a number of different locations, and engaged in a range of activities. Risk-spreading behaviours are, of course, observable in a wide range of migratory contexts and these are typical strategies (de Haas, 2010; Glick Schiller and Faist, 2010). It was generally considered crucial for families to retain a significant investment in agricultural activity, as this was the likely fallback if employment or business activities failed or were cut short.

Where extended families or clans were directed by elder males in the 'traditional' way, some tensions were occasionally visible when younger members were directed to participate in the family venture in ways that they did not favour. After the signing of the CPA in 2005, for example, many young men wanted to set off for Juba, where they hoped they could make their fortunes in the post-conflict soon-to-be capital city. As some Kiryandongo-based elders noted at the time, however, not all able-bodied youths could be spared. Some were needed to provide protection from thieves or interlopers (for example, in the 2000s, refugees were frequently intimidated and harassed by Ugandan pastoral groups who passed through the settlement with cattle, often causing damage to crops and property), and labour for remaining elders, women and children. It was frustrating for one young teacher of my acquaintance to feel that he was missing the best chance that he had of being employed and gaining new skills in an exciting political environment, for example, when he was pressured by elders of his clan to meet the wider needs of the clan and remain in the settlement in 2007. He reluctantly did so, and later returned to rural Eastern Equatoria with his young family, the moment to capitalise on employment opportunities in the new capital having passed in his estimation.

In this context, what was visible was a clan management strategy based on diversifying risk and spreading family resources, in terms of both capital and people across potentially productive spatial lines. Neither national nor

198   *Tania Kaiser*

international borders represented an obstacle to this dispersal, since social and political capital and mechanisms could be employed to navigate these. For the Acholi, the existence of the international border between Uganda and Sudan was simply not considered problematic. In the context of an uncertain post-conflict moment, on the contrary, it could be seen as a valuable form of security for individuals with networks and opportunities potentially available on both sides. Willingness to adopt a both/and attitude to the search for durable solutions – in which families actively explored the possibility of seeking to benefit simultaneously from the different advantages of life in both Uganda and Sudan post 2005 – meant that the teamwork of extended family management was a powerful asset. If we return to the idea that in contexts of exile, the main priority for the family is to reunite as quickly as possible, this outcome may be surprising, even radical. It certainly supports the idea that it may well make sense to conceptualise family units, not only as fragile, vulnerable entities in need of support and protection, but also as vibrant and meaningful social formations which may be one of the solutions to the challenges of forced migration for refugees, given conducive circumstances.

Despite this more nuanced framing of the institution of the family in exile, one also needs to be aware of the social risks consequent to this kind of transformation. One of the inevitable consequences of the dispersal of family members in the ways outlined above was that some refugee settlement households were left composed mainly of the very old, the very young, or the sick or disabled. The absence of many of the workers – male and female – may have secured the extended family financially, but also had implications for the extent to which valued social and ritual activities could take place in their absence. While it is almost certainly the case that the historical practices of child socialisation around the communal hearth or '*wang-o*' had massively decreased during the period of exile, and while it had become relatively common practice to send children to secondary boarding school in Ugandan towns and cities, including Kampala when this was economically viable,[6] the kinds of transformations noted above have had a significant impact on how some refugee children now grow up.

In one fairly dramatic example, almost all of the children of a single relatively wealthy extended family, formerly resident at Kiryandongo, now attend boarding schools in Kampala, Uganda, while their parents are mainly resident in South Sudan. Because the journey between the two is long and expensive, the children make the trip only once a year, spending their school holidays in a private house in Gulu, northern Uganda, under the care of only one of their mothers. The relative distance between the children and their immediate and extended family is therefore great, both socially and physically, and one wonders what consequences may subsequently be visible in terms of intra-family relations and practices. Evidently, we should be wary of ascribing causality for social changes to a single social phenomenon, and this is a topic which will need close observation over time.

Conclusion

Insights produced by ethnographic research with Sudanese Acholi refugees in Uganda over more than 15 years suggest that the notion of 'crisis' may be understood and interpreted rather differently by different social actors. While humanitarian and institutional actors may frame crisis in terms of the immediate physical and security needs of refugee groups and respond with technical and material solutions, refugees' conceptualisations can be seen to be deeper and broader. Findings in the Acholi case suggest that social and intra-familial relations and practices hold a high priority for refugees, and are considered worth protecting in times of crisis, even at the expense of more apparently rational objectives. In a cash-poor environment, for example, it is nevertheless considered worthwhile to invest scarce resources in rather elaborate funeral rituals, in which families perform their unity, position and identities.

Since social relations among the Acholi tend to be mediated by biologically or fictively related people, any crisis – whether political, security-related, livelihood-related or socio-symbolic – will be understood and responded to through the language, structures and priorities of families and clan groups. It is also inevitably the case that within single refugee populations, there will be significant variation in how crisis is defined by groups with different priorities and interests. Equally, even in a single socio-political context, refugee populations are also not all the same and the way that they conceive of themselves as groups may also change over time, including in relation to forms of differentiation such as class, ethnic identity, and socio-economic status, and so on. Both 'family' and 'crisis', then, should be seen as mutable categories which are open to interpretation and challenge. In one notable example, an international NGO which attempted, with only good intentions, to intervene in the settlement with a Sexual and Gender Based Violence Programme (SGBV), found itself precipitating a social crisis in which families were split on their right to intervene, the validity of the message of gender empowerment they wanted to share, and on how gender violence should be defined at all in this context.

Forced migration is recognised to hold the possibility of transformational effects. The relationship between crisis and social upheaval may be seen as providing the backdrop for such social change, which may be expressed in both negative and positive terms by different actors. One important finding of the ethnographic material in the case of the Sudanese Acholi in Uganda is that it suggests that families are likely to look quite different at the end of their forced migration experience, than they did prior to it. However, families do not just react to external changes but the identification and deployment of family networks are key to the process of self-protection, livelihood management, alliance and network building and self-development throughout the period of exile (though in different ways at different times) and into the 'durable solutions' phase (and see also Newhouse, 2012, on post-return strategies in South Sudan). What has been very noticeable in the denouement of the Sudanese refugee story in Uganda has been the dynamism of refugees and former

200   *Tania Kaiser*

refugees. Many still do not reside in South Sudan, or if they do so, they may have moved away from rural areas to cities. Still others have taken up citizenship in third countries, but pursue their South Sudanese identities with enthusiasm from afar. Many intend to return, temporarily or permanently, in the future.

This means that refugees, returnees and others will reside in different spatial configurations, conceive of their social networks and opportunities differently, and have found new ways of identifying and protecting valued social relationships and practices. As the material presented above about the employment of new transnational social formations suggests, one very clear feature is that the family, while transformed, remains a critical and meaningful category in crisis management as in life more generally. For this reason among others, we may view family structures as resources or potential solutions to some of the challenges of forced migration, rather than seeing the reconstruction of families at a literal and physical level as the only required response to them.

Notes

1 The UNHCR's *Handbook* does state with respect to aid distribution that 'The target of the commodity distribution should be towards the family or household unit, however, assumptions should not be made about family size or structure' (UNHCR, 2007: 228).

2 In fairness, it ought to be noted that considerable efforts are carried out by some organisations to understand and work with locally significant social structures and authority holders even in the context of humanitarian work.

3 Thanks are given to funders including the AHRC and SOAS, to the Government of Uganda and the UNCST, staff at UNHCR and NGOs, and, most of all, to all the refugees and Ugandan citizens who generously participated in the research.

4 Kiryandongo's location in Masindi District (now Kiryandongo District), placed it south of the Victoria Nile, a natural boundary between it and rebel-affected territory. As such, it was perceived to be, and was, safer than many of the other refugee settlements closer to the Sudanese border.

5 All names and identifying characteristics have been changed in order to protect the confidentiality of informants.

6 In the early days of the settlement, UNHCR supported a scholarship programme to enable secondary students to pursue their education outside the settlement in the absence of any local opportunities. As the settlement's Self-Help Secondary School became established in the late 1990s, UNHCR shifted to focus on supporting the provision of secondary education mainly in this context. Various other organisations, mainly church groups, continued to provide some scholarships for boarding schools outside the settlement. By the late 2000s, a fair number of children were being sent to private boarding schools funded by the remittances of overseas relatives.

References

Cholewinski, R. (2002) 'Family Reunification and Conditions Placed on Family Members: Dismantling a Fundamental Human Right', *European Journal of Migration and Law* 4: 271–90.

Cresswell, T. (2006) *On the Move: Mobility in the Western World.* London: Routledge.

Crisis? Families and forced migration 201

de Haas, H. (2010) 'Migration and Development: A Theoretical Perspective', *International Migration Review* 44(1): 227–64.

Fourlanos, G. (1986) 'Sovereignty and the Ingress of Aliens', doctoral dissertation, Stockholm, Sweden: Almqvist & Wiksell International.

Glick Schiller, N. and Faist, T. (eds) (2010) *Migration, Development and Transnationalisation*. Oxford: Berghahn Books.

Grove White, R. (2013) 'How the Government's Immigration Rules Are Tearing Families Apart', *The New Statesman*. Available at: http://www.newstatesman.com/politics/2013/06/how-governments-immigration-rules-are-tearing-families-apart.

Horst, C. (2006) *Transnational Nomads: How Somalis Cope with Refugee Life in the Dadaab Camps of Kenya*. Oxford: Berghahn Books.

ICRC (2011) *The International Tracing Service and the ICRC*. International Committee of the Red Cross Resource Centre. Available at: http://www.icrc.org/eng/resources/documents/feature/2011/its-feature-280809.htm.

Jastram, K. (2003) 'Family Unity: The New Geography of Family Life', *Migration Information Source*. Washington, DC: Migration Policy Institute. Available at: http://www.migrationinformation.org/Feature/display.cfm?ID=118 (accessed 25 March 2008).

Kaiser, T. (2006) 'Between a Camp and a Hard Place: Rights, Livelihood and Experiences of the Local Settlement System for Long-Term Refugees in Uganda', *Journal of Modern African Studies* 44(4): 597–621.

——(2007) '"Moving up and Down Looking for Money": Making a Living in a Ugandan Refugee Camp', in J. Staples (ed.) *Livelihoods at the Margins: Surviving the City*. Walnut Creek, CA: Left Coast Press, pp. 215–36.

——(2010) 'Dispersal, Division and Diversification: Durable Solutions and Sudanese Refugees in Uganda', *Journal of East African Studies* 4(1): 44–60.

——(forthcoming) 'Opportunities and Risk: Enacting Socio-Cultural Transformation in Refugee Camps in Uganda', *Social Analysis*.

Lindley, A. (2011) 'Between a Protracted and a Crisis Situation: Policy Responses to Somali Refugees in Kenya', *Refugee Survey Quarterly* 30(4): 14–49.

Long, K. (2011) 'Permanent Crises? Unlocking the Protracted Displacement of Refugees and Internally Displaced Persons', Policy Overview, Refugee Studies Centre, University of Oxford.

Lubkemann, S.C. (2008) *Culture in Chaos: An Anthropology of the Social Condition in War*. Chicago: University of Chicago Press.

Monsutti, A. (2010) 'The Transnational Turn in Migration Studies and the Afghan Social Networks', in D. Chatty and B. Finlayson (eds) *Dispossession and Displacement: Forced Migration in the Middle East and North Africa*. British Academy, Occasional Paper No. 14. Oxford: Oxford University Press.

Newhouse, L. (2012) 'Urban Attractions: Returnee Youth, Mobility and the Search for a Future in South Sudan's Regional Towns', *New Issues in Refugee Research*, Series No. 232. Geneva: UNHCR.

Omata, N. (2011) 'Online Connections for Remittances', *Forced Migration Review* 38.

——(2012) 'Repatriation and Integration of Liberian Refugees from Ghana: The Importance of Personal Networks in the Country of Origin', *Journal of Refugee Studies* 26: 265–82.

Powles, J. and Deakin, R. (2012) 'Seeking Meaning: An Anthropological and Community-Based Approach to Witchcraft Accusations and Their Prevention in Refugee Situations', *New Issues in Refugee Research*, Series No. 235. Geneva: UNHCR.

202 *Tania Kaiser*

Sample, E. (2007) 'State Practice and the Family Unity of African Refugees', *Forced Migration Review* 28: 50–2.

Scott, J. (1998) *Seeing Like a State: How Certain Schemes to Improve the Human Condition Have Failed.* New Haven, CT: Yale University Press.

Staver, A. (2008) 'Family Reunification: A Right for Forced Migrants?', RSC Working Paper, Series No 51.

UNHCR (2007) *Handbook for Emergencies.* Geneva: United Nations High Commissioner for Refugees. Available at: http://www.unhcr.org/472af2972.html.

——(2008) 'Challenges and Opportunities in Family Reunification', discussion paper at the Annual Tripartite Consultations on Resettlement, Geneva, 30 June–2 July 2008. Available at: http://www.unhcr.org/cgi-bin/texis/vtx/home/opendocPDFViewer. html?docid=4fbcf9619&query=family.

——(2011) *Note on Suspension of "General Cessation" Declarations in Respect of Particular Persons or Groups Based on Acquired Rights to Family Unity.* Geneva: United Nations High Commissioner for Refugees. Available at: http://www.unhcr. org/refworld/docid/4eef5a1b2.html (accessed 19 June 2012).

——(2012) *Refugee Family Reunification. UNHCR's Response to the European Commission Green Paper on the Right to Family Reunification of Third Country Nationals Living in the European Union (Directive 2003/86/EC).* Geneva: United Nations High Commissioner for Refugees. Available at: http://www.refworld.org/docid/4f55e1cf2. html (accessed 26 May 2013).

——(2013) *UNHCR Country Operations Profile – South Sudan.* Geneva: United Nations High Commissioner for Refugees. Available at: http://www.unhcr.org/pages/ 4e43cb466.html.

Index

Abu-Lughod, J. L. 26
Aegean islands 30
Afghanistan 161, 163
Africa 26–7, 38–9, 48, 51–2, 56, 59, 63, 122, 127, 166, 196
Africa Day 140
Africa Governance Monitoring and Advocacy Project (AGMAP) 141
African Centre for Migration and Society 137
African National Congress (ANC) 140, 145, 149
African Peer Review Mechanism Monitoring Project 141
African Union 57
Africans 140, 143–4
agriculture 34–5, 37–9, 51–2, 59, 100–1, 127, 191, 196–7
Ahmed, S. S. 57
aid agencies 8, 54, 58–60, 65, 191
Aideed, M. F. 52, 54
AI 73–92
Albania 12, 120, 165
Albuja, S. 14, 64
Alliot-Marie, M. 118
AMISOM 57, 62
Amnesty International 128
Anatolia 27–30
anomie 3, 9
anthropology 5, 185
Anti-Kidnapping Law 80
Apartheid 137, 143–4, 147–9
Arab Gulf 31–2, 36, 38–9, 48, 53
Arab migrations 14, 26, 28, 31, 40
Arab Spring 115, 117–19, 123–6, 128, 131
Arab uprisings 1, 15, 24, 30, 33, 39–40
Arendt, H. 161
Ariel Award 81

Armenians 27, 29–30, 32, 38
ASEAN+3 94
Ashton, C. 118
Asia 26–7, 31, 56, 93–114, 127–8, 130
Asians 145
Assyrians 27, 29–30
asylum seekers 6, 8, 53; Somalia 55, 61, 63; Mexico 84; EU borders 129, 131; South Africa 144–5; border closures 159, 163–4, 166, 170–5, 177; family issues 187
Ataturk, K. 163
Australia 130, 193
autochthony 148–9

Ba'athist regime 32
Bahrain 31, 117
Balkans 27–9, 32, 166, 174
Bangladesh 101, 130
bankruptcy 95, 109
banks 95
Bantu 51–2
Barre, M. S. 47, 49, 51, 64
Baumann, Z. 25
Ben Ali, Z. 118, 125
Berlusconi, S. 24
Black, R. 25
Black Sea 27
Boats4People 117, 130
border closure 15–17, 53, 158–80
border controls 115–35, 143
Bosnia 27
Bosnia and Herzegovina 165
Bouazizi, M. 117
Bourdieu, P. 119
Brassett, J. 7
Britain 6, 28–30, 32–3, 118
British Somaliland Protectorate 48

204 *Index*

Bulgaria 27–8
Bulgarian Turks 164
bureaucracy 8–9, 82, 115, 117, 120, 123–6, 130–2, 159, 165, 182, 187–8, 193–4
Burma 108–10
Burmese 100, 103, 108–9
Burundi 163
Bush, G. W. 171
Busuttil, S. 121–3
Buthelezi, M. 144

Calderón, F. 77, 82, 85–6
Cambodia 100–1, 103, 110
Cameron, D. 118, 121
Canada 84, 130, 193, 195–6
capitalism 3, 33, 93–4, 97–8, 104–5, 110, 127
care chains 101
Caucasia 27–8
Central America 84
Centre for Policy Studies (CPS) 141
Ceuppens, B. 148
Ceuta 120
Chad 130, 163
Chaldaeans 27
Chan, K. W. 104
Chang, D. 15, 17, 93–114
Chatty, D. 28, 30
Chechnyans 30
China 93, 96–9, 101, 105, 110
Chinese 98, 105
Choucha camp 117, 125, 127, 129–31
Christian Aid 13
Christians 27, 29–30, 32
Circassians 28–30, 32
circular migration 38
citizenship 56, 143, 146–8, 161, 176, 200
Citizenship, Democracy and Narco-Violence Survey 74
civil servants 9
civil society 11, 76, 79, 85, 117, 131, 136, 139, 141
civil war 4, 47–9, 51–2, 63, 66, 108, 130, 143, 164
clanship 47–9, 51, 54–5, 65, 189–92, 197, 199
class struggle 3, 33–4, 101, 107, 146, 149
climate change 16
Clinton, H. 86
CNN effect 60
cohesion 136–57
Cold War 47, 52, 64, 116, 160, 162–3
Collier, P. 4

Colombia 75
Colombianisation 86
colonialism 9, 14, 16, 24–6, 28, 30, 32–4, 40, 47–8, 98, 143, 149
communism 140, 162
conscription 9, 27, 188, 194
Consolidated Inter-Agency Appeal 54
constant crisis 14
Convention on the Status of Refugees 158, 177
coping strategies 7, 54, 58–9, 88
corruption 56, 73, 75, 78–81, 88, 105, 144
cosmopolitanism 27
Cossacks 28
crisis: and migration 1–19; political 1–19, 24–6, 29, 46–7, 51–2, 57, 64, 82, 85–7, 158–80; conceptualisation of 2, 25; economic 2–4, 7, 9–16, 18, 24–6, 29, 31–6, 46, 58, 79, 93–114; management of 3, 7, 9–11, 16; categories of 6, 16, 124–31; management 7, 25, 93–114; environmental 12, 16, 46, 59–60, 79, 84; labelling 15, 115–26, 128–32, 158; Middle East 24–45; North Africa 24–45; Somalia 46–72; Mexico 73–4; narratives 78–81; EU borders 115–35; social construction 136–57; manufactured 158–80; responses 170–6; forced migration 181–202
crisis migration 1, 12–13, 18–19, 46, 188
Crisis Migration Project 13
crisis-multipliers 125
Croatia 165
Crusades 24
Curzon, Lord 28

Daarood 49–51, 65
Dadaab camp 130, 174–5
Darfur 130
De Freitas, M. 143
debt 95–6
decoupling 94
democracy 106, 108, 117–18, 140, 142
Democratic Republic of Congo (DRC) 163
Denmark 119
deportation 102–3, 106–9, 141, 144, 169
developmentalism 4, 8, 10–11, 32
diasporas 40, 46, 48, 55–7, 59–62, 69
disasters 2, 4, 12, 60, 63, 136, 144
displacement 1, 5, 8; concepts 12–16, 18; MENA region 25, 28, 30–2, 38, 40;

Somalia 46–7, 49–57, 60–1, 63, 66–8; Mexico 73–92; family issues 181, 190
Dlamini-Zuma, N. 144
downsizing 105
drought 1, 7, 14, 18, 46, 49, 51, 54, 59–61, 64, 66–7
drug cartels 14, 73, 75–8, 80–3, 85–8
Druze 29–30
durable solutions 7, 12, 55, 61, 65, 182–3, 196, 198–9

East 26, 28–30, 40, 98
East Africa 1, 51, 59, 166–7, 185
East Asia 15, 93–114
East Timor 101
economic crises 1, 15, 39, 79, 103–10, 143
Egypt 14, 24, 26, 31–6, 39–40, 117–18, 125, 127, 163
Egyptian Centre for Economic Studies 35
Egyptians 32, 36–7, 39, 129
emergencies 3, 15, 17; MENA region 24–5; mentality 47, 65, 158–82; Somalia 52–5, 60, 65, 68; EU borders 116, 119–22, 124, 132; South Africa 136, 139
employment 13, 31–2, 35–6; MENA region 39–40; Somalia 52, 55–6, 68; East Asia 97, 101–2, 104, 106, 108; EU borders 127; South Africa 144–5, 148–9; families 183, 185, 196–7
encampment policy 55
energy crisis 115
energy resources 25
Enlightenment 29
Entry/Exit System (EES) 123
Eritrea 128, 130, 163
Estrada, L. 81
Ethiopia 48–9, 52–3, 56–8, 61–2, 166
Ethiopians 49
ethnic cleansing 28, 30, 32, 165
ethnography 5, 12, 16, 184–5, 189–90, 199
Europe 6, 9, 24–31, 37–40, 53, 61, 94, 163–4, 166–7, 173
European Border Surveillance (EUROSUR) 123
European Commission 115, 118–23
European Council 119
European External Action Service (EEAS) 118
European Parliament 121–3
European Union (EU) 15, 95–6, 115–35, 173, 177

Europeans 30
exchanges 29–31
exile 196–8

failed states 86
Familia Machoacana 80
families 2–3, 7–10, 12; concepts 16, 18; MENA region 26, 34, 37–8, 40; Somalia 53, 55–6, 60, 67; Mexico 74–5, 80, 82–3, 87; EU borders 130; mass refugee influx 166; forced migration 181–202
famine 46, 51–2, 59–62, 64–6, 68, 166–7, 175
FAO 59
Farouk, King 33
Federation of Asian Domestic Workers Unions (FADWU) 106
femicides 75, 77
Filipino Domestic Helpers General Union 106
Filipino Migrant Workers Union 106
financialisation 11, 16
First World War 26, 28, 30
flash appeals 54
food security 46, 59, 65
forced displacement 51, 77, 79, 82, 85
forced migration 12, 14, 19, 25, 27–8, 30–1, 40, 68, 181–202
foreign direct investment (FDI) 94–5, 100, 110
Foreign Industrial Trainee Programme 100–1, 106–7
Foreign Trainees Programme for Overseas Firms 100
France 28–30, 36, 118–19, 177
Frattini, F. 119
Free Officers Movement 33
Freemantle, I. 15, 136–57, 161
Frelick, B. 168, 171
Friedman, M. 11
FRONTEX 119–23, 126
FRONTEX Risk Analysis Network (FRAN) 120

Gaddafi, M. 39, 118, 127–8
Gaza 163
gender 8, 33, 35, 101–2, 189, 199
General Law for Victims of Crime 80
Geneva Conventions 86
genocide 29
Georgetown University 13
Germany 130
Geschiere, P. 148

206   *Index*

Ghana 130
global economic/financial crisis 1, 6,
    39–40, 93–114
globalisation 11, 25, 64, 106
governance 7, 47, 62, 64
government discourse 136–57
Greece 27, 30, 119–20, 123
Greek language 30
Greeks 29
guest workers 100, 110
Gueterres, A. 175
Gulf states *see* Arab Gulf
Gulf War 36, 53, 163–4, 170

Habar Gedir 54
Habermas, J. 118
habitus 116
Haiti 1
Hammond, L. 14, 46–72, 166
Hanieh, A. 14, 24–45, 125
Hawiye 49–51, 58
hegemony 30, 118
High Level Panel 63
history/historical perspective 2, 9, 14;
    MENA region 25, 41; Somalia 62–5,
    68; Mexico 77, 81–2; East Asia 97,
    106; EU borders 127; South Africa
    147; mass refugee influx 163
hokou 99
Hong Kong 93, 98, 101–2, 105–6,
    108, 110
Hong Kong Confederation of Trade
    Unions 106
hot money 95
Hourani, A. 26
human rights 12–13, 16–17, 66; Mexico
    73, 77, 87; East Asia 106; EU borders
    123; South Africa 136, 141; border
    closures 163, 172; family issues
    185–6
Human Rights Watch 77, 169
humanitarian crises 13, 15–17, 48;
    Somalia 52–3, 58, 60, 65–6, 68; East
    Asia 107; EU borders 121, 129; South
    Africa 141; border closures 158–60,
    167–77; mass refugee influx 162;
    family issues 182
Humanitarian Evacuation Programme
    (HEP) 173–4, 176
Humanitarian Transfer Programme
    (HTP) 173
hurricanes 84
Hussein, S. 32, 163, 171
hyperinflation 58

Ibrahim, S. 31–2
Ider, N. 128–9
imagined threats 158–80
imperialism 25–6, 28
indentures 98
Indians 98
indigenous communities 76, 78
Indochina 163
Indonesia 100–2, 110
Indonesian Group of Hong Kong 105
Indonesian Migrant Workers Union
    (IMWU) 105
Indonesians 106
industrialisation 9, 16, 97–8, 102, 110
infitah 34–6
Institutional Revolutionary Party
    (PRI) 75
integrated border management 121
Integrated Food Security Phase
    Classification (IPC) 59
internal displacement 8, 14, 52, 62, 65,
    67, 73–4, 82–5, 182
internally displaced persons (IDP) 55,
    58, 60–2, 65, 82, 172
International Committee of the Red
    Cross (ICRC) 86
international community 15, 52,
    54, 68, 158, 160–1, 166, 171, 173,
    175–6
International Criminal Tribunal
    for the Former Yugoslavia (ICTY)
    86–7
international humanitarian law (IHL)
    86–7
international law 86–7, 159, 162–3,
    185–7
International Monetary Fund (IMF)
    34–5, 98
International Organisation for
    Migration (IOM) 13, 37, 39, 117, 130,
    193–4
involuntary migration 125
Iran 32, 163
Iran-Iraq War 32
Iranian Revolution 32
Iraq 15, 28–30, 32, 36, 158, 160–1,
    163–4, 165–74, 177
Iraqis 38
irregular migration 100, 103, 123, 127
Islam 24, 29, 32, 56–7, 61, 68, 166, 174
Islamic Courts Union (ICU) 56–7
Israel 31, 163
Italian language 38
Italy 24, 37–8, 118–21, 123, 128, 177

Jackson, S. 148
Janissaries 27
Jankuloski, Z. 172
Japan 97–8
Jastram, K. 186
Jeandesboz, J. 15, 115–35, 159
Jews 27, 29–30
Joint Committee for Migrants in Korea (JCMK) 106
Joint-Operation Hermes Extension 119
Jordan 32, 39–40, 163
Jordan Valley 28

Kadri, A. 36
Kaiser, T. 16–17, 181–202
Kapteijns, L. 51
Kazakhstan 163
Kenya 15, 50, 53, 55–6, 60–3, 130, 158, 162–3, 166–7, 169, 174–7, 190
Kiryandongo Refugee Settlement 184, 188–9, 191–2, 195–8
Korea BorgWarner Changwon Union 107
Korean Confederation of Trade Unions (KCTU) 107
Kosovar Albanians 164–6, 168–9, 176
Kosovo 15, 158, 161, 163–6, 172–4
Kosovo Liberation Army 165
Kurdish Workers' Party (PKK) 164
Kurds 29–30, 32, 162–4, 166, 168, 170–2, 176
Kusakabe, K. 110
Kuwait 31, 39
Kyrgyzstan 101, 163

labelling 15, 115–26, 128–32, 158
labour market 8–10, 16, 33, 36, 99, 101, 144
labour migrants/migration 8–10, 16, 31, 84, 93–114, 184, 189–90
Labour Protection Office 109
Laitinen, I. 122
Lampedusa 118–20
Lao PDR 100, 110
Latin America 77, 86
Latin American Public Opinion Project (LAPOP) 83
Lausanne, Treaty of 30
Law 96 (Egypt) 34–5
Lebanon 28, 30, 163
Lesch, A. 31
LIBE Committee 121
Libya 24, 32, 36, 39–40, 117–21, 125, 127–31

Libyan National Transitional Council 128
Libyans 129
Lindley, A. 11–23, 46–72, 166
livelihoods/livelihood strategies 12, 46, 48–9; Somalia 51–2, 54, 56, 58–9, 61, 64–8; South Africa 136, 139, 141; mass refugee influx 162; families 181, 183–4, 187, 191, 196–7, 199
Long, K. 15, 158–80
Lord's Resistance Army (LRA) 184, 188, 192

Macedonia 15, 158, 160–1, 163–9, 172–4, 176–7
Macedonian Albanians 169
Mae Sot 108–9
Maghreb 27
Malawi 163
Malaysia 96–7, 100, 103–4
Malmström, C. 115, 118–19
malnutrition 52, 54, 59–60, 65–6
Malta 118, 120–1, 123
manufactured crises 158–80
Marfleet, P. 14, 24–45, 125
Margolles, T. 81
Maroni, R. 24
Maronite Catholics 30
Marxism 3, 9
Masebe, T. 141
Masetlha, B. 143
mass refugee influx 15, 60, 82, 158–80
Mazower, M. 27
Mbeki, T. 140
Médecins Sans Frontières (MSF) 62, 168
media 5–6, 25, 62; Somalia 66; Mexico 74, 79, 82, 85, 88; East Asia 105; EU borders 125; South Africa 140; border closures 165, 171, 173
Mediterranean 24, 27, 37–8, 116–20, 122, 124–5, 128–9
Melilla 120
Memoranda of Understanding (MOU) 101
Merida Initiative 86
Mesopotamia 27, 29
Metal Workers Federation 107
Mexican Revolution 81
Mexicans 74, 76–9, 84–5, 88
Mexico 14, 17, 73–92
Middle East 14, 24–45, 61, 128, 162
Middle East and North Africa (MENA) 24–45

Migrant Trade Union (MTU) 107
migration 7–8; and crisis 1–19, 142–5;
  categories of 8, 16, 25–6; workers
  8–10, 15; Middle East 24–45; North
  Africa 24–45; global economic crisis
  93–114; EU border controls 115–35;
  social construction 136–57
military 9, 14, 25; MENA region 27–8,
  32, 34; Somalia 47–8, 62, 65; Mexico
  73, 76, 86; East Asia 108; border
  closures 167–8, 173; family issues 194
millet system 27
Milošević, S. 164, 173
mining 100
Misago, J. P. 15, 136–57, 161
Mitchell, T. 115
mixed flow 125–6
mobility dynamics 47–9, 57–61,
  66–8
Moi, D. A. 167
money transfer system 44, 46, 53, 62
Mongolia 101
Monsutti, A. 188
Montenegro 27
Moore, K. 25
moral panics 6
Morocco 120
Morris, N. 174
mortality rates 52, 54, 65, 191
Movement for Peace with Justice and
  Dignity (MPJD) 74, 77
Mozambicans 138, 148
Mubarak, H. 33–5, 39–40, 118
Muslims 27–8, 30, 32, 59
Myanmar 100–1
Myundong Cathedral 106–7

nakba 30, 32
narco culture 80
Nasser, G. A. 33–5, 37
nation-states 9, 16, 25–30, 49–53
National Action Party (PAN) 76
National Defence Force 139
National Planning Commission 146
National Survey of Victimisation and
  Perceptions of Public Security 74
NATO 165–6, 172–3, 177
Neal, A. 121–2
neo-imperialism 25
neoclassical economics 3, 9, 11
neoliberalism 11, 14, 25–6, 33–40, 93,
  95, 106, 110, 117–18, 125, 127
Nepal 101
Nepalese 106

newly–industrialised economies (NIEs)
  100, 110
nexus hazards 16, 18–19, 24, 26, 31, 40
NGOs 35, 59, 61, 80, 173, 177, 199
Niger 128
Nigeria 130
Nigerians 130
Nile Delta 26, 37, 39
no-man's-land 163
nomads 9, 48, 51, 55, 67
non-crises 136–57
non-refoulement 174–5
North 8, 99, 110
North Africa 14, 24–45, 115, 117–18,
  125–6, 132
North America 39, 53, 61
North-east Asia 97
Norway 130, 173
Nut Knitting Partnership Co 109

OECD 86
Ogata, S. 170
oil 31–2, 48, 61, 115
Omar, F. M. 128–9
ontology 138
Operation Linda Nchi 61
Operation Provide Comfort 171
Opio, J. 195–6
Orientalism 29
Others 27, 51, 148
Ottoman Empire 26–30, 32

Pakistan 101, 161
Palestine 28–30, 117
Palestinians 30–2, 38, 40, 129
Pallister-Wilkins, P. 15, 115–35, 159
Pashtuns 161
passports 131, 193
pastoralism 26, 29, 48–9, 51–2, 54–5,
  59, 197
patronage 30, 32, 40
peace 5, 7, 49; Somalia 52, 64, 69;
  East Asia 108; South Africa
  139–40, 145; mass refugee
  influx 160, 165, 172, 176–7; families
  184, 196
Pearson, R. 110
Peña Nieto, E. 77
permanent crisis 35, 40, 63
permanent migration 36–8
petro-economies 31
Philippines 1, 101–2
pilgrims 29
place 7–8, 17–18

policy failure 11, 62, 64, 85, 139, 141, 144, 149, 177, 182, 196
political economy 4, 26, 63, 74–8
politicisation 16–17
Portugal 27
post-colonialism 30, 32
poverty 13, 33–6, 39; Somalia 49, 67; Mexico 76, 78, 81; South Africa 141–2, 145, 148; family issues 196
privatisation 99
Progres 29
proletariat 101
propaganda 59
protection gaps 12, 17, 19
protection rackets 76
protracted displacement 53–7

Qatar 31

race 30, 137, 144, 146, 148–9
Rahanweyn 51–2
Rapid Border Intervention Team (RABIT) 119
Rapid Task Team 140
recession 93–6, 102–5, 109–10
Red Cross 86, 169
refugees 6–9, 12, 15–16; concepts 18–19; MENA region 28, 30–2, 38, 40; Somalia 46, 48, 50, 52–3, 55–6, 60–3, 65–9; Mexico 84; EU borders 117, 125, 127, 129–31; South Africa 142, 144–5; border closure 158–80; family issues 181–7, 189–94, 196, 198–9; Refugees Act 200
Refugees Act 60
regionalisation 15, 18, 98–9, 101–2, 110
Registered Traveller Programme (RTP) 123
rehabilitation 7, 54
remittance flows 10–11, 32–3, 36–7, 39–40, 46, 51, 55–6, 61–2, 69, 103–4
repatriation 12, 18, 48–9; Somalia 53, 56, 61–3, 68–9; mass refugee influx 173, 175, 177; families 184, 191, 196
resettlement 193–6
Romania 27
Roux-Dufort, C. 138
Rubio Díaz-Leal, L. 14, 64, 73–92
Russian Empire 27–30
Russian Orthodox Christians 29
Rwanda 163

Sadat, A. 34, 36–7
Said, E. 29

Sample, E. 191
Samwoo Precision Industry Union 107
San Andrès Agreements 76
Saudi Arabia 39, 163
Save the Children UK (SCUK) 37
Scandinavia 193
scapegoating 17
Schengen Area 119, 177
Second World War 3, 31
securitisation 11, 17, 116, 121–2, 158, 160, 167, 187
sedentarism 1, 9, 25, 52, 82, 183
Sefardic Jews 27
Self-Reliance Strategy 196
Seoul-Gyeongi Equal Trade Union 107
September 11 attacks 121
Serbia 27, 164–5, 173
Serbs 168
Sexual and Gender Based Violence Programme (SGBV) 199
Al Shabaab 57–62, 64, 66–7
shabka 37
shari'a Muslims 27, 32, 56
shock therapy 3
Sicilia, J. 74
Singapore 96, 98, 102
slavery 51, 98, 101–2, 106
small- and medium-sized enterprises (SMEs) 100–1
smuggling 38, 49, 56, 59, 169
social change/transformation 16
social cohesion 15, 136–57
social construction 136–57
social differentiation 16, 189, 199
socialism 99
Somali Federal Government (SFG) 62, 64
Somali National Movement'(SNM) 48–9
Somali Patriotic Movement (SPM) 49
Somali Salvation Democratic Front 48
Somali-Ethiopian War 48
Somalia 14–15, 17, 46–72, 119, 130, 158, 162–3, 166–7, 170, 174–6
Somalis 49, 55–6, 61, 66–7, 130, 148, 161–2, 169–70, 174–6
Sons of the Soil Land Center 35
South 8
South Africa 15, 17, 136–57
South African Human Rights Commission 141
South African Institute of International Affairs (SAIIA) 141
South Africans 146–9

210 *Index*

South Asia 31
South Korea 93, 96–8, 100–2,
    105–8
South-East Asia 31, 97
Southern African Development
    Community (SADC) 145
Spain 27, 36, 123
Spanish 120
spatialisation 16–17, 64, 117, 148
Sri Lanka 101
state-owned enterprises (SOE)
    35, 99
stateless persons 129
strikes 33, 105–7
structural adjustment programmes
    34–5
struggles of labour 93–114
sub-prime mortgages 96
Sub-Saharan Africa 38, 128, 183
Sub-Saharan Africans 127–8, 130
Sudan 16, 61, 119, 163, 189–90, 192,
    195–8, 200
Sudanese 181, 183–5, 187–92, 194, 196,
    198–9
Sudanese People's Liberation Army
    (SLA) 184
Suez Canal 33, 36
Sunni Muslims 27, 30, 32
survival migration 12
Sykes-Picot agreement 28
Syria 24, 28, 32, 38, 40, 117, 162–3, 177

tahrib 49
Taiwan 96, 98
Tanzania 163
taxation 9, 34, 57, 60
technocracy 116, 185
Thai Migrant Workers Union 106
Thailand 93, 96–7, 100–3, 105,
    108–9
Thais 106, 108
timeframes 14, 63
trade 26–7, 29, 94
trade unions 105–7
Trans-Jordan 28
Transitional Federal Government
    (TFG) 56–8, 60, 166
transnational corporations (TNCs) 96,
    98–9
Tunisia 24, 40, 117–19, 121, 125, 127,
    129–30
Tunisians 118, 120, 126, 177
Turkey 15, 28, 36, 119, 158, 160–4,
    167–8, 170–3, 176–7

Turks 28
Tutu, R. 167

Uganda 181, 183–5, 188, 190–2,
    194–9
Uganda People's Defence Force
    (UPDA) 184
unemployment 13, 36, 39, 56, 97, 102,
    108, 144–5, 148
Union of Nepalese Domestic
    Workers 106
unionisation 100
United Arab Emirates (UAE) 31, 39
United Kingdom (UK) 48, 121, 193
United Nations High Commissioner for
    Refugees (UNHCR) 49, 53, 56;
    Somalia 58, 63, 65–6; Mexico 84; EU
    borders 129–30; mass refugee influx
    158, 162, 164–5, 168–72, 174–5, 177;
    families 182, 186–8, 193–4
United Nations (UN) 52–3, 59–60, 127;
    Regional Offices 36; UNRWA 129;
    Security Council 160, 165, 171;
    Special Envoys 165, 174; border
    closures 169; mass refugee influx
    172, 177
United Somali Congress (USC)
    49, 65
United States (US) 31–2, 39, 52–3;
    USAID 34; and Somalians 56, 58;
    and Mexicans 75, 81–4, 86; and East
    Asians 94–6, 98, 103; EU borders
    121, 130; border closures 163, 167–8,
    171, 173; family issues 193
Universal Declaration of Human Rights
    185–6
Universidad Autónoma de Ciudad
    Juárez 82
University Museum of Contemporary
    Art 81
unmixing 26–30
Uppsala University Conflict Data
    Programme 87
Uzbekistan 101, 163

Vanderbilt University 83
Vaughan-Williams, N. 7
Vietnam 101
violence 49–54, 57–8, 63; Mexico
    73–92; drug-related 75–8; South
    Africa 136–42, 145, 148–9; border
    closures 165, 169; family issues 181,
    188, 199
voluntary migration 125

Wahabis 57
war 3–5, 26, 28; MENA region 30–2,
  36; Somalia 47–8, 51–3, 63–7; Mexico
  78, 86; East Asia 108; EU borders
  116, 130; South Africa 139, 143; mass
  refugee influx 160, 162–4; families
  186, 195
war on terror 61, 64, 118, 167
warehoused refugees 12, 40, 46
warlords 51–2, 64, 66
Weber, M. 119, 123
Weiner, M. 13
West 3, 6, 31; and Somalia 55,
  57–9, 62, 64; and East Asia 98;
  EU borders 127; mass refugee
  influx 159, 163; border closures
  171, 173
World Bank 11, 33–5, 39, 102

World Food Programme 58–9
World Trade Organization (WTO) 106

xenophobia 15, 136–57

Yaung Chi Oo Workers Association 109
Yemen 53, 117, 163
Youngjin Industry Union 107
Youssef, A. 128–9
Yugoslavia 119, 165

Zaire 163
Zambia 163
Zapatista movement 76
Zimbabwe 13, 143
Zimbabweans 148
Zionism 30
Zohry, A. 36, 38